3rd edition

SOCIAL WORK ADMINISTRATION
Dynamic Management and Human Relationships

Rex A. Skidmore
University of Utah

S0-ABB-073

Allyn and Bacon
Boston   London   Toronto   Sydney   Tokyo   Singapore

Vice President, Social Sciences: Susan Badger
Executive Editor: Karen Hanson
Managing Editor: Judy Fifer
Editorial Assistant: Sarah Dunbar
Marketing Manager: Joyce Nilsen
Cover Administrator: Linda Knowles
Manufacturing Buyer: Louise Richardson
Editorial-Production Service: Walsh Associates
Cover Designer: Suzanne Harbison

Copyright © 1995, 1990, 1983 by Allyn & Bacon
A Simon & Schuster Company
Needham Heights, MA 02194

Library of Congress Cataloging-in-Publication Data

Skidmore, Rex Austin, 1914–
    Social work administration : dynamic management and human
relationships / Rex A. Skidmore.—3rd ed.
        p.   cm.
    Includes bibliographical references and index.
    ISBN 0-13-669037-8
    1. Social work administration—United States.   2. Interpersonal
relations.   I. Title.
HV95.S56   1994
361'.0068—dc20   94-3502
                                                                  CIP

Printed in the United States of America

10 9 8 7 6 5 4 3   00 99 98 97 96

To
Social Work Administrators
Who Build Their Staffs
and Work with Them

CONTENTS

PREFACE

The third edition of *Social Work Administration* has been influenced by the wide use of the second edition by social work educators and practitioners. Many of your suggestions have been incorporated into this current edition.

Since the first edition of this book, social work administration has branched out in many directions—many positive, some difficult. On the one hand, several challenging developments have emerged. Government declassification of many social work positions has opened the job market to workers from other fields and disciplines. Competition for positions in social agencies has increased. Budgetary and financial stringencies have surfaced. There are some differences of opinion about whether administration is a social work method and where it fits in the total social work arena.

On the other hand, numerous positive developments have appeared in social work education and practice. By 1992 fifty-five graduate schools of social work in the United States were offering a concentration in the broad field of social work administration, the largest ever. A national sample survey of members of the National Association of Social Workers (NASW) employed full time indicated that between 1981 and 1985 the percentage of social work practitioners in administration increased from 27.8 to 36.5

In recent years new positions and innovations for social work administrators have included appointments as state mental hospital superintendents, state training school directors, and executives of other government and private agencies. Social work administrators have received appointments as presidents of colleges and universities as well as academic deans and vice-presidents. In the business world, social work leaders have been employed as "shadow consultants" to train and help business executives improve their efficiency and effectiveness.

The aim of this book is to provide an overview, mainly for social work students, to help them answer the following questions: (1) Where did social work administration come from? (2) Where is it at present, both in terms of education and practice? and (3) Where might it go in the years ahead? It is my hope that the book will be used by social work students, particularly students enrolled in their first class in administration, to help them understand where administration fits into the scheme of theory and practice.

The book draws on materials from management and human relations, especially from the social work arena. It integrates basic principles, concepts, and processes from management with relationships and skills among executives and staff. The human relations focus is emphasized in particular in the administrative process.

Human relations attach to and involve leaders and followers. Significant data, principles, and skills are presented for both groups. The word *teamship* has been coined as a partner to the word *leadership*. *Leadership* generally has two connotations: ability to lead and the position, function, or guidance of a leader. *Teamship* refers to the ability to be an effective team member and the action of staff members in any agency who work together cooperatively—with one another and with their leader—to their mutual advantage.

This edition includes numerous enriching materials. Of special interest are additions in case management, ethical conduct, time management, shadow consultation, women in management, job opportunities, burnout, and future developments. Throughout the book focused emphasis has been given to human relationships in the administration process.

New references are included at the end of each chapter. They provide excellent resources for additional study of the individual themes presented.

I express sincere appreciation to my colleagues who have made suggestions and offered valuable editorial guidelines and improvements, especially O. William Farley. Kay L. Dea and Milton G. Thackeray have generously shared with me their administrative expertise and understanding, offering suggestions, materials, and professional acumen. Dorthea C. Murdock, Maun R. Alston, and Michael M. Dale have provided significant practice materials that enrich the book. Secretarial assistance, skilled and gracious, has been provided by Neva Nielsen, Mary Broadbent, Sue McIntosh, and Sandy Hiskey.

My deepest thanks and appreciation go to Knell, my wife, who has been a constant inspiration and associate in the formulation, preparation, and revision of this book.

Rex A. Skidmore

1

What Is
Social Work
Administration?

Administration in social work is changing from a pyramid to a circle. No longer does one person at the top have absolute power to dictate and control agency policies and practices. Such power is being shared more and more with staff and clients, who are being challenged to reach for increased knowledge and skills to help plan and facilitate effective services.

In many agencies, in varying patterns, administrators, staff, and clients are working cooperatively together to make decisions and deliver agency services.

In this fast-changing, uncertain world, human services have become a major part of the American way of life. The federal budget uses almost half of its monies for such assistance, and state allocations vary from about one-fourth to one-third of budgetary expenditures. Services for people in need have expanded rapidly in recent years, in public as well as in private agencies. How are these programs administered, how effectively, and by whom?

Social work administration, both in education and practice, has come to the fore in recent years and is recognized as an essential component in the delivery of social services. Administration usually is controlled by leaders in the top echelon of an agency, who facilitate the work of the agency and staff. In actuality it involves *all* staff members at all levels, in either leadership or teamship roles.

A competent administrator can make a social service agency effective and efficient. A capable administrator can bring about desired results; an incompetent leader may block services and thwart the staff. Brief examples follow.

To illustrate an inadequate administrator, let's consider a staff meeting at which an outside guest was invited to present suggestions for possible reorganization of the agency. Mr. A., a competent supervisor, raised questions in the discussion that followed and disagreed in a thoughtful way with some of the recommendations. Soon after the meeting the director of the agency came to the office of Mr. A. and told him his observations were inappropriate. He accused him of being disloyal, unfair, dishonest, and incompetent. Obviously the results of the director's criticisms were negative for Mr. A., and consequently the morale of other staff members diminished when they heard what had happened.

Contrast the foregoing with a somewhat similar incident, which occurred at a staff meeting where there were major differences about plans of action and decisions to be made. Mr. B. disagreed with what the director had presented for approval by his staff. Yet at the end of the meeting the director said, "Apparently we need to meet again to discuss this matter further, so we can obtain consensus regarding what is best." He told them he was hoping to have his recommendation approved but realized there were some angles he had not thought about—and they agreed to meet again. After the meeting was over he went to Mr. B. and said, "I still differ with you on the matter we are discussing, but I respect your opinion and appreciate your willingness to raise questions."

An administrator who gives full support to his or her staff and who tries to strengthen its members can make a difference in their contributions and how they feel about their jobs. In one social service agency where such a pattern existed, an employee wrote to her director, "I just wanted to let you know how much I appreciate your support and encouragement. It always makes me feel good to know you care about me, personally and professionally."

DEFINITIONS

What is social work administration? Although definitions vary, common threads appear in statements by social work leaders. Kidneigh, in 1950, suggested that social work administration is the "process of transforming social policy into social services . . . a two-way process: (1) . . . transforming policy into concrete social services, and (2) the use of experience in recommending modification of policy."[1]

Spencer suggests that there is general agreement that "administration is the conscious direction of the internal relationships and activities of the enterprise toward the achievement of goals." She also adds that it includes "the

---

[1]John C. Kidneigh, "Social Work Administration—An Area of Social Work Practice?" *Social Work Journal* 31 (April 1950), 58.

conscious intervention in the interacting forces operating between the agency and the larger community of which it is a part."[2]

Dunham describes administration as the process of "supporting or facilitating activities which are necessary and incidental to the giving of direct service by a social agency. Administrative activities range from the determination of function and policies, and executive leadership to routine operations such as keeping records and accounts and carrying on maintenance services."[3]

Stein suggests that definitions of administration are numerous, but "central to those most accepted currently is the concept of administration as a process of defining and attaining the objectives of an organization through a system of coordinated and cooperative effort."[4]

Trecker interprets social work administration as a "process of working with people in ways that release and relate their energies so that they use all available resources to accomplish the purpose of providing needed community services and programs." He outlines principles of social work administration defined by several authors, which include common important elements, as follows:

1. Administration is a continuous, dynamic process.
2. The process is set into motion in order to accomplish a common purpose or goal.
3. The resources of people and material are harnessed so that the common purpose or goal may be achieved.
4. Coordination and cooperation are the means by which the resources of people and material are harnessed.
5. Implicit in the definition are the elements of planning, organizing, and leadership.[5]

In summary, social work administration may be thought of as the action of staff members who utilize social processes to transform social policies of agencies into the delivery of social services. It involves executives—the leaders—and all other staff—the followers or team members. The basic processes most often used are planning, organizing, staffing, directing, and controlling, each of which will be described and illustrated in later chapters.

Many social workers and political leaders feel that one of the great

[2]Sue W. Spencer, "The Administrative Process in a Social Welfare Agency," in Ella W. Reed, ed., *Social Welfare Administration* (New York: Columbia University Press, 1961), p. 32.

[3]Arthur Dunham, *Community Welfare Organization: Principles and Practice* (New York: Thomas Y. Crowell, 1962), p. 42.

[4]Herman Stein, "Social Work Administration," in Harry A. Schatz, ed., *Social Work Administration: A Resource Book* (New York: Council on Social Work Education, 1970), p. 7.

[5]Harleigh Trecker, *Social Work Administration: Principles and Practices* (New York: Association Press, 1971), pp. 24–25.

needs and challenges of social work today is to develop more capable, dynamic leaders who can help to formulate and carry out social policies, plans, and decisions that affect the peoples of the world, directly and indirectly. Also, social work educators as well as practitioners advocate that all social work students acquire more knowledge of and skill in administration during their education so that they can make significant contributions in the delivery of social services to disadvantaged people and others.

Social work administration is coming of age. Competent social agency leaders are more and more social work administrators, not administrators with a social work background. Many agency executives and supervisors have received specific training in schools of social work for the positions they hold. Administration as a field in social work has a rightful place, and administration as a basic social work practice method, like casework or group work, has also come to the fore.

Traditionally, caseworkers with experience became the agency executives. Top clinicians surfaced as agency leaders. Today considerable emphasis is placed on students majoring in administration if they wish to become social work executives or managers. It is recognized that administrators should possess a body of knowledge, a cluster of attitudes, and practical abilities to administer in order to develop and provide appropriate social services.

In the present world many business and political science students with MBAs (50,000 graduate each year) and MPAs apply for employment in the social services and are being hired in responsible positions. No longer are administrative positions in social agencies offered only to social workers. All else being equal, most social workers maintain that students trained in social work administration are best qualified for these positions.

Teicher suggests that a qualified social work administrator is preferable to an administrator trained otherwise for social agencies. He maintains that the "true test of administrative success is not the ability to design and respect organization charts. It is the ability to bring to bear on decision making the knowledge and the information which are essential for wise judgments. Such knowledge and information are painstakingly acquired by education, by experience, and by deep immersion in the work of the social agency." He concludes that "the ability to perform well and wisely, to steer the social agency constructively for humane purposes, is best acquired by professional social work education and experience, combined with powerful identification with social work values and ethics. The ability to pull it all together is to be sought in the professional social worker rather than in the professional administrator."[6]

---

[6]Morton Teicher, "Who Should Manage a Social Agency?" in Simon Slavin, ed., *Social Administration: The Management of the Social Services*, 2nd ed., Vol. I, *An Introduction to Human Services Management* (New York: Haworth Press, 1985), p. 49.

NEED FOR SOCIAL WORK ADMINISTRATION

There is a growing need for social work administrators who both care and are competent through knowledge, abilities, and skills in administration. Educators and practitioners recognize that caring is not enough; administrative skills must accompany caring, to provide effective services.

In 1958, at the annual meeting of the Council on Social Work Education (CSWE), held in Detroit, it was reported that only 1 percent of the male students in graduate schools of social work were majoring in administration; yet 54 percent indicated they would like to become administrators in practice within ten years.

It is estimated that within a few years after graduation, more than 50 percent of MSW graduates either will be or will have been in an administrative position. The reality is that those with graduate training in social work drift toward leadership positions, allowing for a high percentage of traditional clinical positions to be filled by undergraduate social work majors. Administrative positions have a strong pulling power, for salaries are higher and there is opportunity to be creative and exercise authority.

Schottland suggests that "human services are the most significant part of our governmental programs, both in terms of their significance and importance to the people of the United States and in terms of their cost." Then he adds, "The administration of these huge programs is complicated and important, and the training of persons in the art and skill of administration, specifically geared to the administration of the human services, is an extremely important and significant contribution."[7]

A study in 1969 by the National Association of Social Workers (NASW) of their members reflected the importance of administration in social work practice. Responses to a questionnaire were received from 2,857 members, most of whom were employed full time. Casework, general administration, and supervision were the most frequently reported primary job functions, carried out by 33.4, 28.7, and 18.8 percent, respectively. Since supervision is often included as a major part of the administration practice, the results indicated that about 50 percent of the members were in administrative positions, especially when those in public relations, personnel work, and staff development were grouped together and added to this category. The study also indicated that the median annual salary for general administration was the highest of any group.[8]

Another factor to consider is that all social workers are part of the administrative process, either in a positive, neutral, or negative manner. Top executives and directors, assistant directors, supervisors, and consultants are

[7]Charles I. Schottland, "Foreword," in Walter H. Ehlers, Michael J. Austin, and Jon C. Prothero, *Administration for the Human Services* (New York: Harper & Row, 1976), p. xi.

[8]Alfred M. Stamm, "NASW Membership: Characteristics, Deployment, and Salaries," *Personnel Information* 12 (May 1969), 39–40.

the formal administrators in an agency. In theory, they are the leaders and in many ways carry the brunt of administrative responsibilities. Nevertheless, if administration is to be effective, all line workers—the caseworker, group worker, and others—need to be actively involved in the administrative process. They are the team members who provide the services for the agency. They can be powerful in a positive way, by making suggestions for improvement and for strengthening administration. When necessary they can insist on and bring about changes in leadership and policies. As leaders and team members work together in a coordinated, integrated manner, they produce the kinds of human services that are desired and needed. The reality is that all levels of staff should participate in the administrative process for the effective delivery of social services.

Another indication of the importance of administration is reflected in the increased numbers of students in graduate school who are majoring in this field. In 1976, according to the CSWE, there were 214 full-time first-year students enrolled with a concentration in "administration, management, social policy."[9] They were in fifteen different schools of social work. At the same time there were 443 full-time second-year students in thirty schools of social work with a similar concentration. These numbers are higher than in previous years; in fact, a few years ago such students were virtually nonexistent. In 1992 there were fifty-five graduate schools of social work offering concentrations in the broad area of administration.

Interest in administration and related areas is indicated by the information in Table 1–1, which shows that in November 1992 there were 4,757 (15.1

TABLE 1-1   Social Work Master's Degree Students Enrolled November 1, 1992, by Primary Methods Concentration

METHODS	NUMBER	PERCENT
Direct practice	16,993	54.0
Community organization and planning	670	2.1
Administration or management	984	3.1
Combination of direct practice with C.O. and planning or administration or management	2,351	7.5
Combination of C.O. and planning with administration or management	752	2.4
Generic	2,800	8.9
Other	798	2.5
Not yet determined	5,140	16.3
None (field of practice or social problem only)	978	3.1
Total	31,466	100.0

Source: *Statistics on Social Work Education in the United States: 1992* (Alexandria, VA: Council on Social Work Education, 1993), p. 34. Reprinted by permission.

[9]*Statistics on Social Work Education in the United States, 1976* (New York: Council on Social Work Education, 1977), pp. 45–46.

percent) social work master's degree students enrolled in graduate programs in administration or management, a combination of direct practice with community organization and planning or administration or management, a combination of community organization and planning with administration or management, or community organization and planning.

Neugeboren suggests that two actions are particularly significant in the increasing enrollment of students in administration in schools of social work: efforts to recruit students into administration programs, with admissions policies giving priority to these students, and the effort to obtain training grants for these students.[10]

BACKGROUND

The proceedings of the meetings of the National Conference of Charities and Corrections, beginning in 1874, reflect that leaders and others were genuinely concerned with people, their social problems, and the delivery of social services. Many of the first papers delivered at meetings sponsored by this organization were related to administrative problems and issues. In 1893 Anna L. Dawes, of Pittsfield, Massachusetts, suggested that schools should be organized to train workers to help give effective social services to those in need. This suggestion was made at the International Congress on Charities, Correction and Philanthropy. Four years later, in 1897, Mary E. Richmond, then general secretary of the Charity Organization Society of Baltimore, Maryland, made a similar suggestion at the National Conference of Charities and Corrections in the United States. Both based their recommendations on the "absence of competent personnel to take the place of the generation then passing off the scene."[11]

The charity organization movement helped to bring into existence schools of social work that taught knowledge and skills related to administration. The beginning of formal education started in 1898, when the New York Charity Organization Society established a summer school for volunteers and others who wanted to "deepen their understanding of the poor people they were dedicated to helping."[12] In 1904 this offering was extended to a one-year program, and to a two-year program in 1910.

At about the same time, educational innovations were appearing in other parts of the country. At the University of Chicago, in 1901, a series of courses in social welfare was offered under the Extension Department. This program was formalized in 1908 with the incorporation of the Chicago School

[10]Bernard Neugeboren, "Systemic Barriers to Education in Social Work Administration," *Administration in Social Work* 10 (Summer 1986), 8, 12.

[11]Frank J. Bruno, "Twenty-five Years of Schools of Social Work," *The Social Service Review* 18 (June 1944), 152.

[12]School of Social Work, *Columbia University Bulletin*, August 5, 1975, p. 10.

of Civics and Philanthropy, the forerunner of the School of Social Service Administration. In 1904 the Boston School for Social Workers was organized through the efforts of Jeffrey R. Brackett, under the joint auspices of Simmons College and Harvard University.[13]

The courses and programs in these pioneering schools of social work provided students with some knowledge about and skills related to administration as part of the general, total curriculum. At first administration was not considered to be separate from direct services and practice. By 1914, however, a course in administration was offered by at least one school of social work. Gradually additions and specific courses were added to the curriculum. World War I and the Great Depression gave added stimulus to more formal education for those who would provide leadership in administering social service programs.

Between 1920 and 1935 the foundations of administrative technical and professional literature were developing. The Cooperative Committee on Administration was established. A special department in the magazine *The Survey* was made available for administrators, volunteers, and others interested in leadership in social welfare. Several national agencies, such as the YWCA, YMCA, and the Family Welfare Association of America, began to set standards and qualifications for their administrators, which gave considerable emphasis to the administrative process. The instigation and enormous expansion of social welfare programs of the New Deal in the 1930s brought many significant developments in social work administration, both in education and in practice.

Street, in 1933, suggested that administration had been overlooked in social work, both in practice in agencies and in educational circles.

> The subject of administration has been much neglected in social agencies. Social workers who are entirely without training in administration, though competent otherwise, are given important executive responsibilities. Their governing boards also, made up of experienced business men and capable women, often know nothing of the problems of administration in the agencies for which they are trustees, and are not willing to give detailed attention to them. The average social agency, public or private, could probably increase its efficiency and economy by fifty percent through utilizing information now readily available on principles and methods of effective administration. This would mean a reduction in cost of service, or an increase in the amount or adequacy of service rendered.[14]

In 1936 a paper on administration was presented for the first time at the National Conference on Social Work. Three years before, an article on administration appeared in the 1933 edition of *Social Work Yearbook*. In

---

[13]Bruno, "Twenty-five Years," p. 152.

[14]Elwood Street, "Social Work Administration," *Social Work Year Book, 1933* (New York: Russell Sage Foundation, 1933), p. 491.

1937 the delegates at the Conference of the American Association of Social Workers gave specific consideration to the administrative process for the first time.

Enough interest in administration had developed so that by 1944, when the new curriculum for the schools of social work was agreed upon, administration was included as one of the "basic eight" adopted by the American Association of Schools of Social Work. This decision was a major push forward in the development of training in administration, with a concomitant attempt to improve administrative services within social welfare agencies in the field.

In 1946 a program section meeting on administration was offered for the first time at the National Conference on Social Work. It is interesting to note the topics that were given individual consideration: process of administration, dynamics of leadership, salaries, job classification, boards, public relations, organized labor and social work, civil service, program development, and retirement planning.

In 1946 Johnson observed that administration had been an important part of social work since its inception.

> Problems of administration are as old as social work. Indeed, the National Conference of Social Work owes its origin to the problems of institutional administration which beset the state boards of charities when they were organized in the last quarter of the nineteenth century. When the representatives of nine states met in New York on May 20, 1874, the first committee appointed was that on uniformity of statistics, a subject on which committees are still meeting.[15]

In 1949 Hamilton made a strong case for more training and development in administration:

> As social work extends with a justified confidence into the newer fields of social welfare, there emerges the demand for a leadership genuinely skilled in administrative process and community planning. There is steady pressure from federal, national and state agencies, chests, councils, federations, and from our own increasing sense of responsibility, for participation in large scale inter-agency and inter-cultural efforts. It has been amply demonstrated that neither the business man nor the caseworker becomes a good administrator by intuition, a pleasant personality, or a head for figures. I do not know which makes the worst administrator, a businesslike authoritarian, or one of those limp creatures who permit an impossible administrative set up to be perpetuated while he holds that the problem will be solved by everyone being nice to one another. Administration is a highly skilled technical process at its best, using the basic philosophy and skill of democratic social work.[16]

---

[15]Arlien Johnson, "The Administrative Process in Social Work," *Proceedings of the National Conference of Social Work, 1946* (New York: Columbia University Press, 1947), p. 249.

[16]Gordon Hamilton, "Education for Social Work–The Inter-action of School and Agency," *Social Work Journal* 30 (April 1949), 85.

The 1952 curriculum policy statement was broadened and more general in nature. The 1962 CSWE statement on curriculum stressed three important areas: (1) social welfare policy and services, (2) human behavior and the social environment, and (3) methods of social work practice. The methods included were casework, group work, and community organization, with research and administration presented as enabling methods.

The 1969 curriculum statement of the CSWE became more general and generic and provided numerous options and programs for the different schools of social work. Administration was not mentioned specifically but could be offered as a "concentration," which schools were invited to provide in keeping with generally sound educational guidelines and principles.

By 1979 thirty-six schools of social work were offering a major in administration. Their patterns differed considerably. For example, the University of Washington offered a two-year major in administration; other schools, such as the University of Utah, offered a generic base during the first year of graduate study and a major in administration during the second year.

A follow-up study at the University of Michigan School of Social Work, with replies from 730 graduates between the years 1968 and 1972, showed that 91 percent of the respondents were employed as social workers. The lowest unemployment rate, 3.3 percent, was found among graduates specializing in administration. Also, it was considered significant that about 40 percent were supervising other people in social work activities.[17] Those who specialized in administration were earning the most money—with more than 40 percent making more than $14,000 a year. In most states in 1995, salaries for social work administrators had increased, so that the majority of salaries were within the range of $25,000 to $60,000 a year.

Scurfield recognizes the trend in social work practice to utilize MSWs in supervisory and management roles rather than as clinicians. He reports that 35 percent of all NASW members in 1960 and 50 percent in 1969 were in supervisory and/or administrative positions, suggesting a real dilemma for social work education. He observes that there is growing criticism of the adequacy of MSW preparation for either clinical or macro-level functions, and that maybe there should be an emphasis on a more "manageable degree of specialization in which students can begin to specialize in a clinical or macro area. There is an alternative approach: to require course work of M.S.W. students in supervision, consultation, administration, and/or organizational theory based on the likelihood that most M.S.W. graduates will be quickly thrust into supervisory or management positions."[18]

Most social work students who graduate with a major in administration accept either full-time or part-time administrative positions. Biggerstaff con-

[17]Norma Radin, "A Follow-up Study of Social Work Graduates," *Journal of Education for Social Work* 12 (Fall 1976), 103–107.

[18]Raymond Monsour Scurfield, "Social Work Administrators: Their Educational Preparation, Value Orientation, Role Transition, and Satisfaction," *Administration in Social Work* 4 (Summer 1980), 56.

ducted a follow-up study of students concentrating in administration in eight schools of social work. The sample, involving graduates from 1970 through January 1977, produced 146 responses. The respondents were currently employed as follows: 22 percent were in top administrative positions, 32 percent held mid-level management positions, 13 percent were line supervisors, and 33 percent were in direct practice.[19]

Course offerings in administration in social work graduate schools are changing rapidly. Gummer reported that a survey by the CSWE found that 46 percent of the eighty-five graduate schools of social work listed some offering in administration during the academic year 1972–1973.[20] By 1988 fifty-three schools of social work were offering a concentration in the broad area of administration, and by 1992 the number had increased to fifty-five.

The CSWE sponsored a study on administration and social work curriculum that focused on ways of enhancing the quality of educational offerings, thus more adequately preparing social work students to administer and/or manage, both of which would be needed to deliver social services. A questionnaire was sent to seventy-eight schools of social work in 1974, and fifty-three (68 percent) responded. This study reflected high agreement among respondents on the content in the administrative curriculum, as follows: (1) personnel—recruiting, selecting, developing, utilizing, leading, mediating, and evaluating; (2) fiscal resources—acquiring, allocating, and controlling; (3) information systems—measuring, analyzing, designing, and operating; (4) social and organizational policies and programs—planning, instituting, monitoring, evaluating, and changing; (5) organizational decision-making and sanctioning systems—creating, using, restructuring, and modifying; and (6) environmental influences—building, challenging, coping, and coordinating.

The study listed three major goals for the administrative component that is emerging:

1. That all students should have some knowledge concerning administration to use in their direct-practice entry positions
2. That all students should have enough knowledge of administration to allow them to move from direct practice into later administrative positions
3. That students choosing to specialize in administration should acquire enough knowledge and skills to allow their entry positions to be in administration[21]

By 1986 interest in administration, community organization, and the whole macro area had developed so that the Community Organization and

[19]Marilyn A. Biggerstaff, "Preparation of Administrators in Social Welfare: A Follow-up Study of Administration Concentration Graduates," *Administration in Social Work* 2 (Fall 1978), 361.

[20]Burton Gummer, "Social Planning and Social Administration: Implications for Curriculum Development," *Journal of Education for Social Work* 11 (Winter 1975), 71.

[21]Kenneth J. Kazmerski and David Macarov, *Administration in the Social Work Curriculum* (New York: Council on Social Work Education, 1976), p. 11.

Social Administration Symposium was held at the CSWE Annual Program Meeting in Miami. The theme of the symposium was the basic issue of legitimation, effectiveness, and even survival of macro education and practice. "It was based on the concern that the political climate of conservatism and retrenchment and declining enrollments in schools of social work and competition from other professions posed a challenge to the survival of macro education and practice."[22] Also significant was the publication of a Special Issue of *Administration in Social Work* (Summer 1987), with papers from the symposium. Although social work administration has numerous problems and challenges, considerable progress has been made in recent years and the future looks promising.

In 1987 Chess, Norlin, and Jayaratne presented a positive statement about the development of social work administration. Their conclusion was based on data obtained from two studies of NASW members, in 1981 and 1985 (with samples drawn from their computerized files), and consisted of members possessing regular and full memberships who resided in the United States.[23] Table 1–2 includes summary data related to practice methods of the NASW members.

A significant finding of this study was that between 1981 and 1985 the percentage of practitioners in social work administration increased from 27.8 to 36.5. Although there were some special factors affecting the results, these

TABLE 1-2 Practice Method of NASW Members Employed Full Time, 1981-1985

	1981		1985	
CATEGORY	NUMBER	PERCENT	NUMBER	PERCENT
Casework	280	41.1	168	29.4
Group work	13	1.9	5	.9
Community organization	8	1.2	7	1.2
Administration	189	27.8	209	36.5
Supervision	70	10.3	49	8.6
Case management			29	5.1
Policy analysis			9	1.6
Teaching			28	4.9
Other	121	17.8	68	11.9
Total	681	100.0	572	100.0

Source: Wayne A. Chess, Julia M. Norlin, and Srinika D. Jayaratne, "Social Work Administration 1981-1985: Alive, Happy and Prospering," *Administration in Social Work* 11 (Summer 1987), 68.

[22]Bernard Neugeboren, "Introduction to the Special Issue: Legitimacy, Effectiveness, and Survival of Macro Education and Practice," *Administration in Social Work* 11 (Summer 1987), 1.

[23]Wayne A. Chess, Julia M. Norlin, and Srinika D. Jayaratne, "Social Work Administration 1981-1985: Alive, Happy and Prospering," *Administration in Social Work* 11 (Summer 1987), 68.

authors concluded that "given the economic and political climate and its implications for the practice of social work administration, the data presented here are generally quite positive. In short, these data suggest that social work administration in 1985 is alive, happy and prospering."[24]

SOCIAL WORK METHODS

Many social work educators and practitioners believe that there are five main social work methods, one of which is administration. Some suggest that there are three primary methods—casework, group work, and community organization—and two enabling methods—research and administration. Others describe one method in social work, the problem-solving method, which encompasses all of the other five, with a focus on understanding and solving problems related to social functioning and social relationships.

A process is a way or manner in which change takes place. In this sense, administration is a significant process. It is in reality a kind of social work practice—the way in which social services can be facilitated and in which the delivery of such services takes place. Whereas casework concerns helping an individual or a family with social relationships, group work uses the group as a tool to do the same; community organization solves social problems through neighborhood and community action; administration is the process of running an agency and involves goals, policies, staff, management, services, and evaluation. Effective administration can make a difference in the delivery of social services.

Casework for many years was almost synonymous with social work. In the 1930s group work came to the fore as an additional method that could be effective in working with people and with their relationships. Before long community organization was catapulted into bold relief as a method of working on social problems involving large numbers of people. Research is related to the other methods and is an attempt to find out facts and truth. What is happening? What could be improved? What could be more effective in producing high-quality social services?

Administration is the method that makes the others possible, the one that helps facilitate the functioning and operation of an agency and its practice methods. Administration and the other methods have much in common: they involve people, encompass relationships and problems, and share many techniques and principles in the helping process. For example, the principle of acceptance is significant in and basic to all five methods. Also, the ability to listen and to participate in communication is shared by all. However, each method has many unique characteristics.

[24]Ibid., p. 76.

COMPARISON WITH ADMINISTRATION
IN BUSINESS AND GOVERNMENT

Administration is not unique to social work; it is an important part of business, government, and the professions. In business, administration is a major interest and focus of training, and business schools offer students numerous managerial courses. In practice, management has become a major part of the business world. In government, similarly, the importance of administration has been recognized at the federal, state, and local levels. Positions for administrators are advertised often, and salaries are among the highest in government or private agencies.

Although there are many differences in administration among social work, business, and government, they also have much in common. Spencer, in the historic 1959 Curriculum Study of the CSWE, listed some common characteristics of all areas of administration:

1. It is primarily a problem-solving process, involving identification of the problem, study of the various aspects of the problem, development of a possible plan for solution, implementation of the plan, and subsequent evaluating of its effectiveness.
2. It is a system or constellation of interrelated and interacting parts.
3. Administration involves use of value judgments in the selection of alternatives.
4. It is seen as an enabling process that makes it possible for individuals and groups to function more effectively.
5. It is concerned to a considerable degree with "futures."
6. It involves the creative rather than the routinized use of knowledge and skill.
7. It is concerned with structuring of program, services, and staff to facilitate optimum efficiency and production of goods or services.
8. It is concerned to a greater or lesser extent with implementing the public will.
9. It involves an appropriate balance between objectifying management operations and the utilization of human resources.
10. It is concerned with the individual staff member in relation to status and recognition, and with the necessity for his or her positive identification with the goals, values, and methods of the organization.
11. Communication, interpersonal staff group relations, and participation in agency administration are major areas of professional concern.[25]

Although social work administration shares many qualities of administration in business and government, as has been indicated, it nevertheless has many distinctive characteristics. A summary of Spencer's pioneering description explains what these are.

1. Administration within social agencies is established to help them meet recognized needs within the community.

[25]Sue Spencer, *The Administration Method in Social Work Education* (New York: Council on Social Work Education, 1959), pp. 21–22.

2. The services provided by these agencies may be classified as falling within three broad categories:
   a. Restoration of impaired social functioning
   b. Provision of resources, social and individual, for more effective social functioning
   c. Prevention of social dysfunction
3. The typical social agency possesses a governing board that generally represents the community.
4. There is an enormous range and variety in the size, scope, structure, and type of programs of organizations in these agencies.
5. The administrator has responsibility for relating the internal operations of the agency to the community.
6. There is a constant necessity for making choices about the use of resources.
7. Social agencies need to avoid using a disproportionate amount of their resources for survival. The principal responsibility for producing, maintaining, and guarding the agency's optimum functions devolves upon the executive.
8. The service performed by social agencies has an increasingly large professional social work component.
9. All levels of staff participate in the administrative process and affect the total agency project to some extent.[26]

SUMMARY

Social work administration is the process of transforming social policies into social services. It is a field and a method, both of which have come into prominence within the past few decades.

Social work administration is a facilitative and enabling method that opens doors to the effective provision and delivery of social services. The need for competent and caring administrators in social work is great.

Training in social work administration is relatively new. The first class in administration in a school of social work was given in 1914.

Social work administration has much in common with administration in business and government. It also has distinguishing characteristics. Together these features balance the principles and techniques of management and the principles and feelings attached to sound human values and relationships. Most social workers prefer their administrators to be trained in social work rather than in business.

QUESTIONS FOR DISCUSSION

1. What is social work administration?

2. Why is there such a great need for well-trained, competent social work administrators today?

[26]Ibid., pp. 22–25.

3. Compare, contrast, and illustrate the social work methods of casework, group work, and administration.

4. What are some of the positive characteristics of social work administration that might appeal to social work students in choosing a major?

5. What have been some of the significant steps in the historical development of social work administration as a method?

6. Compare and contrast the administration process in social work, business, and government.

7. Would you prefer to have an administrator trained in social work in your agency or one trained in business? Why or why not?

8. Where is social work administration likely to be in the year 2000?

SPECIAL ACTIVITIES

1. Visit a social work agency and talk with the administrator about some of the values and problems of social work administration.

2. Read one of the references at the end of the chapter and be prepared to discuss its basic ideas and information.

3. Role-play in class an administrative problem or challenge, for example, firing a staff member, hiring a minority caseworker, planning a budget for a fiscal year, or selecting a case manager.

SELECTED REFERENCES

CHESS, WAYNE A., JULIA M. NORLIN, and SRINIKA D. JAYARATNE. "Social Work Administration 1981–1985: Alive, Happy and Prospering." *Administration in Social Work* 11 (Summer 1987), 67–77.

GARVIN, CHARLES D., and JOHN E. TROPMAN. *Social Work in Contemporary Society.* Englewood Cliffs, NJ: Prentice Hall, 1992.

GUMMER, BURTON. "Are Administrators Social Workers? The Politics of Intraprofessional Rivalry." *Administration in Social Work* 11 (Summer 1987), 19–31.

MIRINGOFF, MARC L. *Management in Human Service Organizations.* New York: Macmillan, 1980.

NEUGEBOREN, BERNARD. "Career Development in Social Work Administration." *Administration in Social Work* 14, No. 1 (1990), 47–63.

PECORA, PETER J., and MICHAEL J. AUSTIN. *Managing Human Services Personnel.* Newbury Park, CA: Sage Publications, 1987.

PRUGER, ROBERT, ed. "Efficiency and the Social Services." *Administration in Social Work* 15, Nos. 1/2 (1991), 1–192.

RESNICK, HERMAN, and RINO J. PATTI, eds. *Change from Within: Humanizing Social Welfare Organizations.* Philadelphia: Temple University Press, 1980.

SCHATZ, HARRY A., ed. *Social Work Administration: A Resource Book.* New York: Council on Social Work Education, 1970.

SLAVIN, SIMON, ed. *Social Administration: The Management of the Social Services,* 2nd ed. Vol. I, *An Introduction to Human Services Management.* New York: Haworth Press, 1985.

STOESZ, DAVID. "Human Service Corporations: New Opportunities for Administration in Social Work." *Administration in Social Work* 13, Nos. 3/4 (1989), 183–197.

2

Social Work and Management

Across the centuries, leaders have been extolled and leadership utilized to reach goals and promote values. More than 2,500 years ago, Lao-tse, in the Book of Tao, *wrote,*

> *A leader is best*
> *When people barely know that he exists. . . .*
> *But of a good leader, who talks little*
> *When his work is done, his aim fulfilled,*
> *They will say, "We did this ourselves."*

In recent decades, particularly in the last twenty-five years, many administrative developments in the fields of business and social work have intertwined. The current challenge in social work is to blend the principles of management efficiency with human relations to bring about the effective delivery of human services. Business-oriented management encompasses the processes of planning, organizing, and directing, in an attempt to increase and improve the operations and products of an organization. In social work, these same processes can be utilized to strengthen agency operations and to enhance social services. This chapter includes selective materials to indicate backgrounds and relationships of both management and social work and to show the beginning of a partnership sharing administrative processes, practices, and skills.

ADMINISTRATION'S ROOTS IN MANAGEMENT

Koontz and O'Donnell define managing as

the creation and maintenance of an internal environment in an enterprise where individuals, working together in groups, can perform efficiently and effectively toward the attainment of group goals. Managing could, then, be called "performance environment design." Essentially, managing is the art of doing, and management is the body of organized knowledge which underlines the art.[1]

In addition, they classify the five main processes that make up the administrative method: planning, organizing, staffing, directing, and controlling. These have been generally accepted by managers and social workers as basic classifications for studying and implementing the total administrative process.

The roots of management go back a long way and involve numerous writers and leaders. In this chapter we shall highlight a few of the pioneers in this field and their contributions while making no attempt to present a history of the development of management theory or practice.

Charles Babbage, who lived in the early nineteenth century, pioneered in applying scientific methodology to the study and implementation of production and administration.[2] Fulmer summarizes his contributions as follows:

Babbage's first contribution to producers was to suggest that various parts of the total job should be assigned to workers on the basis of worker skills.

Division of labor was useful for four reasons . . . : (1) Learning time is reduced because one worker must learn only one skill. (2) Less time is lost in changing from one skill to another during production. (3) Workmen are likely to develop proficiency because they are repeating the same operation time after time. (4) Because the job is broken down into its component parts, special tools and equipment are likely to be developed.

The second area in which Babbage pioneered was in providing guidelines by which managers could weigh the relative values of machine processes versus human operations. The newest machine on the market was an automated pinmaker. Babbage evaluated the machine's product and cost and gave the following questions:

1. What defects is the machine product liable to have?
2. What advantages does the machine product possess?
3. What is the prime cost of the machine?
4. What is the expense of keeping the machine in repair?
5. What is the expense of moving and attending the machine?

[1]Harold Koontz and Cyril O'Donnell, *Essentials of Management* (New York: McGraw-Hill, 1974), p. 1.
[2]Charles Babbage, *On the Economy of Machinery and Manufacturers* (London: Charles Knight, 1832).

... Charles Babbage had a mission: to make tedious computations and production easier for man. Today his pioneering theories are in daily use.[3]

Frederick W. Taylor, often regarded as the "father of scientific management," offered numerous suggestions at the turn of the twentieth century for
improving efficiency and effectiveness. His studies and recommendations
were specific and meaningful. He suggested that efficiency could be obtained
by division of labor, piecework incentive, and careful use of time. He used the
stopwatch to assist with his attempts to become more productive and efficient. In 1903 he produced a handbook, "Shop Management," published
under the auspices of the American Society of Mechanical Engineers.[4] His
philosophy was indicated by the definition he presented of the art of management, "knowing exactly what you want men to do, and then seeing that
they do it in the best and cheapest way." He also suggested "it is safe to say
that no system or scheme of management should be considered which does
not in the long run give satisfaction to both employer and employee."

Taylor advocated the division of labor, getting away from the "single
gang boss" or "military type of organization" and moving toward what he
called "functional management." This meant dividing the work so that each
worker, from the assistant superintendent on down, would have as few
functions as possible to perform and thus could do the work well. His
plan included organizing along the following lines:

(1) Route clerks, (2) instruction card clerks, (3) cost and time clerks, who plan
and give directions from the planning room, (4) gang bosses, (5) speed bosses,
(6) inspectors, (7) repair bosses, who show the men how to carry out their
instructions, and see that the work is done at the proper speed, and (8) the shop
disciplinarian, who performs this function for the entire establishment.
    The greatest good resulting from this change is that it becomes possible in a
comparatively short time to train bosses who can really and fully perform the
functions demanded of them, while under the old system it took years to train
men who were after all able to thoroughly perform only a portion of their
duties.[5]

Taylor demonstrated the practicality of his philosophy and system by
experimenting with the handling of pig iron at the Bethlehem Steel Company
around the turn of the nineteenth century. By substituting piecework for day
work, the workers were able to increase their daily earnings from $1.15 to
$1.88, and the average cost for handling a ton of pig iron was reduced from
seven cents to three cents.[6]

[3]Robert M. Fulmer, *The New Management*, 2nd ed. (New York: Macmillan, 1978), pp. 27–28.
    [4]Frederick W. Taylor, "Shop Management," in Frederick W. Taylor, *Scientific Management*
(New York: Harper & Row, 1911).
    [5]Ibid., p. 104.
    [6]Ibid., p. 54.

While Taylor was making an impression on production in the United States, a contemporary, Henri Fayol, a French mining engineer, was advocating numerous changes to improve production in his country. His philosophy and guidelines were presented in a book published in 1916, *General and Industrial Management*, in which he described and emphasized the following principles of management:

1. Division of work
2. Authority
3. Discipline
4. Unity of command
5. Unity of direction
6. Subordination of individual interests to the general interest
7. Remuneration
8. Centralization
9. Scalar chair (line of authority)
10. Order
11. Equity
12. Stability of tenure of personnel
13. Initiative
14. Esprit de corps[7]

He maintained strong convictions about the importance of his principles of management and claimed that his code was indispensable: "Be it a case of commerce, industry, politics, religion, war, or philanthropy, in every concern there is a management function to be performed, and for its performance there must be principles, that is to say acknowledged truths regarded as proven on which to rely. And it is the code which represents the sum total of these truths at any given moment."[8]

Henry L. Gantt, a contemporary of Taylor, was one of the first persons to pioneer in the "humanizing of the science of management."[9] He opposed dictatorial decisions and autocratic domination, stating that knowledge of human activities was essential for effective management. In 1910 he published a book, *Work, Wages, and Profits*, in which he presented practical ideas about management, including application of the scientific method to labor problems, utilization of labor, advantages and disadvantages of day work and piecework, and rewards for both supervisors and workers. In 1916 he wrote *Industrial Leadership*, in which he stressed his ideas about the importance of the human elements and activities in production. He suggested

[7]Henri Fayol, "General Principles of Management," reprinted in Harry A. Shatz, ed., *Social Work Administration: A Resource Book* (New York: Council on Social Work Education, 1970), p. 145.

[8]Ibid., p. 158.

[9]Fulmer, *New Management*, p. 32.

the famous chart that bears his name, a time chart to help with effective production.

Frank Gilbreth, in the early decades of the twentieth century, made significant contributions to the improvement of scientific management. He conducted motion studies to ascertain the importance of various characteristics of workers and of the various movements they performed. He endeavored to find the most efficient and effective patterns in production and formulated sets of rules to help bring about improvements. In 1908 Gilbreth published his *Field System*, in which he explained many of his basic ideas, rules, and suggestions. He suggested thirty-four "General Rules" for improving production and management, including the following:

> Address all communications to Frank B. Gilbreth, and not to any other name.
>
> Estimates are not to be given by anyone, at any time, without first consulting the Office.
>
> Consult Office about itemizing workman's time so that costs may be compared with similar jobs and with our estimate book.
>
> When men are wanted, ask the Office.
>
> Do not bother the Office unnecessarily.
>
> Union laborers are to be given preference at all times, but no nonsense is to be taken from them.
>
> Blow one blast of whistle at 5 minutes before starting time. Two blasts at starting time. One blast at quitting time. Blasts of whistle to be not over 4 seconds long.
>
> All men are expected to quit work at quitting time as promptly as they began work.
>
> No smoking is allowed on the job except to finish noon smoke—not over one half hour—and no refilling of pipes. All steady pay men must see that this rule is enforced.[10]

Frank and Lillian Gilbreth, husband and wife, made various additional contributions to the fields of scientific management and personnel management. They gained recognition as efficiency experts, in particular through the popular book *Cheaper by the Dozen*, which appeared in 1948 and was written by two of the Gilbreth children.

Fulmer notes that Elton Mayo is often referred to as the "father of human relations."[11] His famous Hawthorne experiments and studies emphasized the importance of human attitudes and feelings in management and production as well as the rights of employees. Various working conditions, such as light, heat, and room color, were studied at the Hawthorne plant of Western Electric, near Chicago. Six of the regular employees were moved to a special location, where careful observation of their actions indicated an

---

[10]William R. Spriegel and Clark E. Myers, eds., *The Writings of the Gilbreths* (Homewood, IL: Richard D. Irwin, 1953), pp. 9–11.

[11]Fulmer, *New Management*, pp. 36–37.

increase in productivity. The studies showed that when workers were given special attention, their productivity increased; what the special attention was mattered almost not at all. Fulmer observed that the Hawthorne studies demonstrated that

1. Man's social and psychological needs are every bit as effective as motivators as money.
2. The social interaction of the work group is as influential as the organization of the actual work task.
3. The human factor cannot be ignored in any accurate management planning.[12]

Although subsequent studies have raised some valid questions about the Hawthorne experiments, their emphasis on the importance of social interaction, special treatment, attitudes toward work, and workers' status has not been renounced. Morale and production level involve social as well as physical factors.

In recent years several writers have made excellent contributions to management efficiency and effectiveness. Douglas McGregor suggested his famous X and Y theories about human performance on the job, based on a comparative study of the operations of management development programs in a number of large companies.[13] In his volume *The Human Side of Enterprise*, he attempted to substantiate the thesis that the "human side of enterprise is 'all of a piece'—that the theoretical assumptions management holds about controlling its human resources determine the whole character of the enterprise."[14]

Theory X describes the working situation in which leaders are authoritative, autocratic, and maintain close control. Workers play a minor role in decision making. McGregor suggested that behind every managerial decision or action, there are assumptions about human nature and human behavior, and the following are significant in relation to Theory X, the traditional view of direction and control.

1. The average human being has an inherent dislike of work and will avoid it if he can.
2. Because of this human characteristic of dislike of work, most people must be coerced, controlled, directed, threatened with punishment to get them to put forth adequate effort toward the achievement of organizational objectives.
3. The average human being prefers to be directed, wishes to avoid responsibility, has relatively little ambition, wants security above all.[15]

Theory Y, diametrically the opposite of Theory X in many ways, stresses a work climate and situation in which democratic participation is practiced

[12]Ibid., p. 37.
[13]Douglas McGregor, *The Human Side of Enterprise* (New York: McGraw-Hill, 1960).
[14]Ibid., pp. vi–vii.
[15]Ibid., pp. 33–34.

and the rights and suggestions of the workers are encouraged and supported. Following are some of the basic assumptions related to Theory Y:

1. The expenditure of physical and mental effort in work is as natural as play or rest.
2. External control and the threat of punishment are not the only means for bringing about effort toward organizational objectives. Workers will exercise self-direction and self-control in the service of objectives to which they are committed.
3. Commitment to objectives is a function of the rewards associated with their achievement. The most significant of such rewards—namely, the satisfaction of ego and self-actualization needs—can be direct products of effort directed toward organizational objectives.
4. The average human being learns, under proper conditions, not only to accept but to seek responsibility.
5. The capacity to exercise a relatively high degree of imagination, ingenuity, and creativity in the solution of organizational problems is widely, not narrowly, distributed in the population.
6. Under the conditions of modern industrial life, the intellectual potentialities of the average human being are only partially utilized.[16]

In recent years a Theory Z has been proposed (along with other approaches) that suggests a middle ground between Theories X and Y.

Another major management development has been MBO (management by objectives), first used by Peter Drucker in his *Practice of Management* in 1954, and since adopted by other management theorists and administrators. The use of this system, with some modifications, has gained momentum, both in government agencies and in the private sector. Odiorne, who has interpreted and popularized MBO, describes its basic premises as follows:

A. Business management takes place within an economic system that provides the environmental situation for the individual firm. This environment, which has changed drastically over the past 30 years, imposes new requirements on companies and on individual managers.
B. Management by objectives is a way of managing aimed at meeting these new requirements. It presumes that the first step in management is to identify, by one means or another, the goals of the organizations. All other management methods and sub-systems follow this preliminary step.
C. Once organizational goals have been identified, orderly procedures for distributing responsibilities among individual managers are set up in such a way that their combined efforts are directed toward achieving those goals.
D. Management by objectives assumes that managerial behavior is more important than manager personality, and that this behavior should be defined in terms of results measured against established goals, rather than in terms of common goals for all managers, or common methods of managing.
E. It also presumes that while participation is highly desirable in goal-setting and decision-making, its principal merit lies in its social and political values rather

[16]Ibid., pp. 47–48.

than in its effects on production, though even here it may have a favorable impact, and in any case seldom hurts.

F. It regards the successful manager as a manager of situations, most of which are best defined by identifying the purpose of the organization and the managerial behavior best calculated to achieve that purpose.[17]

Administrators in many social agencies are utilizing the MBO approach; others question its use in human services. Where it is used, specific objectives are often formulated for departments or divisions and for individual workers, in addition to the agency objectives. In social work, goals and objectives are achieved on a participatory basis, generally involving workers at all levels. After objectives have been formulated, every effort is made to achieve these targets through effective activities and practice. In particular, emphasis is placed periodically on the actual "output" that results from the efforts. The important fact is that appropriate goals or objectives are set and then regular evaluations depict the outcomes. Further goals and objectives are based on these results.

Another significant approach to management is an industrial psychological theory proposed by Frederick Herzberg—the motivation-hygiene theory. The theory was presented in 1959 in *The Motivation to Work*[18] and was further developed in *Work and the Nature of Man*,[19] published in 1966. Herzberg, after his studies on job satisfaction and dissatisfaction of employees in numerous work settings, claimed that many of the traditionally revered factors in the working system—such as salaries and fringe benefits—are not nearly so important in relation to motivation and production as had been thought. He concluded that the following factors could lead to job dissatisfaction: company policy and administration, supervision, interpersonal relations, working conditions, salary, status, and security. In contrast, job satisfaction and concomitant motivation relate especially to opportunities for achievement, recognition for achievement, work itself, responsibility, advancement, and growth. He suggested that the hygiene factors are necessary to prevent discontent with a job; but the second group of factors, which provide for psychological growth, are particularly significant for motivation and effective production.[20]

Management has come a long way from its roots of the past. Today numerous schools of business are offering curricula for training students in management to meet the changing needs of the times.

[17]George S. Odiorne, *Management by Objectives: A System of Managerial Leadership*. Copyright ©1965 by Pitman Publishing Corporation. Reprinted by permission of Pitman Learning, Inc., Belmont, California.

[18]Frederick Herzberg, Bernard Mausner, and Barbara Snyderman, *The Motivation to Work* (New York: John Wiley, 1959).

[19]Frederick Herzberg, *Work and the Nature of Man* (New York: Thomas Y. Crowell, 1966).

[20]Frederick Herzberg, *The Managerial Choice: To Be Efficient and to Be Human* (Homewood, IL: Dow Jones-Irwin, 1976), pp. 49–101.

ADMINISTRATION'S ROOTS IN SOCIAL WORK

Social work as a profession is relatively young. Although disadvantaged people have been aided, directly or indirectly, for centuries by individuals, groups, or organizations, formalized, professional social work education evolved from simple beginnings. At the turn of the nineteenth century, short-term courses were first offered at Columbia University, the University of Chicago, Boston University, and the University of Pennsylvania. Educational and professional associations came into existence gradually, but it was only in 1955 that the National Association of Social Workers was formed, when seven different social work associations joined together. In 1952 the Council on Social Work Education was created and became a viable national educational organization for providing guidelines, accreditation standards and reviews, and resource materials for schools of social work, agencies, and individual members.

In education, as mentioned earlier, a course in administration was offered by a school of social work in 1914. By 1944 the revised curriculum statement for the American Association of Schools of Social Work listed administration as one of the basic eight subjects that should be offered in all schools of social work. Later curriculum statements have become more general and generic and do not specifically require administration. However, schools may offer administration as a concentration or major; fifty-five schools of social work were doing so in 1992.

Social work literature has been limited in the administration area, although many publications about social work knowledge and skills have included materials and cases in this field. Harleigh Trecker, Elwood Street, Ella Reed, and others have provided introductory books on administration.[21] A major theoretical social work contribution was Volume III of the curriculum study of the Council on Social Work Education, which appeared in 1959.[22] This study indicated that administration had reached a significant level in social work education and practice, and it suggested that graduate students could receive sound training for administration positions with two years of graduate study. No attempt was made to distinguish between administration and community organization. The study pointed up the following:

1. The importance of administrative practice to the profession of social work;
2. The necessity that all graduates of schools of social work have preparation sufficient to enable them to fulfill their roles appropriately in the administrative structure and processes of the agency in which they are employed;

[21]Harleigh B. Trecker, *Group Process in Administration* (New York: Woman's Press, 1946); Elwood Street, *A Handbook for Social Agency Administration* (New York: Harper & Brothers, 1947); Ella W. Reed, ed., *Social Welfare Administration* (New York: Columbia University Press, 1961).

[22]Sue Spencer, *The Administration Method of Social Work Education* (New York: Council on Social Work Education, 1959).

3. That this preparation should also be adequate to serve as the basis for further on-the-job and post graduate level training in administration to facilitate promotions to higher level positions and more adequate functioning at lower levels;

4. That the preparation of personnel for direct entry into executive and subexecutive level positions immediately after graduation is an appropriate function in the schools of social work within the Master's level curriculum; and

5. That the matter of who should be admitted to such a program of study (see 4 above) is a career-advising or student-advising function.[23]

In 1970 the CSWE published two volumes on administration that indicated its growing interest in this field: *Social Work Administration: A Resource Book* and *A Casebook in Social Work Administration*.[24] The first volume includes forty articles and reprints from materials relevant to administration and was developed as a resource book for students and practitioners. Up-to-date articles are included, as well as writings from the past, such as Max Weber's "Bureaucracy" and Henri Fayol's "General Principles of Management." The *Casebook*, a companion volume, contains twenty-five examples of practical experience from a variety of settings.

A major step took place in the spring of 1977 with the appearance of the initial issue of a professional journal, *Administration in Social Work*. It is a reputable quarterly publication devoted to the "theory and practice of management and administration in social work and related human services fields."

Philosophically, the basic position of social work in administration is that principles of management, efficiency, and effectiveness should be utilized but must relate to a framework based on sound human relations. The "human" factor in administration is of particular concern to social work. Not only what the worker does is important, but also how he or she feels about it, both in relation to performance and mental well-being. The focus of administration is respect for the integrity of each person, so that each worker will be a key person in the total administration of an agency.

SOME BASIC PRINCIPLES

The following principles are significant in relation to effective social work administration:

Acceptance.   Leaders and staff members are encouraged and expected to accept one another and to act accordingly. The goal is to draw from each staff member his or her best resources and abilities in helping the agency in

---

[23]Ibid., p. 20.

[24]Harry A. Schatz, ed., *Social Work Administration: A Resource Book* (New York: Council on Social Work Education, 1970); Harry A. Schatz, ed., *A Casebook in Social Work Administration* (New York: Council on Social Work Education, 1970).

the delivery of services. This does not rule out evaluations and suggestions for improvements but does mean that all staff members feel a basic security as individuals, with rights as well as responsibilities.

Democratic Involvement in Formulation of Agency Policies and Procedures. Social work suggests that as staff members become a part of participatory administration, they perform better, and so does the agency. They favor the philosophy of McGregor's Theory Y.

Open Communication. Open communication means that a worker may, at almost any time, share ideas and feelings with other staff members and act and react with honesty and integrity. Two-way communication provides a sound framework for the development of efficiency and effectiveness in administrative policies and procedures.

A succinct statement of basic principles of social work administration was offered by Trecker, a pioneer social work administrator:

1. *The principle of social work values*: The values of the profession are the foundations upon which services are developed and made available to persons who need them.
2. *The principle of community and client needs*: The needs of the community and the individuals within it are always the basis for the existence of social agencies and the provision of programs.
3. *The principle of agency purpose*: The social purposes of the agency must be clearly formulated, stated, understood, and utilized.
4. *The principle of cultural setting*: The culture of the community must be understood inasmuch as it influences the way needs are expressed and the way services are authorized, supported, and utilized by people who need them.
5. *The principle of purposeful relationships*: Effective, purposeful working relationships must be established between the administrator, the board, the staff, and the constituency.
6. *The principle of agency totality*: The agency must be understood in its totality and wholeness. It must be seen as a living instrumentality made up of interrelated parts.
7. *The principle of professional responsibility*: The administrator is responsible for the provision of high-quality professional services based on standards of professional practice.
8. *The principle of participation*: Appropriate contributions of board, staff, and constituency are sought and utilized through the continuous process of dynamic participation.
9. *The principle of communication*: Open channels of communication are essential to the complete functioning of people.
10. *The principle of leadership*: The administrator must carry major responsibility for the leadership of the agency in terms of goal attainment and the provision of professional services.
11. *The principle of planning*: The process of continuous planning is fundamental to the development of meaningful services.

12. *The principle of organization*: The work of many people must be arranged in an organized manner and must be structured so that responsibilities and relationships are clearly defined.
13. *The principle of delegation*: The delegation of responsibility and authority to other professional persons is essential.
14. *The principle of coordination*: The work delegated to many people must be properly coordinated so that specific contributions are brought to bear upon the major tasks of the agency and all energy is rightly focused upon the mission to be accomplished.
15. *The principle of resource utilization*: The resources of money, facilities, and personnel must be carefully fostered, conserved, and utilized in keeping with the trust granted to the agency by society.
16. *The principle of change*: The process of change is continuous, both within the community and within the agency.
17. *The principle of evaluation*: Continuous evaluation of processes and programs is essential to the fulfillment of the agency's objectives.
18. *The principle of growth*: The growth and development of all participants is furthered by the administrator who provides challenging work assignments, thoughtful supervision, and opportunities for individual and group learning.[25]

CASE EXAMPLE

In 1970 the CSWE recognized that preparation for administrative practice was emerging as a new or expanding option in the MSW program and that teaching materials were limited in this area. They published a casebook,[26] with twenty-five examples of practical experiences. A brief case is presented from this pioneer book to illustrate some of the factors and feelings involved in an administrative action—promotion of a staff member. Current case materials are offered in other chapters.

SENIORITY VS. ABILITY: A PROBLEM
IN STAFF PROMOTION AND RELATIONSHIPS _____

This case situation is an actual experience of mine as a director of a small agency with a staff of 14 persons. With such a small staff there was an unusual amount of personal interaction—the staff was all female.

I had been on the staff some 45 days when it was apparent that I would have to promote one of the present staff persons to the number-one position. The person in line for promotion because of seniority and educational qualifications was of such a personality, with a forte of being disorganized and not very well liked by several staff members, that I felt it would be extremely difficult to work with her.

[25]Harleigh B. Trecker, *Social Work Administration: Principles and Practices* (New York: Association Press, 1971), pp. 186–194.
[26]Harry A. Schatz, ed., *A Casebook in Social Work Administration* (New York: Council on Social Work Education, 1970).

She had presented me with her resume and I had discussed same with her. I had not been impressed with her job performance, however; she had been with the agency for nearly a year and was a mainstay during the turmoil suffered by the agency because it had been without a director for most of its existence.

The agency exists to provide day care for 160 children, ages one year through twelve. Originally the agency was an extension of the Head Start concept. Instead of providing a setting for children in a centrally housed program, children would be kept in home settings and furnished with educational and recreational activities, combined with nourishing lunches and snacks and a health program.

The agency had been in operation for nearly a year when I was hired as executive director. The staff was confused and there was no real supervision being done by supervisors and everyone was trying to run the agency. The program was suffering from lack of direction and the staff was plagued by constant crises situations.

During my initial briefing by the Board of Directors, I had been told that one of my first tasks would be to hire a person to fill the position of Day Care Counselor. This seemingly simple task was complicated by several factors.

First, the agency served a predominantly Spanish-speaking clientele, which meant that this person must be bi-lingual. My preference was that the person be Puerto Rican. Second, the qualifications for this position and the salary were not at all commensurate.

I went through the process of interviewing and came up with nothing. There were two supervisors on staff, both bi-lingual. One had been there for nearly a year; the other had only been there three months. The supervisor with seniority was the one that had to be seriously considered; but I saw clearly that she just was not the person for the position and I could not in good conscience promote her. The second supervisor, on the other hand, displayed great possibilities for the position. She was conscientious, organized, and in possession of a quality which seemed to me to be tantamount to the position available.

To add to my frustration was the fact that the position should be filled by a person with a college degree plus experience. The supervisor with seniority was receiving her degree in four months and the other supervisor only had three years of college.

I interviewed the supervisor with seniority, then discussed my findings, observations, reservations, and feelings with the Board of Directors. There were several alternatives which could have been pursued in handling the situation. For example, the senior supervisor had expressed her intention to resign in about four months, so I could have simply waited for her resignation; a second alternative would have been to allow the Board of Directors to handle the situation by dictating to me the course of action and, perhaps, finally to have named the senior supervisor as "acting Day Care Counselor" (this was the title of the position open) in hopes that she would resign, because, as acting Day Care Counselor, I could offer her less than the called-for salary.

As a new director and interested in establishing authority and quality relations with staff, I felt that I could not pursue the above alternatives. To have chosen the first would have crippled the services of the agency in that the Day Care Counselor really runs the program and is responsible for recruitment. To choose the second alternative would say to the Board that they had chosen a director who was incapable of handling problems in depth and perhaps would have set a precedent that would have plagued me throughout my employment at the agency. The third alternative would have been a "stop-gap" measure which would have been unsatisfactory to me as well as perhaps affecting the performance of the senior supervisor if she should choose to accept the position as acting counselor. Thus, weighing these points, I felt my only course of action was to promote the other supervisor and deal directly with the repercussions of the senior supervisor and those staff members who were close to her.

With Board approval, I promoted the supervisor who did not have seniority. I was immediately hit by disgruntled feelings on the part of the senior supervisor. Also, several staff persons were raising questions about my decision.

In order to handle the feelings aroused, I called in the senior supervisor and gave her the opportunity to express her feelings to me directly. Then I called in the newly appointed Day Care Counselor, who, incidently, became the supervisor of the woman who had seniority, and laid out the kind of working relationship which I expected to be carried out by them. I followed this up by stating to the senior supervisor that if she felt that she could not abide by my decision and continue to perform her job, I would gladly give her a recommendation for another job at another agency.

Following this confrontation, I called the staff together and heard their feelings on the matter. Then I shared with them the basic details of my decision and told them my expectations relative to their job performance.

Naturally, this did not cause everyone to love me, nor did everyone submit to me as little children—however, that was not what I wanted. What I was interested in was communicating with my staff and keeping lines of communication open so that I could receive feedback. Furthermore, I was interested in the staff understanding that I was forthright and open in my decisions and that I also was able to stand behind such decisions.

Source: Harry A. Schatz, ed., *A Casebook in Social Work Administration* (New York: Council on Social Work Education, 1970), pp. 73-74. Reprinted by permission.

SUMMARY

Although knowledge of and skills in administration have roots in earlier centuries, it is mainly in the nineteenth and twentieth centuries that advancements have been made in education and effective practice.

Management in business was developed by several pioneers in administration, including Frederick W. Taylor, Charles Babbage, Henry L. Gantt, Frank Gilbreth, George Odiorne, and Frederick Herzberg. Their contributions and those of others constitute a science of management that is taught and practiced not only in the business world but also in government and other related fields. Management today has been particularly interested in motivation and accountability, as well as in efficiency and effectiveness.

The roots of social work administration are found in the nineteenth century, but formal developments in education and practice belong to the past few decades.

Management, which stresses production and efficiency, and social work, which underlines human relationships, are coming together in social work administration, and the resulting blend involves the best of each. Social work administration is offered as a major in schools of social work and is considered a significant method in the delivery of social services.

Social workers are beginning to provide significant literature in administration as a practice method. The inauguration of a professional journal in 1977, *Administration in Social Work*, was a major step forward.

QUESTIONS FOR DISCUSSION

1. Compare and contrast administration in social work and business management. What do they have in common?

2. Describe major contributions of the following pioneers in management and administration: Frederick W. Taylor, Henry L. Gantt, Frederick Herzberg, Harleigh Trecker, and Sue Spencer.

3. How do you compare the importance of efficiency in production and the importance of human relationships in the administrative process in social work?

4. Evaluate the famous Hawthorne experiments and studies in relation to the effective delivery of social services.

5. Describe the main characteristics of the X, Y, and Z theories about human performance on the job, and indicate which theory is most applicable to social work.

6. Do you favor "participatory management" in providing social work services? Why or why not?

7. Consider the basic principles of social work administration presented by Harleigh Trecker and pick out two or three you think are particularly significant. Why?

SPECIAL ACTIVITIES

1. Interview a business executive in your community and ask him or her to tell you what some of the most important principles and practices are in successful management.

2. Demonstrate through role playing the importance of feelings in the administrative process in a social work agency.

3. Read the article by Edith Fein and Ilene Staff on the use of time in administration. Do you agree or disagree with their conclusions?

4. Evaluate the case "Seniority vs. Ability." What actions do you agree with? Disagree with?

SELECTED REFERENCES

AUSTIN, DAVID M. "The Human Service Executive." *Administration in Social Work* 13, Nos. 3/4 (1989), 13–36.

BEDEIAN, ARTHUR G. *Management*, 3rd ed. Fort Worth, TX: Dryden Press, 1993.

CARLISLE, HOWARD M. *Management Essentials: Concepts for Productivity and Innovation*, 2nd ed. Chicago: Science Research Associates, 1987.

FEIN, EDITH, and ILENE STAFF. "Measuring the Use of Time." *Administration in Social Work* 15, No. 4 (1991), 81–93.

FULMER, ROBERT M. *The New Management*, 4th ed. New York: Macmillan, 1988.

HART, AILEEN F. "Clinical Social Work and Social Administration: Bridging the Culture Gap." *Administration in Social Work* 8 (Fall 1984), 71–78.

HERZBERG, FREDERICK. *The Managerial Choice: To Be Efficient and to Be Human*. Homewood, IL: Dow Jones-Irwin, 1976.

PATTI, RINO J. *Social Welfare Administration: Managing Social Programs in a Developmental Context*. Englewood Cliffs, NJ: Prentice Hall, 1983.

SLAVIN, SIMON, ed. *Social Administration: The Management of the Social Services*, 2nd ed. Vol. I, *An Introduction to Human Services Management*. New York: Haworth Press, 1985.

TEICHER, MORTON I. "Who Should Manage a Social Agency?" in Simon Slavin, ed., *Social Administration: The Management of the Social Services*, 2nd ed. Vol. I, *An Introduction to Human Services Management*, pp. 44–49. New York: Haworth Press, 1985.

WEINER, MYRON E. *Human Services Management, Analysis and Applications*. Homewood, IL: Dorsey Press, 1982.

3

The Social Work Administrator

Nancy and Jill graduated with MSW degrees in June and accepted posi-
tions in welfare departments located in cities fifty miles apart. Two
months later they met for lunch to talk about their experiences and
futures. Nancy reported that her director was authoritative, rigid, and
demanding and had little respect for her as a person or worker. She had
already started to look for another position. Jill, in contrast, indicated
that her director was the opposite in every way, an executive who showed
interest in her and each member of the staff and who was doing every-
thing possible to facilitate her social work practice. She summarized her
feelings when she noted, "He really cares about us, and this makes all
the difference in the world."

It is obvious that the two working climates were not the same. Admin-
istrators do make a difference. Their abilities and behaviors readily affect
outcomes in the delivery of social services. In many ways, the leader is
the major contributing factor to the success or failure of an agency.

As mentioned previously, sooner or later most MSW graduates become
administrators. What will they be like? What should they be like, to be effective leaders? How do they become executives?

Most social workers who become social work administrators have been
practitioners; relatively few are especially trained for leadership positions,
although the number of students majoring in administration is on the
increase in graduate schools of social work. Some schools provide a two-year
concentration in administration, whereas others offer a generic first year with
a second year devoted to specializing in the knowledge, attitudes, and
methodology of administration. Most graduate schools of social work offer

classes or units in their curriculum in administration, so all students acquire fundamental concepts, principles, and skills related to management and leadership. These can be valuable in the years ahead, especially for those who are appointed administrators.

NASW GUIDELINES

What are the skills and characteristics of successful social work administrators? A committee for the NASW studied this question carefully and concluded that the successful administrator should have the ability to:

1. Think and plan ahead realistically.
2. Assess the feasibility of a particular plan.
3. Consider alternative ways of doing things.
4. Foresee and appraise the likely impact of decisions.
5. Set priorities.
6. Make decisions.
7. Handle multiple roles and tasks simultaneously.
8. Maintain personal equilibrium.
9. Understand the functioning of the bureaucratic systems and of organizational theory and utilize this understanding to achieve agency goals.
10. Get others to work productively utilizing specific talents of individuals and groups and offsetting their limitations.
11. Use and delegate authority constructively.
12. Communicate effectively with others.
13. Act decisively.[1]

Social workers often explain that their education involved the acquisition of knowledge, professional attitudes, and skills. This framework, applied to administrators, suggests an overall description of what a top-notch administrator should be. No administrator is perfect, or even close to it, but the more he or she understands the administrative process and possesses administrative skills, the more likely is the agency and its operation to be effective in the delivery of social services to people in need.

KNOWLEDGE OF THE SOCIAL WORK ADMINISTRATOR

Adequate knowledge of administration is essential for the effective operation of a social work agency. Following are brief descriptions of salient areas of knowledge.

The Administrator Knows the Agency's Goals, Policies, Services, and Resources. The administrator understands clearly the specific targets and

[1]"Social Work Administration" (New York: National Association of Social Workers, 1968), p. 9.

objectives of the agency and is committed to attaining them. He or she is well versed in the policies of the agency, understands them, what they are and what they are not, and does everything possible to carry them out. He or she understands the importance of sound policies and the processes for changing them if such a need arises.

The administrator has a clear understanding of the services that are being performed or might be performed. He or she is aware of the clientele to be served as well as the means for serving them. The executive knows of the current resources, financial and otherwise, of the agency and understands the routes to be taken for increasing resources if the need arises.

The administrator knows the significant details of the agency manuals, historical background, and the highlights of what has happened in the past and is likely to happen in the future.

A successful agency director spends a few hours each week reviewing goals, policies, resources, and challenges; consequently he or she plans effectively for the present and the future.

The Administrator Has a Basic Knowledge of the Dynamics of Human Behavior. This forms a sound base for understanding self, staff, and clients. The administrator knows that people are complex and that their behavior stems from the totality of their component parts, including biological, psychological, social, cultural, and ethical. A leader realizes that human behavior derives from the interaction of individuals with their total environment, especially association with other people.

The administrator knows that staff will act and react in accordance with principles of human behavior and recognizes that to get along effectively with them, he or she will need to keep abreast of the literature about the dynamics of human behavior.

He or she realizes that feelings and emotions of associates are often more important than the knowledge they possess; this, of course, is also applicable to clients who come to the agency.

The Administrator Has a Comprehensive Knowledge of Community Resources, Especially Those Related to His or Her Own Agency. The knowledge of community resources includes a clear understanding of the purposes and services of community agencies, as well as ways of making referrals to them.

Ordinarily, the administrator would have a personal acquaintance and working relationship with executives and other leaders of key agencies in the community, especially those that take referrals from his or her agency. The administrator is acquainted not only with the public and private agencies available but also with professional people in private practice who can be reached if necessary.

Often a major service of social work is to "get Ms. Jones to the proper clinic." This process is facilitated when the administrator knows about and is able to make referrals to appropriate agencies for clients who come to the agency.

The Administrator Understands the Social Work Methods Used in the Agency.   The administrator does not need to be a practicing expert in each method but should have a basic understanding of casework, group work, community organization, and research, in addition to a comprehensive understanding of the principles, processes, and skills of administration. The leader should be aware that the problem-solving process is shared by all of these methods. Case management (see Chapter 4) is a process that is currently receiving considerable attention and use in strengthening social work services. It focuses on planning, coordinating, and integrating the network of services being tapped in the helping process. It derives some principles and skills from casework, group work, and community organization. Case managers are being hired to play significant roles in improving and tightening services in larger agencies.

The administrator knows of resources that can be tapped to improve the skills and abilities of line workers. He or she is aware of staff development programs and techniques, workshop possibilities, and continuing educational programs that are available.

The Administrator Knows Management Principles, Processes, and Techniques.   The administrator has a basic understanding of the five fundamental processes that have been traditionally emphasized in business management: planning, organizing, staffing, directing, and controlling. He or she is aware of the subprocesses involved in each of these categories and is able to use the relevant knowledge in advancing the welfare of the agency through the utilization of management principles and techniques.

The administrator realizes that it is imperative to combine the resources from the areas of management and human relations into an integrated operation involving techniques and skills from each. He or she is conversant with current literature both in management and human relations.

The Administrator Is Well Acquainted with the Professional Associations in Social Work.   The administrator knows about the purposes and activities of the National Association of Social Workers, Council on Social Work Education, and other related national and local organizations. In particular, the administrator is knowledgeable about NASW and is an active member of the local group. He or she realizes the professional association has limitations; but in its relatively short existence, its contributions have been substantial for the advancement and welfare of its members and social work as a whole.

In addition, the administrator is knowledgeable about the professions of psychiatry, psychology, nursing, law, medicine, and others related to social work. He or she knows about their goals, standards, and services and has working relationships with leaders from each group.

The Administrator Understands Organizational Theory. The administrator is aware of different kinds of organizational patterns and can direct them in a competent manner. Such an understanding makes it possible to consider changes in the agency's organization, if that is deemed advisable.

The administrator understands how the organization works and its strengths and limitations. He or she also knows how it fits into the community, structurally and functionally. The leader is aware of other organizational patterns that might be utilized if a need for change arises.

The Administrator Knows Evaluation Processes and Techniques. The administrator knows enough to be able to introduce evaluative research in the agency regarding services being performed and to evaluate staff members and their contributions, both positive and negative.

The administrator realizes that we live in an age of accountability, that social work is being asked, as never before, to demonstrate that it can make a difference in the lives of people through its services. He or she is knowledgeable about MBO, systems analysis, strategic planning, and other management methods, so that these might be used to advantage at appropriate times and places.

Program evaluation is currently recognized as an essential process in providing effective social services. It considers the totality of agency policies and goals and its organization and attempts to find, clarify, and measure the results of its services.

The leader knows what it means to be evaluated as a staff member and works out the best pattern—just and effective—for his or her own staff evaluations. The administrator invites the staff to be part of the system that is agreed upon.

ATTITUDES OF THE ADMINISTRATOR

In addition to substantive knowledge, competent social work administrators possess a cluster of professional attitudes, which are essential for relationships with staff and community. Attitudes are predispositions to act and are intertwined with the feelings of people, which are so important in the administrative process. If a staff member feels unfairly treated, he or she will be likely to respond negatively, regardless of the facts. If an executive feels genuinely positive toward a worker, the message comes through verbally as well as nonverbally.

Some significant attitudes necessary for successful administrators in social work are as follows:

The Administrator Respects Each Staff Member as a Unique Individual. The administrator feels that each person is intrinsically important and deserves the trust and confidence of the leader.

The administrator respects the integrity of each person, his or her privacy when appropriate, and the right to be a self-determining individual within the agency framework.

The administrator thinks that the human personality is the most valuable component in an agency and that staff members can make or break the agency. The administrator recognizes that each staff member is unique, with strengths and limitations, and that he or she should do everything possible to bring out the best in each.

The Administrator Recognizes That No Person Is Perfect and Accepts This Premise Regarding Staff and Self. The administrator accepts each staff member for what that person is and hopes to help each one achieve what he or she wants. Then staff members know they can make mistakes and be understood and helped, rather than be bruised or battered psychologically. Consequently staff members feel that the administrator recognizes self-limitations and is humble about his or her actions. The administrator's attitude is realistic and mature. He or she reaches for the best but acknowledges that no one attains the optimum in knowledge, wisdom, or practice.

The administrator readily admits mistakes, is realistic, and recognizes that he or she is not perfect, any more than are staff members. Such administrators do not pretend to be something they are not.

The Administrator Wishes to Provide a Physical Setting and Emotional Climate That Will Help Bring Out the Best in Each Staff Member. Each staff member senses that the leader will do everything possible to improve physical facilities, if necessary, but in particular will provide an emotional and social climate that will be productive for all concerned.

This climate allows for freedom of expression and activity and for individual growth and development. Staff members feel that the "boss" really cares about each of them in a mature, accepting manner. The administrator feels that his or her job is to help each staff member gain daily satisfaction through achievement and growth, individually and professionally.

The Administrator Is Aware of the Importance of Values. The administrator has convictions about what is right and wrong for self, agency, staff, and other people. The leader does not impose these values on others but respects their values. As far as the agency is concerned, he or she thinks it is important for the staff to understand and agree upon the essential values concerning their operation. Appropriate action and services derive from values that people possess.

The leader brings a sense of dedication to the staff, based on humanitarianism and a notion of what is best for the majority. He or she does not compromise principles, maintains values in times of stress, and realizes that in one sense staff members are the heart of social work.

The Administrator Has an Open Mind and Is Receptive to New Ideas and Facts. Acceptance of reality is more important than trying to justify one's own preconceptions or biases. The leader recognizes that many changes are inevitable and has a positive attitude toward change, although not giving up previous convictions and values without sound reasons.

The administrator values flexibility, and the staff members feel they can adapt to changing situations without difficulty.

The Administrator Recognizes That the Welfare of the Agency Is More Important Than Any Worker, Including the Administrator. If a worker, or even a leader, should need to be replaced for the best interest of the agency, the administrator would not hesitate to help move in that direction. This does not mean that he or she would arbitrarily dismiss anyone. In fact, dismissal would come only after careful consideration and after attempts have been made to help the person who is not performing or achieving adequately.

The staff members feel that their supervisor would step down at any time if he or she felt it was in the best interest of the agency. Knowing that the importance of the agency as a whole supersedes the importance of individual staff members gives a sense of purpose and dedication to the staff.

The social work administrator demonstrates a positive, optimistic attitude toward the agency, staff, and self. He or she exudes a feeling of confidence that everything will work out well. At the same time, the administrator realizes and acknowledges that there is room for improvement and that he or she will do everything possible to help bring about positive change. He or she personifies the feeling that action is possible and rejects pessimism. The leader also trusts that services can be performed well and works for quality as well as achievement.

An effective administrator radiates an optimistic attitude toward social work and relationships with others, particularly staff members, giving them the feeling that policies and practices are basically sound and that together they can accomplish whatever is necessary.

ADMINISTRATORS IN ACTION

In addition to having knowledge and maintaining professional attitudes, effective social work administrators assume many roles and perform many managerial actions. In fact, a capable social work administrator is in motion in a variety of ways most of the time. Again, no one person can do everything that needs to be done—certainly not 100 percent of it—but the more he or she is able to do, the more likely it is that efficient and effective social services will be delivered.

Following are ways in which competent social work administrators can act:

1. Accepting. The social work administrator realistically accepts staff and clients as they are, as well as other professional personnel and leaders in the community with whom he or she works. The leader respects each person as a unique individual with assets and limitations, each striving toward becoming better.

The administrator helps set goals, standards, and guidelines for the staff. He or she encourages individual differences as providing color and warmth in human relationships, and invites each person to be oneself within the framework of the agency, organization, policies, and procedures.

2. Caring. The social work administrator emanates warmth and gives staff members a sense of belonging. Not only are staff members told he or she cares about them, but also, and more important, this is demonstrated by actions. The leader is interested in the staff and does everything possible to help each member develop and achieve. The administrator intertwines thinking and feelings in relationships with the staff. As a result, staff members know and feel they are important and that the administrator will relegate himself or herself to a secondary position vis à vis the employees' welfare. The leader respects and trusts staff members, and they know it. This does not mean that the administrator agrees with and approves of everything that is done but rather that he or she allows for differences and mistakes.

3. Creating. The social work administrator should be creative, one who likes to pioneer or establish innovative policies, methods, and procedures that will improve agency services and staff relationships. Such a person does not hesitate to change his or her attitude if it will bring about a change for the better; in fact, the leader is flexible and periodically spends time alone, as well as with others, endeavoring to find out about new and effective methods and procedures.

The administrator respects the past and gains perspective from it but emphasizes that the present and the future are particularly important. He or she does not hesitate to adopt new and even unusual innovations if they seem significant for the welfare of the agency and the community.

Edwards suggests that "creativity is not the exclusive property of the gifted few. It can be learned. And, once learned, the individual will be able to make a larger contribution to his or her organization."[2] He further explains that creative problem solving has rich possibilities as a management tool.

4. Democratizing. The social work administrator is an advocate of the democratic process. He or she respects the opinions and values of staff and

[2]Morris O. Edwards, "Creativity Solves Management Problems," *Journal of Systems Management* 26 (June 1975), 14.

others, realizing that through participation they can make the agency even better than it is. The leader attempts to involve staff members at all levels. The administrator is the first to recognize that every staff member can make contributions to the welfare of the agency if given a chance. He or she is not a dictator and is not autocratic.

The administrator reaches out for opinions and ideas from the staff and appreciates them. He or she respects the group process and recognizes that cooperation may often be the best way to handle a problem, decision, or planning need.

5. Trusting. The social work administrator has implicit trust in staff members. Their points of view and the opinions and data they present are respected, even though there may be differences between them about what they are doing. The administrator engenders confidence in staff members by not tearing them down, openly or covertly, but rather by manifesting trust and building them up.

Trust, according to Gibb, involves more than confidence. It "implies instinctive, unquestioning belief in and reliance upon something. . . . It is unstrategized and freely given. It is something very much like love, and its presence or absence can make a powerful difference in our lives."[3] He explains further that high levels of trust mobilize forces in persons and can produce the following effects:

BODYMIND PROCESS	HIGH TRUST LEVELS PRODUCE THESE EFFECTS
Motivation	Creates and mobilizes energy, increases strength and focus of motivation.
Consciousness	Unblocks energy flow, expands awareness, makes unconscious more available.
Perception	Increases acuity of perceptions, improves vision and perspective.
Emotionality	Feelings and emotions free to energize all processes of the bodymind.
Cognition	Frees energy for focus on thinking and problem solving.
Action	Release of person for proactive and spontaneous behavior.
Synergy	Total person freed for synergistic and holistic integration.[4]

6. Approving. The social work administrator understands that every person—staff or client—hungers for approval and recognition. He or she concurs with the statement of W. I. Thomas, social psychologist, who concluded

[3]Jack R. Gibb, *Trust: A New View of Personal and Organizational Development* (Los Angeles: Guild of Tutors Press, 1978), p. 14.
[4]Ibid., p. 22.

that "recognition" is one of the "four wishes" shared by all people and is accompanied by "response," another action akin to approval. The administrator gives praise and commendation when deserved, and often. This is done both in writing and verbally. The administrator understands that building up staff members' morale through appropriate approval and recognition benefits not only the staff but the agency as well. The giver of commendation benefits as well as the receiver. Approval is not given unless it is genuine and deserved.

7. Maintaining Personal Equilibrium and Balance. The social work administrator endeavors to live a well-rounded life that includes work, rest, play, and, for most, spirituality. He or she has a high regard for health, mental as well as physical, and endeavors to be as relaxed as possible. The administrator tries to keep frustrations and problems to a minimum so that they are not "taken out" on the staff.

The administrator is industrious and exemplifies the value of labor but takes time to rest and rejuvenate body and mind. He or she participates in recreational pursuits for relaxation and enjoyment, as well as to gain a renewal of energy. Golf, tennis, or other activities may be a regular part of a weekly regimen.

8. Planning. The administrator is proficient at utilizing the planning process and realizes that administrators either plan or perish. He or she knows from experience that effective planning can bring desired results and that lack of planning can weaken and destroy an agency or its services. The leader utilizes planning to help reach specific targets and agency goals. He or she encourages staff members to formulate individual objectives, department goals, and objectives for the agency as a whole.

9. Organizing. Effective organization follows sound planning; otherwise, the agency will be ineffective. A capable administrator has the ability to organize the agency and does so with the help of the board, staff, and clients. The agency is thus an efficient structure, with effective lines of authority and responsibility. He or she delegates some authority, but not too much, ordinarily giving each leader no more than five or six persons to direct.

The administrator provides a structure that allows for communication to flow in all directions, from top to bottom, bottom to top, and side to side. Authority is also granted to carry out assigned responsibilities.

10. Setting Priorities. The effective social work administrator understands that some goals and objectives are more important than others and that the selection process is a significant one. He or she is able to compare, contrast, and weigh the significance of each goal or operation proposed and come to a sound decision regarding its importance. The leader is able to explore various alternatives and determine the value of each in relation to the agency's services.

The administrator understands that some goals are short term and others are long term and that the difference has to be kept in mind as decisions are made.

11. Delegating. An efficient social work administrator realizes that agency responsibilities should be shared and welcomes the opportunity to give assignments and authority to other staff members. When a responsibility is delegated, so is the authority to carry it out. The administrator does not make assignments and then decide to handle them, unless there are extenuating circumstances, and even then the staff member involved must concur.

12. Interacting with the Community and Professions. The administrator has good relations with the public. He or she interprets the agency's organization and services to the community to engender attitudes and actions favorable to the agency. Staff members are encouraged to remember that what they do and say is the first line in public relations.

The administrator has effective working relationships with workers from psychiatry, psychology, nursing, medicine, law, and other helping professions. He or she helps them understand the roles and services of social work, particularly those of his or her agency.

13. Decision Making. The social work administrator is challenged by the decisions that have to be made. The entire process and individual steps to be taken to implement decisions that will benefit the agency and the community are understood. The leader marshals the facts, looks carefully at alternatives, anticipates the likely outcomes of each, and makes what seems to be the best choice. He or she realizes that some mistakes will be made but has the courage to make decisions whenever necessary. The administrator is willing to take risks and involve staff in the decision-making process.

14. Facilitating. The social work administrator does everything possible to open psychological doors for staff members so they can move in the directions in which they wish and need to go. He or she is sensitive to their individual plans and needs and does whatever possible to help them move ahead. The leader does not try to direct their actions but stays in the background, giving support.

15. Communicating. One of the most important actions of a social work administrator is communication—sending and receiving messages and signals, ideas as well as feelings. The administrator understands that listening is particularly important for a leader and that a person can listen with both "ears and eyes." It is understood that nonverbal signals are often more accurate and significant than spoken words. The leader carefully observes facial expressions, posture, body movements, gait, and other expressions of feeling.

16. Timing. Capable administrators have the ability to act at the appropriate moment to further their plans and decisions. Ineffective executives may act for the right reason but at the wrong time, and nothing significant ensues. Proper timing is involved in working with staff, other agencies, and the community as a whole.

17. Building. Administrators differ considerably in the way they treat staff members. Some build them up; others bruise them or at times even batter them psychologically. Some administrators are jealous of their staff members and often hold them down or belittle them. Effective leaders do all they can to encourage initiative, innovation, and achievement. They reward staff members, giving them full recognition for accomplishment. They gain much of their own satisfaction vicariously, through achievements of their staff.

Effective administrators do all they can to make their employees feel important, particularly through their accomplishments. They give recognition in writing and verbally, individually and before others, for what staff members do. When members of the staff feel good, they will accomplish more—for themselves and the agency. Production in the delivery of human social services increases as staff members feel wanted and needed and become contributors to a successful team.

18. Motivating. Finally, the effective social work administrator has the ability to motivate and even inspire staff members in using their talents and in carrying out agency functions.

The administrator understands the wishes and needs of staff members and the agency and does everything possible to encourage them to use their abilities in implementing agency services. The leader realizes that his or her actions make a difference—the higher the morale, the better the delivery of social services.

ETHICAL CONDUCT

Professional social workers are genuinely concerned that their leaders and managers know what is right and do what is right, particularly in the agencies in which they serve. Dishonesty, coverups, and the denial of realities readily lessen trust and cause people to shun services. Likewise, staff members are repulsed if their leaders are unethical. Particularly in this uncertain world with its many pressures for unethical behavior, social work leaders who will maintain integrity and trust are needed as never before.

Lewis reaffirms the importance of ethics in social work administration and suggests "that managers must evidence adherence to the values that justify their organizational goals. Such adherence should be demonstrated by ethical imperatives that justify practice principles. When these imperatives are not identified and subscribed to in both word and deed, the manager may justifiably be judged an unprincipled practitioner."[5]

Levy suggests that whatever, by way of ethical conduct, is expected of social workers in their relationships to clients "would be expected of administrators in their work and with administrative groups. All of the humanistic and humanitarian considerations applicable to social workers in their relationships to clients apply to the administrator's relationships with board members, committee members, volunteers, and so on."[6]

The 1990 NASW Delegate Assembly revised the Code of Ethics[7] adapted by the 1979 Delegate Assembly and specified the professional relationships and standards as follows:

1990 NASW Code of Ethics—Summary of Major Principles

I.   THE SOCIAL WORKER'S CONDUCT AND COMPORTMENT AS A SOCIAL WORKER
    A. *Propriety.* The social worker should maintain high standards of personal conduct in the capacity or identity as social worker.
    B. *Competence and Professional Development.* The social worker should strive to become and remain proficient in professional practice and the performance of professional functions.
    C. *Service.* The social worker should regard as primary the service obligation of the social work profession.
    D. *Integrity.* The social worker should act in accordance with the highest standards of professional integrity.
    E. *Scholarship and Research.* The social worker engaged in study and research should be guided by the conventions of scholarly inquiry.
II. THE SOCIAL WORKER'S ETHICAL RESPONSIBILITY TO CLIENTS
    F. *Primacy of Clients' Interests.* The social worker's primary responsibility is to clients.
    G. *Rights and Prerogatives of Clients.* The social worker should make every effort to foster maximum self-determination on the part of clients.
    H. *Confidentiality and Privacy.* The social worker should respect the privacy of clients and hold in confidence all information obtained in the course of professional service.
    I. *Fees.* When setting fees, the social worker should ensure that they are fair, reasonable, considerate, and commensurate with the service performed and with due regard for the clients' ability to pay.

---

[5]Harold Lewis, "Ethics and the Managing of Service Effectiveness in Social Welfare," *Administration in Social Work* 11 (Fall/Winter 1987), 283.

[6]Charles Levy, "The Ethics of Management," in Simon Slavin, ed., *Social Administration: The Management of the Social Services,* 2nd ed., Vol. II, *Managing Finances, Personnel, and Information in Human Services* (New York: Haworth Press, 1985), p. 292.

[7]*Code of Ethics* (Silver Spring, MD: National Association of Social Workers, n.d.), pp. 1–2.

III. THE SOCIAL WORKER'S ETHICAL RESPONSIBILITY TO COLLEAGUES
  J. *Respect, Fairness, and Courtesy.* The social worker should treat colleagues with respect, courtesy, fairness, and good faith.
  K. *Dealing with Colleagues' Clients.* The social worker has the responsibility to relate to the clients of colleagues with full professional consideration.
IV. THE SOCIAL WORKER'S ETHICAL RESPONSIBILITY TO EMPLOYERS AND EMPLOYING ORGANIZATIONS
  L. *Commitments to Employing Organizations.* The social worker should adhere to commitments made to the employing organizations.
V. THE SOCIAL WORKER'S ETHICAL RESPONSIBILITY TO THE SOCIAL WORK PROFESSION
  M. *Maintaining the Integrity of the Profession.* The social worker should uphold and advance the values, ethics, knowledge, and mission of the profession.
  N. *Community Service.* The social worker should assist the profession in making social services available to the general public.
  O. *Development of Knowledge.* The social worker should take responsibility for identifying, developing, and fully utilizing knowledge for professional practice.
VI. THE SOCIAL WORKER'S ETHICAL RESPONSIBILITY TO SOCIETY
  P. *Promoting the General Welfare.* The social worker should promote the general welfare of society.

This code gives the administrator a societal compass. It helps the leaders, and workers, to have a responsible interest in and compassion for people, their problems, and their relationships with others. It is a fundamental guideline for all agency staff members.

A current positive development is the establishment of ethics committees in social work. Reamer reports that this movement is bringing significant changes in human service agencies and that these committees are assisting in educating staff, formulating policies, and reviewing cases that contain complex ethical issues.[8]

SUMMARY

Modern social work emphasizes the significant role of the administrator in the delivery of effective social services. The administrator must know basic administrative processes to understand human behavior, formulate sound social policies, and encourage skillful social work practice.

Professional attitudes of social work administrators are particularly significant in providing an emotional climate conducive to the effective delivery of social services.

Specific actions of effective social work administrators are numerous and include the following: accepting, caring, creating, democratizing, trust-

[8]Frederic G. Reamer, "Ethics Committees in Social Work," *Social Work*, 32 (May–June 1987), 188.

ing, approving, maintaining equilibrium, planning, organizing, setting priorities, delegating, interacting with community and professional persons, decision making, facilitating, communicating, timing, building, and motivating. The 1990 NASW Code of Ethics is a helpful guide for administrators and workers—it outlines and defines ethical principles in their daily work.

QUESTIONS FOR DISCUSSION

1. Evaluate the 1968 NASW guidelines for a successful social work administrator in relation to your present situation.

2. Why should the social work administrator have a comprehensive knowledge of community resources?

3. Do you agree that the social work administrator should belong to the NASW and be active in the local unit? Discuss your opinion.

4. Why is case management being introduced in an increasing number of social work agencies?

5. How important is "trusting" between administrators and staff?

6. Think of five specific ways in which an administrator might "build" his or her staff.

7. Evaluate the 1990 NASW Code of Ethics, including its positive qualities and its limitations.

SPECIAL ACTIVITIES

1. Interview a case manager in a social work agency concerning his or her responsibilities and challenges.

2. Role-play the importance of recognition by the administrator that no staff member is perfect and acceptance of this premise for staff and self.

3. Arrange a panel on the 1990 NASW Code of Ethics, discussing its strengths and limitations.

4. Read and evaluate the book by Felice D. Perlmutter.

SELECTED REFERENCES

AUSTIN, MICHAEL J. "Executive Entry: Multiple Perspectives on the Process of Muddling Through." *Administration in Social Work* 13, Nos. 3/4 (1989), 55–71.
BARBEAU, ERNEST J., and ROGER A. LOHMANN. "The Agency Executive Director as Keeper of the Past." *Administration in Social Work* 16, No. 2 (1992), 15–26.
BERLINER, ARTHUR K. "Misconduct in Social Work Practice." *Social Work* 34 (January 1989), 69–72.
EZELL, MARK. "Administrators as Advocates." *Administration in Social Work* 15, No. 4 (1991), 1–17.

HOLLAND, THOMAS P., and ALLIE C. KILPATRICK. "Ethical Issues in Social Work: Toward a Grounded Theory of Professional Ethics." *Social Work* 36 (March 1991), 138–143.

LEWIS, HAROLD. "Ethics and the Managing of Service Effectiveness in Social Welfare." *Administration in Social Work* 11 (Fall/Winter 1987), 271–284.

NEUGEBOREN, BERNARD. "Career Development in Social Work Administration." *Administration in Social Work* 14, No. 1 (1990), 47–63.

PECORA, PETER J., and MICHAEL J. AUSTIN. *Managing Human Services Personnel.* Newbury Park, CA: Sage Publications, 1987.

PERLMUTTER, FELICE DAVIDSON. *Changing Hats: From Social Work Practice to Administration.* Silver Spring, MD: NASW Press, 1990.

RESNICK, HERMAN, and RINO J. PATTI, eds. *Change from Within: Humanizing Social Welfare Organizations.* Philadelphia: Temple University Press, 1980.

WIEHE, VERNON R. "Evaluating the Executive Director's Performance." *Administration in Social Work* 8 (Winter 1984), 1–12.

4

The Planning Process

Once upon a time a Sea Horse gathered up his seven pieces of eight and cantered out to find his fortune. Before he had traveled very far he met an Eel, who said, "Psst. Hey, bud. Where 'ya goin'?"

"I'm going out to find my fortune," replied the Sea Horse, proudly.

"You're in luck," said the Eel. "For four pieces of eight you can have this speedy flipper, and then you'll be able to get there a lot faster."

"Gee, that's swell," said the Sea Horse, and he paid the money and put on the flipper and slithered off at twice the speed. Soon he came upon a Sponge, who said, "Psst. Hey, bud. Where 'ya goin'?"

"I'm going out to find my fortune," replied the Sea Horse.

"You're in luck," said the Sponge. "For a small fee I will let you have this jet-propelled scooter so that you will be able to travel a lot faster."

So the Sea Horse bought the scooter with his remaining money and went zooming through the sea five times as fast. Soon he came upon a Shark, who said, "Psst. Hey, bud. Where 'ya goin'?"

"I'm going out to find my fortune," replied the Sea Horse.

"You're in luck. If you'll take this short cut," said the Shark, pointing to his open mouth, "You'll save yourself a lot of time."

"Gee, thanks," said the Sea Horse, and zoomed off into the interior of the Shark, there to be devoured.

The moral of this fable is that if you're not sure where you're going, you're liable to end up someplace else—and not even know it.[1]

---

[1]Robert F. Mager, *Preparing Instructional Objectives*, 2nd ed., p. vii. Copyright © 1975 by Pitman Learning, Inc., Belmont, California. Reprinted by permission.

Planning is essential in social work administration. As one agency director said, "Plan or perish." Planning is needed at all levels of operation and should be part of every worker's daily routine.

For years business has emphasized the importance of planning and has stressed MBO and other systems as a means of planning effectively and achieving desired results. In the last two decades, social work has developed a genuine interest in the planning process. It is a major component of social work practice and is considered essential in the operation of social agencies and in the delivery of social services.

In their best-seller, *Managing*, Harold Geneen and Alvin Moscow stressed the importance of having objectives: "A Three-Sentence Course On Business Management: You read a book from the beginning to the end. You run a business the opposite way. You start with the end, and then you do everything you must to reach it."[2]

WHY PLAN?

Planning is advocated in social work for several important reasons:

1. Efficiency
2. Effectiveness
3. Accountability
4. Morale

Efficiency is desirable in every administrative operation, whether in business or in social work. The aim is to achieve goals with a minimum of cost and effort. This occurs only through careful planning, which is an anticipatory process. In social work, staff and resources are limited, so it is particularly important to provide services as efficiently as possible.

Effectiveness is also extremely important. If activities are not planned, the desired results may not be achieved. In social work, the main goal is, of course, to help people in need. If staff efforts and agency resources are diffused and planning for unity of purpose and integration of effort does not occur, the level of achievement is low.

Planning is needed for evaluation and accountability. Today public-spirited citizens, legislators, and community leaders are asking valid, pointed questions: What are the results of social work and social work services? Can we afford them? Can we improve them? These and other questions can be answered only as social work administrators plan carefully in relation to specific objectives and evaluation procedures for measuring their programs and services. The new sunset laws, tax cuts, and related legislation are attempts

---

[2]Harold Geneen and Alvin Moscow, *Managing* (New York: Avon Books, 1984), p. 35.

to force social work and other professions to justify public expenditures for their services or see them terminated. Proper planning makes it possible to carry out objective research and evaluation of experimental demonstrations as well as of regular services.

Careful planning is essential for the morale of an agency. Staff members need feelings of achievement and satisfaction to perform their best. Such feelings are engendered when executives and staff members jointly plan the total operation of the agency, making it possible for each staff member to feel needed and effective. An agency that makes it possible for each staff member to understand exactly what to do and how to do it provides an emotional and administrative climate that is conducive to high morale. How the staff feels will make a difference in the delivery of social services.

THE PLANNING PROCESSES

Planning is the process of anticipating goals or targets and then preparing a plan for reaching them. It means looking at where you are, where you want to go, and how to reach your destination. Both management and social work recognize that effective planning is essential for the production and delivery of social services. Schaffer suggests that

> corporate planning—that collection of methods, departments, functions, tools, and activities which companies buy or create to help assure their future— has acquired an enviable reputation in books, articles, management seminar programs, and business courses. But this reputation or "image," like the visible part of an iceberg, is only part of the story. Very little attention has been paid to the submerged part of the iceberg.[3]

He explains that there are widespread reports of disappointments and frustrations among some companies that have used long-range planning. He lists four classic steps in corporate planning:

1. Research—to analyze corporate strengths, weaknesses, and other factors, and to determine the opportunities and risks created by external trends.
2. Formulation of objectives—to define what the company should become in the long-term future.
3. Strategic planning—to develop an overall framework outlining how the corporation will move to its ultimate objectives.
4. Operational planning—to create steps that each department and function should take in order to carry out the strategic plans.[4]

---

[3]Robert H. Schaffer, "Putting Action Into Planning," *Harvard Business Review* 45 (November–December 1967), 158.

[4]Ibid., p. 69.

BASIC PLANNING STEPS

In social work and in social service agencies, planning is recognized, as never before, to be an essential ingredient in the effective delivery of services. The planning process in social work is basically similar to the planning process in management, but there are some different emphases. Seven steps and their related activities are particularly important in the planning process in social work.

1. Select objectives.
2. Consider agency resources.
3. Enumerate the alternatives.
4. Anticipate the outcomes of each alternative.
5. Decide on the best plan.
6. Plan a specific program for action.
7. Be open to change.

Each of these steps is crucial for social work planning, and together they can bring efficiency and effectiveness to the delivery of social services. Each will now be considered briefly.

Select Objectives

Objectives are destinations, goals, or targets. They relate to the purposes and policies of agencies. There are two kinds of objectives: (1) overall and long-range and (2) specific and short-range.

The overall goals concern why the agency was established and its purpose for existing. The goal of a child-placement agency for example, is to help place disadvantaged children into homes where they may receive love and guidance. A comprehensive mental-health center comes into existence to provide services that will help reduce mental illness, prevent mental problems, and enrich daily living. These are long-range objectives. Planners in an agency need to understand clearly the aims and purposes of the agency charter and policies.

Short-term or specific objectives involve the present and immediate future. Planning is an anticipatory process, and as such it is most effective when the targets are specific, simple, and attainable. Most objectives are short-term. The objective concerns what might happen in a given day or within a week or other short period of time. This kind of objective deals with the immediate present and is particularly important in the daily administration of a social work agency.

Long-range goals involve overall targets of the agency and may encompass a period of months or even years. Five-year plans are an example of this kind of planning. On nearly every level, this kind of goal setting is important—for the individual worker, the department, and the agency as a whole. Such goal setting invites creativity and dreaming for the future.

In social work, as in many professional areas, overall and specific objectives for the agency are often formulated by joint participation of administration and staff, on a democratic basis. Although leaders may present suggestions for consideration, staff involvement in the formulation of agency goals and specific targets usually pays big dividends.

Agencies vary considerably in involving staff members and persons other than administrators in the planning process. Jansson and Taylor surveyed 167 executives of social agencies in Los Angeles County and discovered that there was, at best, "uneven use of planning—and planning often appears to be dominated by executives and to make little use of data and committees."[5] They noted that actual participation in program planning involved the following groups and percentages:

Agency administrator	90%
Supervisory staff	68%
Service staff	49%
Board members	37%
Consumers of service	27%

Management by Objectives. As mentioned earlier, for some years business has been utilizing management by objectives (MBO), introduced by Peter Drucker, George Odiorne, and others in an attempt to become more efficient and effective. Social work has also developed a strong interest in this approach.

Management by objectives is a systems approach to improving operations. It includes inputs, activities, and outputs (see Figure 4–1). Input has to do with beginnings, resources, goals, objectives, and related operations. Activities refers to the actual doing and achieving. The objectives are defined in the input stage, and the attempt to achieve the objectives is part of the activities step. Output has to do with results. What happened? Were the objectives reached or attained? If not, the system has not been effective.

Experts in MBO describe *input traps* and *activity traps*, which hamper the process. An input trap is an introductory action or situation that limits or hampers agency operation or production of services, for example, vague or abstract goals, overdirection or underdirection of staff, and excessive demand for paper work. An activity trap is doing things just to keep busy. It may include overemphasis on reports or busy work or getting overinvolved in

FIGURE 4-1 Management by Objectives

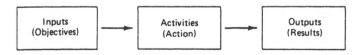

[5]Bruce S. Jansson and Samuel H. Taylor, "The Planning Contradiction in Social Agencies: Great Expectations versus Satisfaction with Limited Performance," *Administration in Social Work* 2 (Summer 1978), 176.

personality discussions and isolated incidents. This kind of activity involves professional irresponsibility. Overstressing activity and doing niggling or irrelevant work tends to reduce the self-esteem of workers.

There are two main kinds of goals and objectives: strategic and operational. *Strategic goals* are concerned with developing new ideas and with overall or long-range planning, and they invite creativity and innovation. *Operational goals* or objectives tend to be specific and measurable. Where are we now? What are the trends? How are we doing?

In social work, MBO is becoming a practical tool for streamlining the operations of an agency and focusing its services. Many public and private agencies are incorporating MBO into their operating procedures. More agencies are asking individual staff members to set specific objectives for a given time, often a year, and are asking department heads to do the same. Specific objectives are being formulated for the agency as a whole so that the input can be focused and practical.

Raider suggests that "MBO is a very simple system in theory. Basically, it is an approach to management in which agency staff participate in the process of specifying long-range goals and short-range objectives to be achieved within an established time period. Success in achieving these agreed-upon goals and objectives is evaluated periodically."[6]

According to Raider, there have been three primary reasons for failure in the use of MBO by social work administrators:

(a) agencies did not understand what they were getting into and as a consequence did not do adequate preliminary analysis and planning;
(b) agencies sought to implement a model of MBO that had not been sufficiently tailored to reflect the unique needs and characteristics of social agencies;
(c) a poorly conceived strategy was used to implement the system.[7]

Raider offers a four-phase approach for installing MBO in social agencies: (1) careful self-study, looking at agency instability, environmental instability, position discontinuity (frequent replacement of personnel or changes in staff responsibilities), and unmediated competition (lack of established channels within an agency for mediating competing objectives or goals); (2) implementation strategy, which would include training for all who would be using MBO; (3) system design, tailored for the individual agency; and (4) developing a long-lasting commitment, with an emphasis on flexibility, personal growth, and frequent two-way feedback.[8]

Pecora and Austin suggest that a refinement of the MBO approach—the MOR, or management by objectives and results—can be an important cost-effective performance appraisal method. This method differs slightly from

[6]Melvyn C. Raider, "Installing Management by Objectives in Social Agencies," *Administration in Social Work* 1 (Fall 1977), 235.
[7]Ibid., pp. 235–236.
[8]Ibid., pp. 236–243.

MBO as it emphasizes key results areas, performance indicators, and standards. These authors maintain that among the advantages of MOR "is its flexibility and ability to incorporate performance targets for both job output and personal development."[9]

Strategic Planning. This is one of the newer concepts that is being used in social service agencies as well as in business and other areas. It puts a major focus on looking ahead realistically, as much as possible, and includes specific long-range goals. To illustrate, United Way of America, in 1985, agreed on five core strategies in looking ahead:

> (1) A focus on community health- and human-care problem solving; (2) inclusiveness of people, agencies, and natural geographic areas; (3) a single communitywide campaign for health- and human-care services; (4) a year-round communications program of education and involvement at the workplace and communitywide; and (5) a fund-distribution system that is accountable to donors, accommodates donors' choice as to who should receive their gifts, and provides for flexible funding for venture support and problem-solving initiatives.[10]

Behavioral Objectives. In recent years social work education and practice have focused on the behavioral/nonbehavioral dichotomy in an attempt to strengthen the educational and practice processes. A behavioral objective is specific, usually simple, observable, measurable, and realistic. Its specificity is important because it narrows one's target and one's vision. Simplicity allows for clarity of understanding and procedure. The behavioral objective must be observable so it can be measured; otherwise an evaluation cannot take place. It needs to be realistic or it has little value or pragmatic meaning.

A nonbehavioral objective tends to be general, vague, and unobservable, and it cannot be measured. For example, a nonbehavioral objective would be the following: "I will become a better social worker." Although this may be a desirable overall goal, it cannot be observed and measured. Translation into a behavioral objective might take the following form: "I will read professional journals on social work practice fifteen minutes a day to become a better social worker." This objective can be observed and measured and is likely to bring results in the direction of the desired goal.

When an administrator in a social work agency says, "I am going to be a better administrator," he or she is describing a nonbehavioral objective. If he or she had defined a specific action, that would be a move in the right direction. For example, an administrator might specify the following: "I will talk with each of my staff for fifteen to thirty minutes each week, giving them

[9]Peter J. Pecora and Michael J. Austin, *Managing Human Services Personnel* (Newbury Park, CA: Sage Publications, 1987), p. 68; for a description and examples of MOR see pp. 68–77.

[10]*Rethinking Tomorrow and Beyond* (Alexandria, VA: United Way of America, 1985).

the opportunity to make suggestions regarding their own work and the work of the agency." Another example of a behavioral objective would be for each staff member to spend fifteen minutes daily in creative contemplation and planning to improve agency services.

Programmed Instruction. Another current development in planning is the use of behavior objectives in programmed instruction. Ehlers, Austin, and Prothero have pioneered in this field with their introductory text, *Administration for the Human Services.*[11] They present specific behavioral objectives that are available as guidelines and targets for those studying the program.

Consider Agency Resources

The second step in planning is to consider an agency's economic and physical resources as well as its personnel and staff. It is essential to relate targets to plant facilities, the budget and monies available, and community support for the services.

Equally important is the staff available. Not only does the number of staff members need to be considered but also their quality. What are their competencies, attitudes, and feelings? Is adequate staff available for the goals to be achieved? Is money available to hire new staff if the answer is no? What are the attitudes and feelings of the staff toward the objectives that have been set? If the answers are basically affirmative, the administrator has been given a signal to proceed; if not, other resources may have to be obtained.

Enumerate the Alternatives

After the targets have been set and agency facilities and staff have been surveyed, it is important to consider different ways in which the desired objectives might be achieved. A poor administrator may take the first path he or she sees; a good administrator will ordinarily consider numerous paths and carefully describe and anticipate each.

During this stage, creativity may play a significant role. Freewheeling group discussions and/or talks with individuals allow the opportunity to think of new possibilities and usually pay big dividends in terms of meaningful alternatives.

Anticipate the Outcomes of Each Alternative

Again, the planning process is an anticipatory process—looking ahead to the future to try to estimate what is likely to happen if a particular action occurs. Since we cannot look into a crystal ball, we need to anticipate from various vantage points what is likely to happen. As we look at possible outcomes of a variety of alternatives, we can weigh the choices and come up with the one

[11]Walter H. Ehlers, Michael J. Austin, and Jon C. Prothero, *Administration for the Human Services: An Introductory Program Text* (New York: Harper & Row, 1976).

that is best. In particular, we have to anticipate the economic and political future.

Decide on the Best Plan

After the alternatives have been enumerated and studied carefully, especially in relation to future developments, data and thinking need to be pooled in an effort to compare and contrast the different possible routes. After such careful examination, a decision can be made about what is the most sensible choice. It is of course hoped that the decision will bring about the desired results.

Priorities. One of the challenging aspects of planning is setting priorities. When alternatives are listed and possible choices of objectives are realized, it is then necessary to weigh them for significance and feasibility. Some are more important than others; some need immediate action, whereas others may be wisely postponed.

The importance of setting priorities is illustrated by the action of an efficiency expert who, as reported by Covey, outlined his firm's services to the president of a large steel corporation. The president had requested help in improving the corporation's efficiency and effectiveness. The consultant said, "I can give you something in a few minutes to increase your doing and action fifty percent. First, write on a blank sheet the six most important tasks you have to do tomorrow. Second, put them in the order of their importance. Third, pull this sheet out the first thing tomorrow morning and begin working on item one. When you finish it, tackle item two, then item three. Do this until quitting time. Don't worry if you finish only two or three or even if you finish one item. You'll be working on the most important ones. Fourth, take the last five minutes of each working day to make a 'must' list for the next day's tasks."[12] According to the report, the president sent the consultant $25,000 for the idea—$1,000 for each of the twenty-five minutes of the visit.

Plan a Specific Program for Action

This is the time to formulate a specific program to reach the agreed-upon target(s). This is the blueprint or mapmaking stage, in which step-by-step action is outlined and recorded. A time chart for achieving the objectives is essential. Priorities need to be decided on. This is essential; otherwise, one is acting like a pilot trying to reach a small island in the Pacific without a flight plan. It is important to program specific time for completing the project, allowing for periodic study and reports of progress. Specific time must be allocated so that urgent matters do not overshadow it.

Planning a timetable is helpful in making a blueprint come alive and in effectively implementing plans. A variety of time-scheduling patterns have

[12]Stephen R. Covey, *How to Succeed with People* (Salt Lake City: Deseret Book Co., 1971), pp. 96–97.

been introduced and are in use, along with individual variations. A few of the main ones are described briefly.

In about 1910 H. L. Gantt, a pioneer in business management, formulated the Gantt chart, which has been widely used as a planning and control technique in nonrepetitive operations. Carlisle's example of a Gantt chart (Figure 4–2) illustrates its two-dimensional pattern, with time on the top scale and the operations or activities on the vertical axis. In this figure, the sequence of operations necessary to develop and produce a new product is indicated—the development of hydraulic stools for dentists, draftsmen, or secretaries. This type of chart has been used to some extent in social work. It is a relatively simple way of looking ahead and charting services to be performed.

Although business management has introduced a variety of other kinds of time-scheduling devices, including milestone charts, and impact charts, the first network system, PERT (Program Evaluation and Review Technique), is being used extensively by social work administrators. PERT was developed in 1958 by a team of representatives from the Special Projects Office of the U.S. navy, industrial contractors, and a group of consultants. They were working on the planning and control system for the Polaris missile to be used on nuclear submarines. Through this technique, it was claimed that "over two years were saved on the development of this weapon system."[13]

Be Open to Change

Flexibility is essential in the total planning process. The original plan should be followed unless the facts have changed or better procedures for moving

FIGURE 4-2 **Example of a Gantt Chart.** Adapted from Howard M. Carlisle, *Management Essentials: Concepts for Productivity and Innovation,* 2nd ed., p. 214. Copyright © 1987 by Science Research Associates, Inc. Reprinted by permission of the publisher.

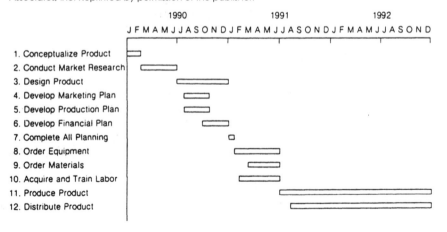

[13]Howard M. Carlisle, *Management Essentials: Concepts for Productivity and Innovation,* 2nd ed. (Chicago: Science Research Associates, 1987), p. 221.

ahead have been developed. However, change often occurs as planning is programmed specifically and implementation takes place. Competent administrators advocate changing plans at any moment along the way *if* the change will bring in facilitative resources and alterations. The incompetent administrator is one who sticks to the original plan even though it is outmoded and changes would be productive. Elasticity in implementation is essential.

The seven basic planning steps do not always occur in a linear fashion; sometimes there is a good deal of jumping and crossing back and forth. Thus, flexibility is fundamental in planning; rigidity is unacceptable.

CASE MANAGEMENT

Case management, with an emphasis on effective planning, is fast becoming a major component in social work practice, especially in larger agencies and in intervention with complex and fragmented services. Although rooted in casework, group work, and community organization, its approach is unique—assessment of clients' problems and needs, integration of planning, coordination, linkage of resources, monitoring of services, and follow-up to reach specific goals and effective results. Case management has surfaced in recent years because of our increasingly complex society, depersonalization, and more specialized social work practice with some fragmented services. It is also considered a way to achieve better cost effectiveness and cost control.

The board of directors of NASW in June 1992 described case management intervention as "a method of providing services whereby a professional social worker assesses the needs of the client and the client's family, when appropriate, and arranges, coordinates, monitors, evaluates and advocates for a package of multiple services to meet the specific client's complex needs."[14]

Vourlekis and Greene define case management by presenting and describing eight "practice key skills" that are particularly significant: client identification and outreach, individual and family assessment and diagnosis, planning and resource identification, linking clients to needed resources, service implementation and coordination, monitoring service delivery, advocacy to obtain services, and evaluation.[15]

The position of case manager has come to the fore as a result of the increase in case management practice. Men and women who are employed in this role usually have a limited caseload, preferably fifteen to twenty cases. The case manager's challenge is to individualize the total intervention process. He or she helps to identify the client's problems and needs, plans for treatment and services, monitors the process, and follows through carefully

[14]National Association of Social Workers, "Case Manager's Role Clarified by Guidelines," *NASW NEWS* 37 (September 1992), 7.

[15]Betty S. Vourlekis and Roberta R. Greene, eds., *Social Work Case Management* (New York: Aldine de Gruyter, 1992), pp. 183–188.

so that the client is not lost along the way. The case manager has a dual role of providing some casework services, if needed, as well as coordinating the network services that are appropriate.

Administrators should be aware of the growing interest in case management. The fragmentation and depersonalization of many of our social service systems have created an urgent need for individual case managers who help vulnerable people in our society receive the services they need. Following is a vignette illustrating the role of the case manager.

CASE MANAGEMENT

John is a twenty-four-year-old male who has been diagnosed with a serious mental illness. He completed two years of college but then became quite dysfunctional. His parents tried to help him in the first few months of his difficulty but soon asked a mental-health center for assistance. The center's personnel placed him on medication, which helped him to stabilize. Also, John was asked to come to psychotherapeutic counseling interviews twice a month. For a period of two years, the personnel encouraged John to stay on his medication and attend his counseling sessions. John responded only partially to his treatment regimen, and the quality of his life did not improve significantly. He would miss some of his appointments and several times refused to take his medications.

A new administrator was appointed to develop case manager services within the mental-health system. The administrator was an MSW professional who had worked with individuals with serious mental illnesses for a number of years. He hired three case managers and trained them to be advocates of individuals who were not responding well to the traditional mental-health system.

One of the case managers had John in his caseload of twenty. He arranged to meet John several times and formed an excellent relationship with him. After the relationship was formed, the case manager asked John to define some specific goals he would like to pursue. John said he would like to learn to cook and to get a job in the food-preparation industry. Also, the case manager offered to help John get to his counseling appointments at the mental-health center.

John responded well to the individualized approach taken by the case manager. The case manager helped John register in an apprenticeship cooking class offered by a local college. John's attendance at his counseling sessions improved, as did his attitude about taking his medications, because of the psychological support given to him by the case manager. John still has problems to solve, but the quality of his life has improved considerably because of the case manager's total, integrated approach. John is now able to live independently.

INTERAGENCY PLANNING

In addition to planning within agencies, a significant current development in the delivery of social services has been the increased emphasis on planning and community organization, involving many agencies in a given community. Basic principles and processes pertaining to intra-agency planning are also applicable to interagency planning.

Several schools of social work provide training in community organization and social planning, offering such concentrations for students who wish to obtain positions with agencies that coordinate and plan for the welfare of communities, for example, a community welfare council and United Way. Other agencies, including private, state, and federal, also employ social work graduates, full time and part time, in social planning, particularly for interagency coordination and teamwork.

Another significant planning development is the increase in the number of social planners in government, both federal and state, and in private corporations and agencies. An example is Planned Variations, a program of the Department of Housing and Urban Development (HUD) that was designed to grant more authority to local executive leadership.[16] Gilbert, Rosenkranz, and Specht studied this program and observed that social planning includes the cycle of competition among three primary societal values—participation, leadership, and expertise.[17] They stated that *participation* "extols the virtue of each man's being directly involved in making meaningful decisions that affect his welfare," *leadership* is the "antithesis of participation," and *expertise* "elevates rationality to the supreme criterion for decision-making." One of their major conclusions was that from a "dialectical perspective, the competition among participation, leadership, and expertise is seen not as a dilemma, but as a dynamic, necessary, and continuously unfolding process."[18]

Several schools of social work now offer a program that provides specific training, in classwork and in the field, for social planners. As a result, many graduates from MSW and DSW programs are being hired in government, private agencies, and in some businesses as social planners.

SUMMARY

Planning has become a major process in social work education and practice. It can increase efficiency, effectiveness, and accountability and improve morale.

Management by Objectives, MOR (management by results), strategic planning, behavior objectives, and other planning approaches are being utilized by social workers to improve the delivery of social services.

The planning process includes seven basic steps:

Select objectives.
Consider agency resources.

[16]Neil Gilbert, Armin Rosenkranz, and Harry Specht, "Dialects of Social Planning," *Social Work* 18 (March 1973), 78.
[17]Ibid., pp. 79–80.
[18]Ibid., p. 84.

Enumerate the alternatives.
Anticipate the outcomes of each alternative.
Decide on the best plan.
Plan a specific program for each action.
Be open to change.

Case management, although rooted in social work practice of the past, is gaining in popularity and use; it emphasizes planning, coordination, integration of network services, monitoring, and follow-up.

Interagency planning is essential for the coordination and cooperation of agencies in communities to bring about the optimal delivery of social services. Competent administrators welcome the opportunity to plan with other administrators to enhance social work practice, avoid unnecessary duplication, and fulfill community needs.

QUESTIONS FOR DISCUSSION

1. Evaluate the statement of the philosopher who said, "Plan or perish."

2. How does planning affect social work practice in relation to efficiency, effectiveness, accountability, and morale of staff?

3. Describe the seven planning steps in this chapter and the meaning of each.

4. Do you favor the use of MBO in social work agencies? Why or why not?

5. How important is interagency planning in the delivery of social services? Can you illustrate your point of view by an experience in your own community?

6. Why is there an increase in case management in social work today?

7. What are the roles of the case manager in the provision of social services?

SPECIAL ACTIVITIES

1. Write a brief account of an experience in your life that illustrates the importance of planning.

2. Invite a representative of the United Way or Community Services Council in your community to relate to your group facts and experiences about the importance of interagency planning.

3. Role-play a possible first interview of a case manager with a client in a county welfare department agency.

SELECTED REFERENCES

BEDEIAN, ARTHUR G. "Planning." *Management*, 3rd ed., pp. 120–233. Fort Worth, TX: Dryden Press, 1993.

BILLIS, DAVID. "Planned Change in Voluntary and Government Social Service Agencies." *Administration in Social Work* 16, Nos. 3/4 (1992), 29–44.

DINERMAN, MIRIAM. "Managing the Maze: Case Management and Service Delivery." *Administration in Social Work* 16, No. 1 (1992), 1–9.

FULMER, ROBERT M. *The New Management*, 4th ed. New York: Macmillan, 1988.

GENKINS, MARY. "Strategic Planning for Social Work Marketing." *Administration in Social Work* 9 (Spring 1985), 35–46.

MOORE, STEPHEN. "Case Management and the Integration of Services: How Service Delivery Systems Shape Case Management." *Social Work* 37 (September 1992), 418–422.

PATTI, RINO J. "The New Scientific Management: Systems Management for Social Welfare." In Simon Slavin, ed., *Social Administration: The Management of the Social Services*, 2nd ed. Vol. II, *Managing Finances, Personnel, and Information in Human Services*, pp. 184–198. New York: Haworth Press, 1985.

PATTI, RINO J. *Social Welfare Administration: Managing Social Programs in a Developmental Context.* Englewood Cliffs, NJ: Prentice Hall, 1983.

RESNICK, HERMAN, and RINO J. PATTI, eds. *Change from Within: Humanizing Social Welfare Organizations.* Philadelphia: Temple University Press, 1980.

VOURLEKIS, BETSY S., and ROBERTA R. GREENE, eds. *Social Work Case Management.* New York: Aldine de Gruyter, 1992.

WALDEN, THEODORE, KATIE HAMMER, and CAROL H. KURLAND. "Case Management: Planning and Coordinating Strategies." *Administration in Social Work* 14, No. 4 (1990), 61–72.

5

Decision Making

Ted Jones had been the director for fifteen years of a marriage and family counseling agency in a large metropolitan area. When Ted retired, the board hired a replacement it supposed was competent. He had an MSW degree and an impressive academic record.

At the first meeting of the staff the new director stated that he was pleased to join their important agency and was looking forward to working with them individually and collectively. He said he preferred to operate on a democratic basis and would need the help of all staff members in making decisions.

Within a short time it was clear that the new director did not truly mean what he had said. Although he prided himself on being democratic and involving staff members in decision making, he made decision after decision entirely on his own. He assigned responsibilities but would not give the staff authority to make decisions and carry them out. Soon staff morale ebbed to its lowest level in years, and agency services diminished.

Decision making is very important in administration, particularly in social work, where decisions daily affect the lives of individuals, groups, and communities and staff as well as clients. Levy stressed the importance of decision making in the following jocular comment:

> Scarcely anything will offend one so much as the charge that he is indecisive. The truer the charge, the more prompt and definite the reaction. Call a man wife-beater, embezzler, pervert, liar, loafer, knave, and expect a disappointed pout. Say he is indecisive, and seismographs quiver. Accuse him of being

insipid, dull, tedious, overbearing, arrogant, egotistical, and with a conde-
scending smirk he will ask if you aren't being just a trifle petty. Tell him he can't
make a decision and he will turn blue with rage.[1]

Management has been defined as the process of making decisions and
implementing them. Certainly decision making is the essence of management
in many ways and affects what goes on in every agency. Administrators make
many decisions daily, each of which may alter services of agencies directly or
indirectly. Both quantitatively and qualitatively, decision making is a major
component of administration in every social agency.

The significance of decision making is illustrated in an unusual family-
counseling situation. A man had an alcohol problem for many years and had
many personal and family difficulties. He sought counseling and attempted
to give up alcohol. He would not drink for long periods of time and then go
on a bender. Finally his wife went to the counselor also. She was encouraged
to be accepting of her husband, virtually no matter what he did. She agreed
not to criticize him. One evening while preparing supper, she realized there
was no bread in the house. She turned to her husband and casually said, "We
need some bread. Would you go to the store and get some?" He agreed. On
the way to the shopping center, he ran into one of his buddies, who said invitingly, "Let's have a beer." He did not return home for two days. When he
finally entered the front door, his wife looked at him and merely said, "Oh,
where's the loaf of bread?" He has not touched liquor since.

Decision making is important in social work because it affects the lives
of individuals, families, groups, and communities. It is a major component of
the treatment process. In administration, also, decision making is significant
because it affects the morale of the staff and the eventual delivery of social
services.

WAYS OF MAKING DECISIONS

If you ask the typical administrator of an agency how he or she makes decisions, the answer will probably be, "I study the facts carefully and make a
rational choice." Actually, this rarely happens. Decisions are usually made on
the basis of a combination of facts and feelings, often more related to the latter. A caseworker may be hired because the director likes this person more
than other candidates, even though the other candidates have better qualifications. Another administrator may criticize staff members because it makes
him or her feel superior. One can build up one's ego at the expense of others.

[1]Charles S. Levy, "Decisions! Decisions!" *Adult Leadership* 11 (May 1962), 10.

This happens in the business world as well as in social agencies. Competent administrators recognize this situation and endeavor to make allowances for feelings if they are blown out of proportion, which they often are.

There are various ways of making decisions. Carlisle draws on the field of management and suggests that there are three types of decisions: intuitive, judgmental, and problem solving.[2]

Intuitive decisions are tied to feelings rather than to rationality. The action decided on relates to what the person feels to be right or best, to "hunches" or "gut feelings." Social workers use this method often, particularly when they work with a client. It involves their feelings and information. In administration, this kind of decision is often made. Impressions of others and what they are doing play a vital role in the hiring and firing of staff and in making decisions for the welfare of the agency.

Judgmental decisions are based on knowledge and experience. According to Carlisle

after a person becomes familiar with an organization setting and its operations, decisions that were once new become routine. A supervisor becomes so familiar with the operations of the work unit that he or she can accurately predict what will happen if a particular course of action is pursued. Supervisors make many decisions each day, especially in working with subordinates, where little mental reflection is required because they are sufficiently informed about the operations to know exactly what should be done. At least 95 percent of the decisions made by supervisors are judgmental. Rarely do they have to stop and get more information on a topic unless the problem is new or their experience does not cover the issue.[3]

A third method of decision making is *problem solving*, which involves situations in which quick judgments are not adequate. More information is needed, and such decisions usually require some time, allowing for study, analysis, and reflection. This rational method ordinarily involves an objective or scientific approach and is especially used for solving complex problems involving several choices.

GUIDELINES FOR DECISION MAKING

Although business and management have led in suggesting procedures and guidelines for the decision-making process, social work is developing rapidly

[2]Howard M. Carlisle, *Management Essentials: Concepts for Productivity and Innovation* 2nd ed. (Chicago: Science Research Associates, 1987), pp. 112–113.

[3]Ibid., p. 113.

in this regard. The following is a set of guidelines for decision making that are relevant for social work administration and practice.

1. Define the Situation or Problem. Social psychologist W. I. Thomas introduced the concept of *defining the situation*, which implies that to understand people and their behavior, it is imperative to understand the varying problematical situations in which they find themselves, as well as their interpretations and feelings about them. In other words, it is important to know "where a person is" at a given moment; what psychological, sociological, and cultural factors and forces are involved; and what the feelings of that person and relevant others are about the total situation. It is also necessary to understand what the problem actually is and to understand its setting.

The 1988 Accreditation Standards of the CSWE recognized the need to understand the diversities of people and situations; they require the schools of social work to "have stated affirmative procedures and a stated policy against discrimination on the basis of race, color, creed, gender, ethnic or national origin, or age." CSWE's 1992 Curriculum Policy Statement for the MSW degree goes further, requiring the programs of social work education to "present theoretical and practice content about patterns, dynamics, and consequences of discrimination, economic deprivation, and oppression. The curriculum must provide content about people of color, women, and gay and lesbian persons. . . . In addition . . . include, but are not limited to, those distinguished by age, ethnicity, culture, class, religion, and physical or mental ability."[4]

One must get at the heart of the problem. Often, superficialities are exchanged that cover up the real situation, and decisions based on false premises may not be germane. Effective administrators try to define the situation, including both facts and feelings, and to come as close as they can to actuality. They look not only for what is on "top of the table" but for what is "under the table" as well. They realize, for example, that a staff member who is suggesting changes in the administrative structure of an agency in reality is asking for more responsibility, authority, or recognition. Administrators also recognize that workers' feelings are often more important than their thoughts, suggestions, or requests, and that it is extremely important to define the situation both by verbalizing the facts and comprehending the emotional climate. An example of defining the situation can be seen in the hiring of a new staff member. It is important to ascertain what the prospective employee really thinks and feels about the opportunities the agency offers, not just what he or she says.

[4]*Curriculum Policy Statement for Master's Degree Programs in Social Work Education* (Alexandria, VA: Council on Social Work Education, 1992), p. 8.

2. Collect and Study the Facts.   A major step in the decision-making process is collecting and studying data germane to the situation or problem. The collection of facts can take place in many ways. Ideas and feelings may be obtained from the person who asks for a decision. Data may be acquired, of course, from that person's associates and family members. Records may be checked to see what the objective data are regarding a person or situation. The collection of facts is an approximation because it is usually impossible to collect all pertinent data that exist. Nevertheless, basic facts should be ascertained to give meaning to the decision.

Studying the facts is essential in decision making. This means that the data need to be scrutinized carefully and objectively, and their importance must be weighed. The importance of facts is often relative, and careful study and analysis of information inevitably help to set priorities.

If one does not possess enough information to make an informed decision, additional information must be sought. This process can be illustrated by a hypothetical situation. A director of a community services council has a decision to make. The local United Way has raised serious questions about the contributions of the agency to the welfare of the community. Before the director decides what to do, he has to find out the details of the charges against him and his agency, including their possible meaning. These might be obtained from the administrators of the United Way or board members as well as from others in the power structure who might know what is going on behind the scenes. The director may also want to hear opinions of people who have been serviced by his agency. With the additional information, he can then make a sound decision.

3. Formulate Choices.   The process of making decisions is like being at a crossroads and having to decide which highway to take. Sometimes there may be only two choices; at other times, numerous alternatives may exist. It is important to recognize and understand the different alternatives that are available. Each one needs to be clarified and understood. Although all roads may lead to Rome, there is probably one route that is the best from a given location.

For example, consider a confrontation with staff members who are not performing well. The director or administrator may consider one or several of the following alternatives:

Fire them immediately.
Talk to them and encourage them to do better.
Talk to them and try to train them to do better.
Invite their colleagues to work with them and help them to do better.
Move them to other positions where they might function more efficiently.
Change the organizational pattern of the agency to accommodate their abilities and interests.

Although other possibilities might exist, these are common in this kind of situation. It is up to the administrator to understand fully the choices available in making an intelligent, fair decision.

4. Anticipate Likely Results of the Choices.   In addition to understanding different choices and priorities, it is essential to anticipate likely outcomes. Each alternative must be considered in regard to what would be likely to happen if a particular direction is chosen. Additional questions that need to be considered concerning a specific alternative are these: When would it happen? Where would it happen? How would it happen? In addition, what are the anticipated results in terms of the individual(s) involved, others, and the agency? In some ways, anticipated outcomes are most important because staff members in an agency are there to carry out the agency's goals and to maintain its values and services.

An example of this process might involve granting additional responsibility and authority to a supervisor. The two alternatives would be either to do it or not to do it. Not to do it would mean that the agency's work would go along as usual. To change might bring about a variety of outcomes. It might be advantageous to the delivery of services in the agency. It might slow down services. It might strengthen the individual supervisor, who would have ego satisfaction and feelings of accomplishment. The choice then might be between increasing responsibility and authority to build up the individual or leaving things as they are, supposedly for the welfare of the agency. The goal presumably is to make changes in responsibility that will benefit both the agency and individual. Timing is also important. The alternative most appropriate for the present or the future is the one to understand and to adopt.

5. Consider Feelings.   Theoretically, as mentioned earlier, decisions are made on a rational basis, after careful consideration of facts, alternatives, and anticipated outcomes. In reality, feelings and emotions often color, affect, and alter rational reasons for action. Certainly in the decision-making process, consideration of individual feelings about different choices is paramount.

Administrators who look at facts showing rather clearly that someone deserves to be promoted but who hesitate because they feel negatively about this person need to take a careful look at how they feel and why. They may find that their feelings have a flimsy foundation; if they view the situation objectively, their feelings may shift and become consonant with rationality. They may, however, find that their feelings are based on facts that they had not considered previously. On the basis of these, they will make a decision that might be entirely different from that which appeared to be rational at the outset.

It is important to recognize that all administrators have a variety of feelings, each of which may be significant in making a specific decision. Feelings such as fear, hate, uncertainty, anger, and trust need to be scrutinized and understood if effective, sound administrative decisions are to be made.

6. Choose Sound Action.   After the above-mentioned steps have taken place, it is up to the administrator to make the decision—to choose the path that seems appropriate and makes the most sense.

Administrators need to recognize that they will make mistakes in making decisions, that sometimes they will make a wrong choice. In fact, this occurs to all administrators and recognizing it can facilitate the decision-making process. There is no perfection in decision making, just as there is no perfection in other aspects of human relationships.

It is usually important to avoid postponing decisions for too long. Procrastination can be debilitating to the administrative process, and administrators who procrastinate too often are basically incompetent. However, care should be taken not to move too fast, too soon. Sometimes considerable time is needed for sound decision making.

7. Follow Through.   Once a decision is arrived at, every effort should be made to support it and to do what must be done to carry it out. Half-hearted support or neglect may doom a decision to failure. Following through requires the personal support of the administrator and staff members when needed. All staff members should be made aware of the decision in order to understand and support it. Sometimes a decision needs to be carried out by one person, with the cooperation and assistance of other staff members. Either those in administrative roles or those on the firing line may assume the initiative or be asked to lead.

It is important not only to make a decision but also to sustain the support that will guide it on its journey to its destination—just like a rocket that has been launched from the pad at Cape Canaveral. This necessitates interest, enthusiasm, back-up, time, and sharing responsibility and authority with others.

8. Be Flexible.   Flexibility is critical in decision making and in making an outcome effective. It is necessary to have an open mind in case an error has been made or another alternative becomes more desirable or advantageous. A decision should not be firm for the sake of firmness. It should be carried out only if it seems to be best and no valid reasons arise for changing it.

Since it is impossible to anticipate every possible outcome of a particular decision, sometimes the result is not what was anticipated. Then it is necessary to alter plans and procedures. For example, in a large, comprehensive mental-health center, it was decided, after careful consideration, to send out a weekly newsletter to keep the staff apprised of developments and actions. After two editions, it was clear that it would take too much time and effort and thus not be worthwhile to publish the newsletter this often. The decision was made to publish a monthly newsletter, which was more practical and meaningful for all concerned.

9. Evaluate Results. Careful evaluations should be made to ascertain developments that have followed the decision. Usually it is helpful to make a tentative analysis soon after action has been taken. At a later date a more comprehensive evaluation should be done so that changes may be made if necessary.

EVALUATING DECISIONS

The quality of decision making is another significant factor. Janis and Mann suggest that an examination of procedures used by the decision maker is one means of predicting whether a given decision is likely to lead to satisfaction or regret. From an extensive review of the literature, they identify seven major criteria to determine the quality of decision-making procedures. They conclude, "Although systematic data are not yet available, it seems plausible to assume that decisions satisfying these seven 'ideal' procedural criteria have a better chance than others of attaining the decision maker's objectives and of being adhered to in the long run."

The decision maker, to the best of his or her ability and information-processing capabilities, does the following:

1. Thoroughly canvasses a wide range of alternative courses of action;
2. Surveys the full range of objectives to be fulfilled and the values implicated by the choice;
3. Carefully weighs whatever he knows about the costs and risks of negative consequences, as well as the positive consequences, that could flow from each alternative;
4. Intensively searches for new information relevant to further evaluation of the alternatives;
5. Correctly assimilates and takes account of any new information or expert judgment to which he is exposed, even when the information or judgment does not support the course of action he initially prefers;
6. Reexamines the positive and negative consequences of all known alternatives, including those originally regarded as unacceptable, before making a final choice;
7. Makes detailed provisions for implementing or executing the chosen course of action, with special attention to contingency plans that might be required if various known risks were to materialize.[5]

[5]Irving L. Janis and Leon Mann, *Decision Making* (New York: Free Press, 1977), p. 11.

TECHNIQUES OF DECISION MAKING

Individual or Group

Decisions may be made by individuals or by groups. In social work, many decisions that affect agencies' policies and procedures are shared by several members of the staff. Certain powers inhere in group relationships that are absent in individual behavior, and these can be used to advantage in the decision-making process.

Usually a few key individuals influence the thinking and feeling of others and are really the powerhouses in decision making. Hubert Humphrey, former vice president, at a public lecture in 1970 observed, "Consensus is decided by a working minority" rather than the majority—"the majority does not get things done."

Power and creativity are inherent when staff members meet to consider problems and alternatives and then make decisions. Modern social work is increasingly using the group process to crystallize decisions about problems and plans of action. Committee action has increased in use, along with involvement of clients and public-spirited citizens who serve on advisory committees and boards that guide the destinies of agencies.

When ideas and interests of a larger group are wanted the *Delphi method* is often used as a procedure for obtaining opinions and information from a group of experts or involved persons. Questionnaires are sent to these people, and their answers are tabulated and analyzed. Then new questionnaires are sent, asking for their reactions to information that has been summarized from the first round and played back to them. This system derives from the early practice of the priestess at Delphi, who sent runners to different parts of the country to gather opinions from various wise men. Today computers and other kinds of equipment simplify and speed up the process.

Webber indicates that opinions differ on how to obtain the best thinking of a group. Group action is slower, not as accurate as that of the most acute individuals, but more accurate than that of most individuals. That is, the group process is usually a leveling one. Webber reports that five-person groups take longer than individuals working alone (50 percent longer), but most groups perform better than persons working alone.[6]

The advantages and disadvantages of group decision making are summarized by Bedeian[7] as follows:

ADVANTAGES

1. Acceptance by those affected is increased.
2. Coordination is easier.

[6]Ross A. Webber, *Management* (Homewood, IL: Richard D. Irwin, 1975), p. 527.

[7]Arthur G. Bedeian, *Management*, 3rd ed. (Forth Worth, TX: Dryden Press, 1993), pp. 216–217.

3. Communication is easier.
4. Greater number of alternatives can be considered.
5. More information can be processed.

DISADVANTAGES

1. Group decisions take longer to reach than individual decisions.
2. Groups can be indecisive.
3. Groups can compromise.
4. Groups can be dominated.
5. Groups can play games.
6. Groups can fall victim to "groupthink" (where the drive to achieve consensus becomes so powerful that it overrides independent, realistic appraisals of alternative actions).

Programmed or Nonprogrammed

Traditionally, a variety of techniques has been used in the decision-making process. Recently, with the advance of electronics, computers, and other innovations—mechanical and psychological—new means have come to the fore. Simon divides types of decisions into two categories, programmed and nonprogrammed. The programmed is the regular, organized, formal kind of situation; the nonprogrammed is at the other end of the continuum, along with informal, spontaneous, and ill-structured types of situations.[8] Simon suggests that we have a long way to go in developing effective decision-making techniques (see Table 5–1).

Social workers are using a variety of traditional techniques. Many larger social agencies are utilizing computers and other scientific devices to assist with the decision-making process.

Fulmer suggests asking certain basic questions to help with preventive problem solving. He states that answers to the following questions can be of genuine help in making sound decisions:

1. What is right?
2. What can go wrong?
3. What could cause this problem to occur?
4. What preventive action can I take?
5. What is my contingency plan?
6. When will my alternative plan go into action?[9]

[8]Herbert A. Simon, "Traditional Decision-Making Methods," in Harry A. Schatz, ed., *Social Work Administration: A Resource Book* (New York: Council on Social Work Education, 1970), p. 190.

[9]Robert M. Fulmer, *The New Management*, 4th ed. (New York: Macmillan, 1988), pp. 50–54.

Preventive decision making inheres in the anticipatory process of looking ahead and thinking of what might occur. By looking ahead, the decision may be held in abeyance or changed.

TABLE 5–1.   Traditional and Modern Techniques of Decision Making

TYPES OF DECISION	TECHNIQUES	
	TRADITIONAL	MODERN
PROGRAMMED Routine, repetitive decisions Organization develops specific processes for handling them	1. Habit 2. Clerical routine: Standard operating procedures 3. Organization structure: Common expectations System of subgoals Well defined infor- mational channels	1. Operations research: Mathematical analysis Models Computer simulation 2. Electronics data processing
NONPROGRAMMED One-shot, ill-structured, novel policy decisions Handled by general problem-solving processes	1. Judgment, intuition, and creativity 2. Rules of thumb 3. Selection and training of executives	Heuristic problem- solving techniques applied to: (a) training human decision makers (b) constructing heuristic computer programs

Source: Adapted from Herbert A. Simon, *The New Science of Management Decision,* rev. ed. (Englewood Cliffs, NJ: Prentice Hall, 1977), p. 48. Reprinted by permission.

PITFALLS IN DECISION MAKING

Carlisle suggests numerous restrictions in management problem solving, four of which are especially important:

1. People have limited rationality and knowledge.
2. Lack of time often prevents intensive analysis.
3. Goals sought are generally not maximal.
4. Pressures brought by others are often more significant than "the facts" collected to support each alternative.[10]

There are many dangers and pitfalls in the decision-making process. Some of the more important ones are the following:

[10]Carlisle, *Management Essentials,* p. 123.

1. Procrastination. It is easy to let matters slide, in the hope that problems will resolve themselves or go away. Sometimes time will take care of or solve a difficult situation. Often, however, stalling only complicates the problem. Competent administrators believe in and practice the prime motto "Do it now."

2. Oversimplification. There is a tendency to follow simple steps in problem solving and/or decision making, believing that such action will solve the problem. Usually it is not that easy. Sherman dramatizes oversimplification as follows:

> A . . . pitfall is oversimplification. If my experience has taught me anything, it is that the "192 principles" of organization that can be extracted from the textbooks do not begin to answer even the least complex organization problems. Why? There are many reasons. Values differ, conditions change, all the facts are rarely (if ever) available, non-rational as well as rational factors influence the decisions made. But the most pervasive reason is that organizing involves people. And people react on the basis of an almost infinite number of stimuli. I have yet to participate in the discussion of a concrete organization problem in which we did not spend more time discussing how a key figure would react, and the abilities, prejudices, likes and dislikes, and strengths and weaknesses of the principal executives involved than all the time (if any) spent discussing "unity of command," "span of control," the "scalar principle," and the "general staff concept."[11]

3. Irrational Behavior. There is always the possibility that decisions will not be made on an objective, fair basis. Complexities and feelings, as well as differences in people, cause many detours from sound decisions.

As mentioned earlier, traditional economic and managerial theories imply that rationality rules in the decision-making process, that administrators consider problems, look at facts and alternatives, and then make sound decisions about what is best. It is also recognized that decision making is often a challenging process that is very complex and difficult, as no administrator knows all the facts and relationships in a given situation. Also feelings often surface that influence the decision more than do the facts.

4. Mistakes Bring Discouragement. Executives and staff members who participate in decision making in an agency constantly need to keep in mind that mistakes will be made and will have to be lived with. Even when the best problem-solving techniques are used, errors creep in because of the complexity of social relationships and changing social and emotional situations.

Administrators and staff members need to be accepting of one another when mistakes occur. Errors should be rectified as soon as possible, but they

[11]Harvey Sherman, *It All Depends: A Pragmatic Approach to Organization* (University: University of Alabama Press, 1967), pp. 104–105.

should not be punished. A competent administrator realizes that no one is perfect, or even nearly so, and that an accepting attitude is paramount in the administration of a social service agency.

SUMMARY

Effective decision making is vital in social work administration. It affects the delivery of social services and the lives of individuals as well as groups and communities. Following are basic guidelines for decision making:

1. Define the situation
2. Collect and study the facts
3. Formulate choices
4. Anticipate likely outcomes of the alternatives
5. Consider feelings
6. Choose sound action
7. Follow through
8. Be flexible
9. Evaluate results

Pitfalls in decision making include these:

1. Procrastination
2. Oversimplification
3. Irrational behavior
4. Mistakes that bring discouragement

Some decisions are best made by individuals, others by group interaction.

QUESTIONS FOR DISCUSSION

1. Why is decision making so important in social work administration?

2. How effective is intuition in making staff decisions? Illustrate your position.

3. What did W. I. Thomas mean by "defining the situation"? Interpret this concept in relation to a beginning step in the decision-making process.

4. Present the nine guidelines for decision making in this chapter. Evaluate and illustrate one of them.

5. What kinds of decisions are best handled individually and what kinds are best handled by groups?

6. Why is decision making such a difficult process, especially in social work administration and practice?

7. Tell the class the process you went through in deciding about your interest in social work. How difficult was it?

SPECIAL ACTIVITIES

1. Read the chapter by Bedeian on decision making and present to the class the view of business management in this current, popular business text.

2. Role-play consideration of a decision of your choice, involving two or three college students, to illustrate challenges and problems that may arise in such a process.

3. Invite a social work agency director to make a presentation to your class, discussing challenges and problems in decision making on the job.

SELECTED REFERENCES

BEDEIAN, ARTHUR G. "Managerial Decision Making." *Management*, 3rd ed., pp. 200–233. Fort Worth, TX: Dryden Press, 1993.

CARLISLE, HOWARD M. *Management Essentials: Concepts for Productivity and Innovation*, 2nd ed., pp. 109–136. Chicago: Science Research Associates, 1987.

FALLON, KENNETH P., JR. "Participatory Management: An Alternative in Human Service Delivery Systems." In Simon Slavin, ed., *Social Administration: The Management of the Social Services*, 2nd ed. Vol. I, *An Introduction to Human Services Management*, pp. 251–259. New York: Haworth Press, 1985.

HERZBERG, FREDERICK. *The Managerial Choice: To Be Efficient and to Be Human*. Homewood, IL: Dow Jones-Irwin, 1976.

PACKARD, THOMAS. "Managers' and Workers' Views of the Dimensions of Participation in Organizational Decision-Making. *Administration in Social Work* 17, No. 2 (1993), 53–65.

PACKARD, THOMAS. "Participation in Decision Making, Performance, and Job Satisfaction in a Social Work Bureaucracy." *Administration in Social Work* 13, No. 1 (1989), 59–73.

POPPLE, PHILIP R. "Negotiation: A Critical Skill for Social Work Administrators." *Administration in Social Work* 8 (Summer 1984), 1–11.

RESNICK, HERMAN, and RINO J. PATTI. *Change from Within: Humanizing Social Welfare Organizations*. Philadelphia: Temple University Press, 1980.

SLAVIN, SIMON, ed. *Social Administration: The Management of the Social Services*, 2nd ed. Vol. II, *Managing Finances, Personnel, and Information in Human Services*. New York: Haworth Press, 1985.

TAYLOR, RONALD N. *Behavioral Decision Making*. Glenview, IL: Scott, Foresman, 1984.

THOMAS, JOHN CLAYTON. "Public Involvement and Governmental Effectiveness: A Decision-Making Model for Public Managers." *Administration and Society* 24 (February 1993), 444–469.

WERNET, STEPHEN P., and DAVID M. AUSTIN. "Decision Making Style and Leadership Patterns in Nonprofit Human Service Organizations." *Administration in Social Work* 15, No. 3 (1991), 1–16.

6

Financial
Management

The director came to work early and went home late. During the day he seemed sullen, uncooperative, and uninterested in his staff. Someone asked him late in the afternoon, "What's the matter, boss?" He retorted, "Don't bother me; I'm working on budgets."

It is often difficult to cope with the financial aspects of social work administration, especially with present-day changes, rollbacks, and the termination of programs. Yet these factors can decide the fate of an agency.

Competent administrators are aware of different resources they can tap to obtain funds for their agency. They know the value of a carefully planned budget. After financial resources have been allocated, they need the ability and skills to implement the budget in an effective, efficient manner. Administrators need to look at money matters and budgets philosophically as well as pragmatically. Too often they become confused. The following three factors are particularly important financially in a social work agency:

1. The attitude of the administrator and the staff members toward money and budgets
2. The amount of income and money available to the agency
3. The effective (or ineffective) use of the money available

The attitude toward money is particularly important; it can make or break an agency. Agency income is important, but not all-important. A competent administrator recognizes and maintains a realistic attitude toward obtaining and dispensing funds. Administrators and staff can be appreciative or critical toward funds allocated to them, and the position they take does make a difference. If administrators and staff are realistic about the money available, they are likely to achieve better results in the delivery of social services. Administrators who overemphasize the value of money in their agencies may have morale problems and difficulties with staff that surpass their financial realities. The caseworker who is constantly critical about budgetary matters will hurt the agency and lessen his or her contribution to it. This does not mean that financial questions should not be raised and budgetary suggestions made. In fact, in the money arena, all staff members are needed to help develop resources for the agency, make suggestions about the budget, and help maintain efficiency and effectiveness in implementing financial plans.

A carefully planned budget is of the utmost importance for the welfare of a social agency. The director or budget officer may have the major responsibility for planning the budget, but it is best that the democratic process be invoked to obtain suggestions and reactions from staff members at all levels. This does not mean leaving the final decisions to staff members or giving them all the details to work out—individual salaries, for example—but it does involve open, two-way communication in budgetary planning.

On the one hand, the amount of money available to an agency is important because it sets the parameters of agency operation. On the other hand, it is of interest that some agencies provide similar services and yet have different incomes. An agency's services are not always in direct proportion to the amount of money in the budget.

Efficient and effective use of the money available is of the utmost importance. Two agencies with basically the same income and services to perform may vary considerably in their delivery of social services, depending on how they use or waste their financial resources.

BUDGETING

Financial Resources

Social work agencies obtain money from a variety of sources, both public and private. Many receive federal allocations, some get state money, some county funds, some city allocations. Private sources include foundations and corporations as well as individuals who are interested in the services of a given agency. Administrators who plan carefully can usually derive income from several sources. For example, the director of an alcohol-treatment center indicated he was receiving funds from twenty-six different sources, both public and private, to operate his agency.

If administrators wish to receive government funds, they need to plan a long time before the meeting of the legislature, the commissions, or the advisory committee to be able to justify their request. They need a well-prepared explanation of their needs, services, and specific plans. They may have to prepare brochures, which should be clearly worded and attractive. Personal contact is particularly important. Decisions are often made by a few key people who participate in the legislative process, not by the total body. Appropriate contacts, made on a personal, meaningful basis, often produce desired results.

Persistence and patience are essential. Many requests have been turned down once, twice, or three times, and then finally been approved because of the persistence of competent administrators. Ordinarily, administrators should not take no for an answer *if* what they are requesting is significant.

Definitions

The word *budget* derives from an old French term, *bougette*, which means a "little bag," a sack or pouch. "The British adopted the word to describe the motion engaged in by the chancellor of the exchequer when he presented his annual financial statement to Parliament. He was said to open his 'budget' or bag which contained the various financial documents."[1]

The importance of the budgeting process in both public and private agencies and organizations is interpreted by Carlisle:

> The budget is the most universally used, comprehensive, formal management system for planning and controlling operations. Not all organizations have formal plans, but, with few exceptions, all have budgets. Furthermore, most planning and control systems cover only one aspect or function of an organization because their different activities cannot be equated. However, budgets encompass all elements, and appropriate comparisons can be made using the dollar as the common denominator.
>
> The significance of the budget does not stop here. Those who control the purse strings hold the power in the organization. A program or unit cannot function without resources, and it is the budget that makes obtaining resources possible. The budget is a valve that management uses to let resources flow to functions or programs, depending on which they want to emphasize. No other internal tool is as effective in expressing the will of management. The annual budget decisions are some of the most significant that management makes and should receive thorough care and consideration. Each subunit fights for its share of the budget pie, because resources provide the capacity to pursue opportunities. Without adequate resources, no organization can perform at its full potential.
>
> Budgeting is usually more critical for public than private institutions.[2]

Gross suggests that the budget is a plan of action: "It represents the organization's blueprint for the coming months, or years, expressed in monetary terms."[3] The budget has two main functions: to record in monetary

[1]*Budgeting: A Guide for United Ways and Not-for-Profit Human Service Organizations* (Alexandria, VA: United Way of America, 1975), p. 3.

[2]Howard M. Carlisle, *Management Essentials: Concepts for Productivity and Innovation*, 2nd ed. (Chicago: Science Research Associates, 1987), pp. 249–250.

[3]Malvern J. Gross, "The Importance of Budgeting," in Simon Slavin, ed., *Social Administration* (New York: Haworth Press and Council on Social Work Education, 1978), p. 233.

terms realistic goals or objectives of an organization for the coming year and to provide a monitor for the financial activities throughout the year. The objectives need to be specific and realistic and must be approved by the board or other governing body. For the budget to serve effectively on the monitoring level, the following elements must be present:

1. The budget must be well-conceived, and have been prepared or approved by the board.
2. The budget must be broken down into periods corresponding to the periodic financial statements.
3. Financial statements must be prepared on a timely basis throughout the year and a comparison made to the budget, right on the statements.
4. The board must be prepared to take action where the comparison with the budget indicates a significant deviation.[4]

TYPES OF BUDGETS

In many nonprofit and social work agencies, budgets have not been prepared and used in a significant way. Traditionally, the line-item budget has been used the most; however, in recent years it has come under fire because it does not depict efficiency, effectiveness, priorities, or programs of the agency. Consequently, other strategies and patterns are utilized in increasing numbers by social service agencies.

Social work agencies extensively utilize four formats or combinations thereof: line-item budgeting, program budgeting, functional budgeting, and zero-based budgeting. They are not mutually exclusive and can be combined in various ways to bolster administrative effectiveness in an agency. Table 6–1 presents a hypothetical budget prepared by the United Way of America to illustrate salient factors related to each of the first three patterns.

Line-item Budgeting

The line-item budget is the most elementary and most used format in private and public social work agencies. It is based on line-item accounting and incremental increases in projecting ahead for a year or more. This system indicates how the money is to be spent but does not depict what the agency does. It is not program oriented. The proposed expenditures for each department or unit are listed for a specific period of time. It does not present agency goals, targets, programs, or results.

The line-item system is illustrated in Table 6–1 by the specific items listed in the left margin, with total amounts indicated in the right margin. Also, as in this table, estimates are often made for a year ahead. In this instance the salaries for the first year are $243,300 and for the next are

---

[4]Ibid., p. 234.

TABLE 6-1 Family Service Agency of Utopia, Inc.

	PROGRAM SERVICES				SUPPORTING SERVICES			TOTAL PROGRAM AND SUPPORTING SERVICES EXPENSES	
	ADOPTION	FOSTER HOME CARE	COUNSELING	TOTAL	MANAGEMENT AND GENERAL	FUND RAISING	TOTAL	19X2	19X1
Salaries	$ 33,600	$ 25,100	$126,900	$185,600	$33,100	$36,800	$ 69,900	$255,500	$243,300
Employee benefits	1,800	1,400	6,400	9,600	2,200	1,500	3,700	13,300	12,500
Payroll taxes, etc.	3,000	2,300	12,400	17,700	3,000	3,100	6,100	23,800	21,500
Total salaries and related expenses	38,400	28,800	145,700	212,900	38,300	41,400	79,700	292,600	277,300
Professional fees	63,000	300	61,200	124,500	2,600	800	3,400	127,900	125,300
Supplies	3,900	21,300	1,300	26,500	1,800	1,700	3,500	30,000	27,100
Telephone	9,500	1,000	1,100	11,600	1,500	2,300	3,800	15,400	16,800
Postage and shipping	2,900	1,300	8,900	13,100	1,000	9,000	10,000	23,100	18,000
Occupancy	2,550	21,100	11,250	34,900	1,500	1,350	2,850	37,750	36,300
Interest	—	—	100	100	800	—	800	900	200
Rental and maintenance of equipment	3,550	1,100	1,250	5,900	1,500	1,350	2,850	8,750	9,300
Printing and publications	5,400	400	6,400	12,200	300	1,600	1,900	14,100	15,800

Travel and transportation	12,500	2,000	2,200	16,700	2,300	3,000	5,300	22,000	31,300
Conferences, conventions, & meetings	3,700	7,100	2,000	12,800	4,500	400	4,900	17,700	20,600
Specific assistance to individuals	16,500	24,300	5,000	45,800	—	—	—	45,800	48,400
Membership dues	500	—	—	500	—	—	—	500	500
Awards and grants—									
To national organization	10,000	—	3,000	13,000	—	—	—	13,000	14,200
To individuals and other organizations	11,000	11,900	—	22,900	—	—	—	22,900	26,300
Insurance	10,450	10,100	5,100	25,650	600	50	650	26,300	21,000
Other expenses	1,250	500	400	2,150	100	2,050	2,150	4,300	5,600
Depreciation of buildings & equipment	700	600	2,900	4,200	600	400	1,000	5,200	4,600
Total functional expenses	$195,800	$131,800	$257,800	$585,400	$57,400	$65,400	$122,800	$708,200	$698,600
Payments to national organization								12,400	15,400
Total expenses								$720,600	$714,000

Source: United Way of America, *Accounting & Financial Reporting* (Alexandria, V.A.: United Way of America, 1989), p. 149. Reprinted by permission.

increased to $255,500. The total expenses for the agency amount to $714,000 for the first year and, projected for the year ahead, to a total of $720,600.

Stretch highlights essentials of line-item budgeting, defining it as an approach that allows for

> a very tight degree of managerial control over each major significant resource item allocated through the budget decision process. The main feature and advantage of the line budget approach is its reliance on explicit categories of expenditures to insure justification. Suffice it to say that when human services managers usually think of "the budget," they are most probably thinking of the typical item-by-item line control budget where such key expenditure categories as personnel, rent, utilities, and so forth, are explicitly defined and authorized in terms of what can be spent on each line item.[5]

Program Budgeting

Program budgeting includes services offered by the agency. Goals and objectives are a significant part of this system. Such a budget may cover several years, particularly as a program is offered and approved for a specific amount of time. Cost estimates and specifics of each program are included. In Table 6-1 the Program Services section illustrates this approach. The Family Service Agency has three programs: counseling, budgeted at $257,800; adoption, budgeted at $195,800; and foster-home care, budgeted at $131,800. The total for program services is $585,400, which leaves a balance of $122,800 for supporting services.

Stretch suggests that "program budgeting as an additional management strategy is closely allied with the objective of effective monitoring of fiscal and human resources as these are targeted to achieve program objectives." He explains the salient characteristics of this system as follows:

> Program budgeting considers expenditures in light of the major program components operative in the human service agency's mix of services. Program budgeting has been found to be a useful management tool in monitoring the effect of key allocation decisions as these affect the level of program quality. Program budgeting is essentially output oriented. A program budget is constructed by regrouping all line item expenditures into their respective program area. For example, the line items of personnel, rent and utilities would be regrouped according to some rational formula of direct and indirect cost factors to reflect the various programs that these resources support.[6]

An example of program budgeting is PPBS, or planning, programming, and budgeting systems. This term came into popular use, particularly in federal and state governments, in the 1960s. In 1965 President Lyndon Johnson

[5]John J. Stretch, "Seven Key Managerial Functions of Sound Fiscal Budgeting: An Internal Management and External Accountability Perspective," *Administration in Social Work* 3 (Winter 1979), 445.

[6]Ibid., p. 447.

recommended to all federal government agencies that they use this system. According to Fulmer, this pattern

> emphasized that programs had to be planned and budgeted as units, even when they shared many support functions. The system requires the identification of programs and all their associated costs. Budgets are developed for the entire project, though it may span several years. . . . The system affords new perspectives on accountability, and results in a beneficial use of cost analysis and system-effectiveness studies. PPBS is no cure-all, but it has proven effective in stimulating interest in reality-based budgeting.[7]

Functional Budgeting

This system encompasses program services but emphasizes the supporting administrative services that are needed for operating an agency. Programs and services are put into categories that can be monitored on a functional accounting basis. This is a system that lists all revenues and expenditures, particularly as they relate to management and general functions, fund-raising functions (if any), and identifiable programs offered by the agency. In Table 6–1 the programs absorb most of the budget money, but the supporting services require $122,800 of the total $714,000. Most federal grant applications use a modified version of this system.

Zero-based Budgeting

Zero-based budgeting (ZBB) has gained much attention and momentum, particularly in government agencies. This is an attempt to tighten budget strings and to require agencies to justify their expenditures in relation to services and outcomes. Zero-based budgeting operates on the premise that an agency must start from scratch and each year justify every financial request it makes. In other words, the agency starts with no money each year and describes and justifies all expenditures that are claimed for the ensuing year, whether they have existed before or not. This process means that some agencies' allocations are cut back and some agencies or programs are abolished. For most, however, it means more careful scrutiny is made of where the money is spent and why, particularly in regard to specific needs for the present and future. Zero-based budgeting has received considerable support from top government officials and those in private enterprise, even from presidents of the United States and many governors. It is a comprehensive consideration of each item in the budget with no part being guaranteed for the future.

Otten suggests that we should not be too harsh "in rendering premature judgment on ZBB. The concept squarely addresses many of the shortcomings

---

[7]Robert M. Fulmer, *The New Management*, 2nd ed. (New York: Macmillan, 1978), p. 148.

of the traditional budgeting approach. . . . Certainly, it presents a unique challenge for those who advocate accountability, and it offers an even greater challenge to those committed to delivering more effective services to the impoverished and disadvantaged of our nation."[8]

Another innovation during the past few years has been the passing of *sunset laws* by numerous legislatures. These laws provide money for an agency for a given length of time, at the end of which an agency may be discontinued. This has meant that some agencies or programs have been abolished at the end of two, three, or five years. For most agencies and programs, however, it has meant careful scrutiny, analysis, and justification of their budget needs.

BUDGETING AND FINANCIAL PLANNING

Preparing a budget in a social work agency is a challenging opportunity that ordinarily comes once a year. In actuality, it is a process that needs to be worked on throughout the year to be effective and meaningful. Historically, budgets were prepared by the administrator and handled by agency boards, with little staff involvement. Today, many budgetary matters are shared with the staff, and relevant guidelines are suggested by staff members. Details of the budget are usually left to administrators, who may be knowledgeable about the agency's total financial picture.

Budgeting is recognized as one of the important responsibilities of and opportunities for administrators in social agencies. Well-prepared budgets can and do make a tremendous difference in the delivery of social services. Poorly prepared budgets may result in the receipt of fewer funds, thus handicapping the agency.

Traditionally, budgeting has been the process of asking for a percentage increase over the offer in the previous year, with specific justification for innovative requests. Agency needs are explained and interpreted as part of the budget procedure.

In budget planning it is important to be realistic, flexible, and able to compromise at times. The competent administrator realizes that being realistic about financial requests is essential. There is seldom enough money to do what needs to be done. Also, in budget negotiations with boards or other higher authorities, it is important to be flexible yet firm in asking for allocations. Compromise invariably has to play a part in working out differences; the administrator who is too rigid will ordinarily end up with fewer funds.

---

[8]Gerald L. Otten, "Zero-Based Budgeting: Implications for Social Services?" in Simon Slavin, ed., *Social Administration: The Management of the Social Services*, 2nd ed., Vol. II, *Managing Finances, Personnel, and Information in Human Services* (New York: Haworth Press, 1985), p. 136.

Two other factors are relevant in budget planning. Wise administrators do not pad their requests in anticipation of having them cut and ending up with what they need. This action often backfires, to the detriment of the agency. Also, in most agencies it is advisable to request that a limited contingency fund be available for emergencies and unexpected developments.

The Budget-making Process

The budget-making process involves the following main steps:

1. Setting specific goals related to the needs of the agency
2. Ascertaining facts regarding the agency's operation
3. Looking at specific alternatives for the operation of the agency, particularly in terms of money
4. Deciding on priorities for the agency
5. Finalizing decisions regarding the budget
6. Providing adequate interpretation and public relations

First, in budget construction it is particularly important for the administrator and those assisting with budget formulations to look at the specific needs and goals of the agency. Goals for the future may be basically the same as those of the past, or they may be different. To set meaningful goals, it is important to review the basic policies and procedures of the agency and make objectives as specific as possible, within time-framed parameters. The goals and objectives ought to be observable and measurable so that evaluations can take place periodically to ascertain how the agency is performing in the delivery of social services.

The second major step is to collect and study basic information regarding the current and past operation of the agency, including what has and has not been accomplished. Facts need to be looked at both in relation to the agency as a whole and on an individual basis for staff and professional workers. Of course, building resources and facilities need to be taken into consideration.

Third, it is necessary to look at alternatives, different ways of using the money that may become available during the year. Competent administrators are creative and, one hopes, innovative as they anticipate possible alternatives to the path ahead. They do not cast aside current programs just because they are no longer new, but they try to look at new possibilities in order to open new vistas for the agency in terms of services.

One of the most important parts of the budget process is for administrators to study different alternatives and list them in order of priority. Ordinarily there are more needs than can be met, and an agency has to decide which are most important at that time. Again, in establishing priorities, the fourth step, it is essential to look at agency policies and goals to see which are most financially compatible with the agency.

Fifth, actual decision making is usually the toughest part of the budgeting process. Administrators and other key personnel who help with budget formulation need to use the previous steps to gather pertinent data and then take all factors into consideration in making final decisions. Care has to be taken to look at needs and potentials both of the agency as a whole and of the individuals who work there. In social work agencies it is particularly important to consider the welfare of clients along with the efficiency of the agency's operation.

Sixth, after the budget blueprint has been adopted, competent administrators interpret it to those in positions of power so that they fully understand the reasons for specific requests. The better the job of public relations and interpretation to those who give the final budget approval, the more likely it is that positive results will ensue.

The United Way of America suggests eight major steps in the total budget-making process: preplanning, launching, data gathering and analysis, setting objectives, programming the objectives, preparing and testing the budget, modifying the budget, and adopting a balanced budget. These are highlighted, with major actions appropriate to each, in Figure 6–1.

Financial Operations

In addition to tapping resources and preparing the budget, another main component in agency financial operations is spending the money that is allocated or available. Certain basic principles and procedures are significant in this process.

A competent administrator periodically checks resources, budget allocations, and expenditures. During a given year, he or she may run into difficulty in any one of these, or even in all three. Also, as the year proceeds, the situation may need to be altered for any one of these factors.

Periodic checks are helpful, particularly for understanding what money is still available. This process opens up opportunities for improving agency services by utilizing total resources in a given period of time. Table 6–2 illustrates the monthly budget review process of a private agency, a Travelers Aid Society in a metropolitan area. Board members find this kind of financial report helpful, for it includes the total budget for the year, current monthly expenditures, totals spent to date, and percentage of budget expended to date for line items.

Ordinarily the money should be used as approved in the agency budget. If a basic shift of emphasis is contemplated, it should be cleared with the governing board. If the change in expenditures is of minor significance, the administrator may make the decision and handle the alteration. Financial

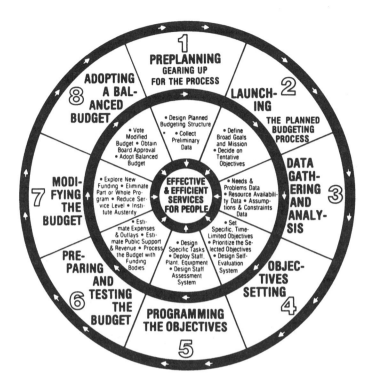

FIGURE 6-1 **Program-planning and Budget Cycle.** From *Budgeting: A Guide for United Ways and Not-for-profit Human Service Organizations* (Alexandria, VA: United Way of America, 1975), p. 16. Reprinted by permission.

flexibility is important, which means that there may be some transferring of funds from one part of a budget to another to take care of emergencies or other needs. Shifts in staff or programs may also necessitate this.

Usually it is important for an administrator to stay within budget allocations. When emergencies arise, sometimes a shift has to take place. Competent administrators usually work with the available funds. If they need more, they try to obtain additional financial resources in the year ahead by increasing their requested budget, giving adequate justification and interpretation.

Many administrators are trying to improve their financial operations and resources by utilizing improved methods in cost reporting. Gross suggests that this is an indispensable link to accountability and that administrators should be concerned about developing more measurable ways of expressing and describing output as well as inputs and costs. He suggests five alternative methods of cost reporting that may be used to advantage, depending on individual financial situations: reimbursable cost reporting, average per-person cost reporting, functional cost reporting, unit cost reporting, and

TABLE 6-2. A Monthly Budget Review

	REVENUES	BUDGET FY 1992–1993	CURRENT MONTH	YEAR TO DATE	PERCENT OF BUDGET RECEIVED TO DATE
4100	United Way	181,244.00	15,108.00	141,962.00	78
4200	Federal	223,671.00	17,721.50	154,684.55	69
4300	State fees	33,600.00	2,640.50	16,311.98	49
4310	State grants	322,830.00	49,074.85	298,036.26	92
4320	State Medicaid	35,000.00	2,965.28	17,015.54	49
4400	County grants	157,110.00	12,757.13	147,424.87	94
4410	County, other	100,000.00		100,000.00	100
4500	SLC grants	168,650.00	20,917.09	130,730.18	78
4600	Local grants, WVC	17,000.00	0.00	15,000.00	88
4610	Local grants, WJ	11,000.00	0.00	5,000.00	45
4700	Contributions, general	270,000.00	51,112.13	212,709.44	79
4710	Contributions, restricted	86,000.00	2,185.32	50,129.38	58
4720	Contributions, designated	160,000.00	4,796.44	186,121.61	116
4730	Contributions, events	66,500.00	50.00	85,052.82	128
4740	Contributions, endowments	70,000.00	0.00	8,000.00	11
4800	Revenue, fees	3,600.00	333.00	1,832.20	51
4810	Shelters	23,400.00	2,272.76	17,565.98	75
4900	Reimbursements, travel	7,500.00	241.40	5,663.05	76
5000	Interest	7,700.00	294.30	1,919.85	25
5100	Miscellaneous	10,000.00	180.53	17,660.01	177
5200	Contingency	149,797.00			
	TOTAL REVENUES	2,104,602.00	182,650.23	1,612,819.72	77%

TABLE 6-2. A Monthly Budget Review (continued)

EXPENSES		BUDGET FY 1992–1993	CURRENT MONTH	YEAR TO DATE	PERCENT OF BUDGET EXPENDED TO DATE
6050	Salaries, administration	325,865.00	26,358.91	245,473.18	75
6100	Salaries, program	926,535.00	83,993.37	702,614.86	76
6200	Vacation pay	1,450.00	0.00	0.00	0
6300	Payroll taxes	125,250.00	12,672.77	96,855.94	77
6350	Health/life insurance	105,250.00	10,066.29	90,120.24	86
6400	Interns	3,700.00	0.00	3,000.00	81
6450	Professional fees	9,450.00	359.85	6,185.35	65
6500	Travel, employees	3,950.00	220.80	2,118.02	54
6550	Conferences, meetings	7,275.00	773.05	2,587.78	36
6560	Membership dues	430.00	0.00	195.00	45
6570	National dues	6,600.00	632.41	5,691.75	86
6600	Supplies	52,298.00	4,924.70	29,588.95	57
6700	Telephone	21,475.00	2,108.58	16,880.76	79
6800	Utilities	124,690.00	10,980.06	90,677.78	73
6850	Repair/maintenance	70,728.00	3,393.23	50,741.28	72
6870	Operational expenses	14,781.00	572.00	10,378.83	70
6900	Vehicles	11,400.00	563.20	7,585.95	67
7010	General insurance	22,125.00	1,661.75	15,479.87	70
7500	Special assistance	111,800.00	11,654.10	81,043.65	72
7700	Restricted	35,500.00	1,728.34	27,464.47	77
7710	Special projects	7,000.00	0.00	0.00	0
7770	Fundraising	27,825.00	1,342.89	27,847.39	100
7850	Public relations/education	5,350.00	1,158.34	3,728.80	70
7950	Buildings	11,500.00	0.00	0.00	0
7960	Equipment	30,850.00	0.00	4,946.83	16
8000	Depreciation	28,100.00	4,378.18	35,694.09	127
8900	Miscellaneous	13,425.00	126.19	5,991.79	45
	TOTAL EXPENSES	2,104,602.00	179,669.01	1,562,892.56	74%

Source: Travelers Aid Society, Income Statement and Budget Comparison, April 30, 1993 (Fiscal Year July through June).

needs cost reporting. Gross observes that the "crucial role played by the cost reporting approach chosen points out the need for social worker administrators' involvement in choosing the appropriate cost reporting method to be used in analysis."[9]

Teaching Fiscal Management

In this fast-changing world, curricula in training social work administrators are shifting often. A current thrust is teaching fiscal management in schools of social work. For example, a few years ago a new course in financial management became a requirement for students in the social administration sequence at the Columbia University School of Social Work. The justification for this innovation was based on both program and fiscal accountability because of the following current developments: quantification and costing out of many elements of agency plans, operations, and services; increasing emphasis on accounting standards, auditing procedures, and financial reporting; required tracking of resources consumed in agency operations; multiplicity of city, county, and state funding streams for agencies; sophisticated developments in technology applied to financial management; and administrative sophistication needed to manage large-scale contracts for service delivery.[10]

Diversity of Staff

Staff members are particularly important in financial planning and in the implementation of financial decisions. The hiring, directing, and even firing of staff are among the greatest challenges that administrators face. More and more staff members are involved in the financial operations of social service agencies, especially in planning, in decision making, and in carrying out agency practice.

Social work educators and practitioners recognize that diversity in staff is not only desirable but also important for the effective use of professional employees and in servicing those who come for assistance. Successful administrators agree with the current guidelines of CSWE in their accreditation and curriculum standards, which state that the educational institution shall have affirmative action procedures and a stated policy against discrimination on the basis of race, color, creed, gender, ethnic or national origin, handicap, or age. Effective administrators utilize affirmative action in hiring and maintaining staff and in the services they provide for clients.

[9]Arnold M. Gross, "Appropriate Cost Reporting: An Indispensable Link to Accountability," *Administration in Social Work* 4 (Fall 1980), 31–41.

[10]James O. F. Hackshaw and Nicholas Robertshaw, "Teaching Fiscal Management," *Administration in Social Work* 12, No. 1 (1988), 13–14.

Successful administrators accept the diversities of staff members and tap their individual abilities and resources to provide high-quality services. Discrimination is avoided at every turn. Equality, fairness, and justice are sought in financial operations, especially for salaries, promotions, and other available rewards.

Contracting Services

In recent years, service contracting has become an important part of financial operations in numerous social work agencies, mainly in government but also in private ventures. Administrators are using this resource to acquire various kinds of services rather than handling them under the agency umbrella.

This system, of course, requires a clear understanding of what service is to be performed, the costs involved, the professional skills available, and the timetable for operation. Wise administrators weigh carefully the advantages and disadvantages of performing specific services within their own operations or offering the work to other professionals, individuals or agencies.

Grantsmanship

Within the past four decades, a whole new process has been introduced in obtaining and budgeting funds for social services—grantsmanship, that is, obtaining grants from government agencies, particularly the federal government, and from private corporations and individuals. Applications for grants are usually made in accordance with printed guidelines supplied to help applicants define their objectives, describe their framework and methodology, and include a systematized, built-in evaluation procedure.

Books and pamphlets have been written providing guidelines and suggestions for those who apply for grants. Workshops and seminars are sponsored by universities and commercial organizations to train people in how to apply for and get grants. This is an area that requires knowledgeability, and administrators who are interested in obtaining grant money should increase their understanding of it.

Obtaining grants is usually dependent on the following: (1) a clear understanding of the guidelines and specific instructions, (2) careful formulation of the application, and (3) effective submission of the application to the granting agency and its representatives. Careful reading of the announcements and guidelines is essential in the grantsmanship process. The clearer the understanding of what is suggested and what is possible, the more likely the application will be appropriate. The better the preparation for the proposed action, the more likely it will be accepted.

The application needs to be written in a clear, interesting, and forceful manner. It must be well organized and related to the objectives of the granting agency. The more the application touches on specific areas, the more likely it is to be approved. Since so many applications are ordinarily received for most grant programs, the more unique and ingenious the application, the better. Whenever a new approach can be introduced with anticipated pragmatic results, the more likely it is to be accepted. Creativity and organization are paramount.

Moreover, if personal contacts can be made, allowing for the expression of enthusiastic interest and comprehensive knowledgeability of the field being considered, the more likely the grant will be obtained. Person-to-person clarification before and during the grant's preparation is desirable and may make the difference.

SUMMARY

Financial operations in social work agencies include (1) obtaining financial resources, (2) budgeting and planning, and (3) expending the money available. Funding for social work agencies may derive from public or private sources or both.

In the main, four kinds of budgeting are used by social workers in the delivery of social services: line-item, program, functional, and zero-based. Each of these patterns has advantages and disadvantages, and they are commonly combined. Budgets are being tied to performance and results in social work practice as never before.

Budgeting and financial planning processes include setting goals, ascertaining facts, describing alternatives, setting priorities, making decisions, and carrying on effective public relations. It is important that the administrator periodically check the agency's budget to ascertain the balance between income and expenditures. Flexibility in the operation of a budget is essential within the framework of agency policies. Grantsmanship skills are important for present-day administrators.

QUESTIONS FOR DISCUSSION

1. How important is the attitude of staff toward money and budget matters in the operation of a social work agency?

2. Describe and evaluate the advantages and disadvantages of the four types of budgets presented in this chapter.

3. If you were a director of a public welfare department, what criteria would you use in making recommendations for salary increases?

4. What suggestions do you have for reducing financial discrimination based on race and gender in social work agencies?

5. Describe and evaluate the advantages of contracting for services in a mental-health agency.

6. What are the most important procedures in applying for a grant?

7. What do you think are the most pressing financial problems for social work today? What suggestions do you have for reducing these problems?

SPECIAL ACTIVITIES

1. Draft a grant proposal for an agency of your choice and ask for $100,000 annually for a five-year period.

2. Arrange an interview with an agency director to discuss the major financial problems and challenges in that agency.

3. Role-play a caseworker in a veterans hospital asking her supervisor for a 20 percent increase in salary for the year ahead.

SELECTED REFERENCES

FRANK, RICHARD. "Cost-Benefit Analysis in Mental Health Services: A Review of the Literature." *Administration in Mental Health* 8 (Spring 1981), 161–176.

GROSS, MALVERN J. "The Importance of Budgeting." In Simon Slavin, ed., *Social Administration: The Management of the Social Services*, 2nd ed. Vol. II, *Managing Finances, Personnel, and Information in Human Services*, pp. 11–25. New York: Haworth Press, 1985.

HACKSHAW, JAMES O. F., and NICHOLAS ROBERTSHAW. "Teaching Fiscal Management: A Live Case Approach." *Administration in Social Work*, 12, No. 1 (1988), 13–14.

HARDINA, DONNA. "The Effect of Funding Sources on Client Access to Services." *Administration in Social Work* 14, No. 3 (1990), 33–46.

KARGER, HOWARD JACOB. "The Common and Conflicting Goals of Labor and Social Work." *Administration in Social Work* 13, No. 1 (1989), 1–17.

KARGER, HOWARD JACOB. "Social Service Administration and the Challenge of Unionization." *Administration in Social Work* 13, Nos. 3/4 (1989), 199–218.

KETTNER, PETER M., and LAWRENCE L. MARTIN. "Purchase of Service Contracting: Two Models." *Administration in Social Work* 14, No. 1 (1990), 15–30.

MORRISON, JOHN D. "Making the Most of Federal Block Grants: Implications from a Prototype Program." *Administration in Social Work* 9 (Summer 1985), 73–84.

OTTEN, GERARD L. "Zero-Based Budgeting: Implications for Social Services?" In Simon Slavin, ed., *Social Administration: The Management of the Social Services*, 2nd ed. Vol. II, *Managing Finances, Personnel, and Information in Human Services*, pp. 126–137. New York: Haworth Press, 1985.

SHERRADEN, MICHAEL W. "Benefit-Cost Analysis as a Net Present Value Problem." *Administration in Social Work* 10 (Fall 1986), 85–97.

STRETCH, JOHN J. "What Human Services Managers Need to Know About Basic Budgeting Strategies." *Administration in Social Work* 4 (Spring 1980), 87–98.

VINTER, ROBERT D., and RHEA K. KISH. *Budgeting for Not-for-Profit Organizations*. New York: Free Press, 1984.

7

Accountability and Evaluation

A few days before Christmas several staff members of a public welfare office were eating lunch. Their conversation turned to their agency and its accomplishments. Overheard were these comments: "We have done a fine job this year." "Our agency has been operating on two cylinders since June." "From what I've heard, we are providing more and better services than ever before." "Just the other day the staff researcher told me we had served only two-thirds as many clients as last year."

Who was correct? What were the facts? In fact, all the comments were partly erroneous. None of the workers knew exactly what the agency had accomplished.

In our fast-moving world, public-spirited citizens, legislators, clients, and others are raising more and more questions about social work agencies and the services they deliver: "Do these services really make a difference?" "Is money wasted?" "Are they providing too many services?" "Are they not providing enough?" "Where do we draw the line?" "Shouldn't we discontinue some agencies?"

Social agency administrators are aware, as never before, of the need for program evaluation and accountability. Biggerstaff suggests that program evaluation

> has become a built-in professional responsibility for social agencies. Evaluation affects directly the agency's purpose and operation, and it has major implications for public accountability. In many agencies it is necessary to employ an evaluator or consultant for the evaluation task, since few administrators and

staff members have the required skills. But the administrator does need to know what questions to ask and how to utilize the evaluation results.[1]

Turem suggests that we may advance administration in social work through more interest and action related to accountability. This should be based on

> something other than the level of effort, elegance of style or good intentions. To get to such standards requires that each manager review information on who is doing what to whom for what end, to what effect and at what cost. Then some manager must decide if it is to continue. Automation is making it increasingly easy to do this and so cost effective that one can even hope for a growth in the numbers of social workers who manage agencies.[2]

The clamor for effectiveness and efficiency has brought efficiency experts, systems analysts, and other management scientists into the social services. Gruber poses the question, When the technocrats take over the planning and administration of services, what happens to the people who are serving and the people served? He responds with positive suggestions for social service agencies:

> A first step in refurbishing a democratic welfare state is to rescue the concept of accountability from the narrow confines of audits and counts. No matter how sophisticated they are, techniques like PPBS and MBO are simply devices for internal reckoning. Accountability in the larger sense involves the government's reckoning with the people, the organization's reckoning with the community. If social planners neglect this broader view, they will aggravate social atomization, public cynicism, and mistrust, which in turn will trigger more monitoring and more control. Thus the crux of the issue is to create community within pluralism and to restore the prerogatives of the people by reviving the political concept of accountability as distinct from the corporatist concept of efficiency.
> Also, it is possible to use the newer social techniques and systems to benefit rather than to dehumanize man. Take for example, management information systems. Only the public's enfeeblement and its conquest by technocrats prevents the turnabout of technological controls.
> Why not use high-speed telecommunications systems to give citizens the best available information about the way social institutions perform? Or is that information exclusively for the managers?
> Why not devise dialogue models of planning, using the best available technology, that will provide guidelines for citizens to work with systems planners, social scientists, social work practitioners, engineers, and managers? Data gathering, data transmission, cable television, and other technical processes could surely be useful. Techniques like these could even bring meetings for public decision-making into the living room with direct citizen vote.

[1]Marilyn A. Biggerstaff, "The Administrator and Social Agency Evaluation," *Administration in Social Work* 1 (Spring 1977), 71.

[2]Jerry S. Turem, "Social Work Administration and Modern Management Technology," *Administration in Social Work* 10 (Fall 1986), 24.

The possibilities for a stronger public and an informed citizenry beckon invitingly. If such opportunities are not seized, the likelihood is continued enervation of the people and then gradual envelopment in a smooth, banal tyranny that conquers not through whips and wages, but through total administration and forms of corporatist-statist oppression as yet foreseen only in imaginary technological nightmares.[3]

Questions have been raised about the cost of social work services and the effectiveness of social service agencies. In the past, we have operated on the assumption that the costs are justified to help disadvantaged people. As for effectiveness, we have listed statistically the numbers of clients we have interviewed and claimed rather smugly that this "proves" that our services are important, even essential. Today a blunt question is being asked: Is this going far enough? Social work is expected not only to be accountable for what it spends and why but also to indicate more objectively what actually takes place, if anything, as a result of such services. The reality is that we live in an age of accountability, and social workers need to understand this and respond to it realistically and forthrightly.

A new model of social work administration has been described by many professional social workers, stressing that its central mission is the production of desired client outcomes or results. Rapp and Poertner suggest that "not to monitor client outcomes substantially and use that data to improve operations is tantamount to managerial irresponsibility, incompetence, and unethical conduct."[4] Doueck and Bondanza reflect the thinking of most present-day social work administrators, as well as political and community leaders, that we live in an era of accountability and diminishing resources, and "it becomes increasingly important for human services agencies to demonstrate the efficacy of their programs."[5]

ACCOUNTABILITY

Agency Accountability

Accountability is applicable to both the agency and individual staff members. As far as the agency is concerned, many bona fide efforts are being introduced to establish program evaluation and undertake other kinds of research to ascertain what occurs in the delivery of social services. Some administrators and agencies have protested this kind of action, saying that everything cannot be measured in social work practice. They claim, for example, that one cannot

[3]Murray Gruber, "Total Administration," *Social Work* 19 (September 1974), 635. Copyright © 1974 National Association of Social Workers, Inc. Reprinted with permission.

[4]Charles A. Rapp and John Poertner, "Moving Clients Center Stage Through the Use of Client Outcomes," *Administration in Social Work* 11 (Fall/Winter 1987), 35.

[5]Howard J. Doueck and Ann Bondanza, "Training Social Work Staff to Evaluate Practice: A Pre/Post/Then Comparison," *Administration in Social Work* 14, No. 1 (1990), 119.

measure feelings or scientifically ascertain everything that takes place in an interview or in other social work relationships. Everyone who understands evaluation research agrees that no evaluation can conclusively measure all facets of human relationships. Nevertheless, most professional experts agree that there is much more that can be measured and understood than has been in the past. As we attempt to measure what is actually happening, we are more likely to improve our services and help disadvantaged people.

Program Evaluation

Program evaluation is a relatively recent function of administration; yet it is already highly significant. Poland suggests numerous difficulties in implementing program evaluation: (1) the random allocation to experimental and control group, so necessary to sound research design, is difficult; (2) administrators may influence an evaluation; (3) administrators may resist the controls demanded in an experiment; (4) administrators may suppress unfavorable evaluations.[6]

Although these difficulties may be serious, they are not insurmountable. Capable administrators either hire program evaluators from outside the agency or develop employees of their own who are qualified to help with this newer aspect of administration. The trend in larger agencies is to employ competent social work personnel who can carry out program evaluation. In many agencies this is not feasible, so people from allied disciplines, such as psychology and business, are requested to provide this service.

The MBO approach is used extensively in some social work agencies to help with program evaluation and accountability. This means, of course, that the agency needs to work out specific, time-based objectives that can be observed and measured. At the end of a period of time agreed upon by those in authority, outcomes are ascertained by evaluating what has occurred. Recently, the focus of evaluation has been shifting from a mere tabulation of case interviews or case numbers to a consideration of results, actual changes in people's behavior and in their relationships.

Such a process cannot cover the total arena in social work. Some components in human relationships cannot be measured objectively, particularly those related to changes in feeling that take place in social relationships. Also, there is the danger, in this approach, of becoming too impersonal and cold, doing away with sensitive support, the strength of the social work approach.

Biggerstaff underlines the importance of social agency evaluation:

> Evaluation of programs has become a specific task of social agencies in recent years, because evaluation is now mandated for most programs funded by public monies. The social agency administrator must be equipped to manage the evaluation of service delivery programs or agency operations in his or her

[6]Orville F. Poland, "Program Evaluation and Administration Theory," *Public Administration Review* 34 (July/August 1974), 334.

domain. In addition, every social worker, regardless of role or setting, needs to be alert to the reciprocal implications of program purpose, functioning, evaluation, and accountability. . . .

Evaluation is viewed as a panacea by some and a threat to agency operations by others. It should be regarded as neither, but rather as a tool that enables administrators to make more reliable decisions about present and future agency operations and services.[7]

Piliavin and McDonald recognize that some social workers question the benefits of evaluative research but suggest that when research is properly designed and implemented, findings can be useful in improving and refining social services. They illustrate their position with the following case example:

Two years ago a Milwaukee social agency (along with many other agencies across the nation) received federal funds for a summer job program for poor delinquent youths. The wage of each participant was about fifty dollars per week, and the program was ten weeks in duration. Aside from income redistribution, considered by agency personnel as an automatic benefit, it was also expected that participants would lessen their criminal activities following their program involvement. This expectation was based on the hypothesis that experience with the program would lead the delinquents to find legitimate work available and more rewarding than crime. Unhappily, the evaluation of this program came up with the finding that experimentals (the program participants) and controls had similar crime patterns during the summer but that in the subsequent fall the experimentals committed crime significantly in excess of controls. The researchers argued that the post-program crime upsurge by experimentals resulted from the living standards these youths were provided during the summer. When their comparatively "heady" income was stopped, they increased their crime in order to maintain their new and more costly tastes. Meanwhile, controls did not vary their crime rate to any significant degree because their tastes remained the same. In effect, then, the researchers argued that the summer job program was geared to backfire. Armed with this information, the agency was able to obtain money from funders for more permanent part-time employment efforts.[8]

Effectiveness in providing social work services is becoming more and more important in today's world, wherein money is limited and results are recognized as particularly significant. Patti observes that the past approach of counting the work performed is not enough. "This can and frequently does lead to the anomalous situation in which the agency is 'well' managed, but has little demonstrable impact on the clientele it serves."[9] He proposes a management approach that seeks to build practice around the central criterion of service effectiveness, which is reflected in three kinds of outcomes: the extent

---

[7]Biggerstaff, "The Administrator," pp. 71–72.

[8]Irving Piliavin and Thomas McDonald, "On the Fruits of Evaluative Research for the Social Services," *Administration and Social Work* 1 (Spring 1977), 67–68.

[9]Rino J. Patti, "Managing for Service Effectiveness in Social Welfare: Toward a Performance Model," *Administration in Social Work* 11, Nos. 3/4 (1987), 8.

to which the agency is successful in bringing about desired changes in or for the client systems it serves, service quality, and client satisfaction.

Grasso and Epstein suggest that the traditional program evaluation approach based on a retrospective, purely quantitative focus is inadequate even though it results in statistical indicators such as the number of units of service delivered, the number of closed cases, the average length of service, the number of successful program completions, and the number of recidivists. They recommend a new developmental approach that considers five primary stages of client-agency involvement that evaluation can address: referral, intake, intervention, program completion, and program follow-up. Grasso and Epstein conclude that

> developmental program evaluation relies on both qualitative and quantitative data for making future-oriented clinical and programmatic decisions. Using the individual case as the primary unit of analysis . . . this approach not only guides future program decisions, but also helps direct service workers manage their cases. It provides a method for assessing client change across different stages of agency involvement and, as a result, helps workers focus their interventions more precisely on specific client needs.[10]

Individual Accountability

In addition to agency performance being measured, evaluated, and held accountable, there is also a thrust toward evaluation and accountability of individual staff members. In universities and professional schools this is accomplished in part by anonymous student evaluations, which are administered at the end of each quarter or semester. In agencies this evaluation takes place in a variety of ways.

Self-evaluation, periodically participated in, can be helpful to individual staff members in many ways. Peer evaluations are used in some agencies; associates of a given worker offer observations and suggestions, both positive and negative, about that worker's performance.

Many agencies provide for oral evaluations by an administrator to individual workers; they focus on positive contributions as well as limitations. Basic questions often considered are these: What is the worker doing well? What could be improved? Many agencies provide for two regular oral evaluations each year. Some conclude the process with a written summary of the verbal evaluation and other pertinent comments and suggestions supplied by the administrator. These evaluations are often facilitated by workers preparing in advance what they see as personal objectives for service in the agency as well as preparing a self-evaluation. Many agencies encourage their employees to list at least once a year their specific targets and objectives for the year ahead.

---

[10]Anthony J. Grasso and Irwin Epstein, "Toward a Developmental Approach to Program Evaluation," *Administration in Social Work* 16, Nos. 3/4 (1992), 199–200.

METHODS

A variety of methods are used in evaluative program research in social work agencies. As we discussed in Chapter 4, management by objectives is a process that addresses inputs, activities, and outgo or results. It encompasses specific targets and goals in a time frame, with observations made and measurements taken to ascertain outcomes. Activity traps may divert energies and abilities and prevent employees from accomplishing their objectives.

Another approach is to get feedback from clients about what they think of the services they receive. Weissman points out that an effective management information service has been developed by researchers at the Henry Street Settlement in New York City, which has stimulated management and staff to examine program objectives to "develop indices of success, and to carry out exploratory studies of program effectiveness." He mentioned that in these studies, a pattern providing for systematic feedback of clients' perceptions of services has had significant impact on the workers' behavior and attitudes.[11]

Various information systems have been and are being designed to assist with program evaluation planning and with decision making in the delivery of social services. Computers and other technical means are increasingly utilized in social welfare agencies. Weirich suggests that information systems need to be understood within their organizational contexts:

> Service administrators will have to consider organizational factors as well as technical ones in their decisions to initiate, implement, and routinize new systems. Information systems can be magnificent, but they are not magic. The service administrator need not be mystified by their hardware, for in the end it is the administrator's hard work that will determine the system's usefulness. Although the computerized information system can certainly contribute to decision-making, it is no substitute for administrative judgment.[12]

Hirschhorn believes that program evaluation is coming into its own in social work administration and offers ways to further its effectiveness:

> Administrators, evaluators, planners, and professionals all stand at a crossroads. No less is at stake than the character and potential of today's social agency. Increased accountability at all levels of service, funding, and planning, is fundamental for sustaining the democratic character of post-industrial society. We are too interconnected today to tolerate monopolies on decisions that affect us all. Administrators and evaluators must place appropriate limits around the classical evaluation model and must in turn develop a broad participatory planning framework in which process, context, and system become the

    [11]Harold H. Weissman, "Client, Staff, and Researchers: Their Role in Management Information Systems," *Administration in Social Work* 1 (Spring 1977), 43.

    [12]Thomas W. Weirich, "The Design of Information Systems," in Felice Davidson Perlmutter and Simon Slavin, eds., *Leadership in Social Administration* (Philadelphia: Temple University Press, 1980), p. 155.

key organizing terms. Only in this way can they surmount the dangers and emerging reality of austerity, narrow measurement, and workload politics. Only in this way can they help resolve the current crisis in social service.[13]

Hawkins and Sloma emphasize that evaluation research in social work administration is applied research and should contribute to the programs studied. They state that evaluation studies have been "plagued by major problems including methodological rigor, discovery of unanticipated consequences and nonutilization of findings." These authors propose steps in an "interactive strategy for designing, mounting, carrying out, and reporting evaluation studies. The steps include identifying evaluation audiences, grounding and negotiating evaluation designs, involving practitioners in operationalizing variables and developing data collection instruments, and providing oral feedback of results to evaluation audiences."[14] They suggest that this approach can minimize unanticipated findings and ultimately increase the likelihood of the utilization of results.

Evaluation may be used as a change agent, which in a sense runs counter to the accepted value of organization stability. Poland suggests that organizations often have a limited tolerance for change and may reactively suppress program evaluation.[15]

Rock reports a study of Goal Attainment Scaling (GAS) in a large social work department in an urban teaching medical center. He concludes that outcome measurement has inherent limitations but with care in methodology, "important patterns can be identified, which should be useful to practitioners, administrators, and evaluators."[16] Although social work administration has a long way to go, it is moving in the direction of objective evaluation of services in relation to client outcome. Effective administrators are aware of these developments and are tapping the resources of client outcome research.

Evaluation Process

Ward emphasizes that evaluation of social work services is predicated on the notion that research into social interventions can point to underlying cause-effect relationships that can be understood and changed to produce increased effectiveness for a larger number of people in need. He lists the following steps in the development and execution of evaluation:

1. Determining the program's goals
2. Allocating financial resources for conducting the evaluation

[13]Larry Hirschhorn, "Evaluation and Administration: From Experimental Design to Social Planning," in Felice Davidson Perlmutter and Simon Slavin, eds., *Leadership in Social Administration* (Philadelphia: Temple University Press, 1980), p. 191.

[14]J. David Hawkins and Donald Sloma, "Recognizing the Organizational Context: A Strategy for Evaluation Research," *Administration in Social Work* 2 (Fall 1978), 283.

[15]Poland, "Program Evaluation," pp. 337–338.

[16]Barry E. Rock, "Goal and Outcome in Social Work Practice," *Social Work* 32 (September-October, 1987), 397.

3. Hiring technical staff (may be done in house if qualified persons are available)
4. Contracting with consultants
5. Translating the goals into measurable indicators of goal achievement
6. Training management and staff in the concepts of evaluation
7. Designing the evaluation system
8. Developing, validating, and implementing the information system
9. Collecting data on indicators of the consumers receiving the services and possibly on an equivalent group that does not receive the services
10. Comparing the data on the two groups with goal criteria
11. Coordinating the activities of these multidisciplinary actors in the development and implementation of the evaluation
12. Reporting on evaluation results[17]

Rosenberg and Brody suggest that emphasis on accountability in the social services introduces both threats and challenges. Their conclusions contain guidelines for a professional approach to this development:

> The two major threats seem to be that the new models use management concepts that emphasize evaluation and measurement, and de-emphasize the central role of psychosocial diagnosis and long-term casework counseling. . . . Management concepts, if humanely applied, can be powerful tools for delivering more effective services. Evaluation and client feedback are not only necessary for effective service delivery, but are an ethical requirement of the profession. Systematic methods must be developed that assess whether social workers are helping, harming, or doing nothing for the people they serve.[18]

Ward observes that friction is likely to develop between social service staff and the evaluators because of conflicting values and frames of reference. Service workers, for instance, are primarily

> concerned with services to individuals, families, and groups, whereas the evaluator's role is to determine the degree to which improvements are occurring in the consumer's condition as a result of the receipt of the service. Intellectually, service workers may understand and accept the explanation that the evaluation will improve future program and budgetary decisions; pragmatically, they may resist it. The service workers may feel they need consumer-specific information offering assistance in their day-to-day activities, but the evaluators and management may tend to favor aggregate information expressed in statistics—means, correlations, coefficients, percentages. . . . Service workers are likely to envision little value in such information for their use and may question the value of the entire evaluation.
>   To overcome friction emanating from conflicting values and frames of reference, further orientation on the roles and responsibilities of the informational needs of different actors may be necessary. In addition, top management may

[17]James H. Ward, "An Approach to Measuring Effectiveness of Social Services: Problems and Resolutions," *Administration in Social Work* 1 (Winter 1977), 410.
[18]Marvin L. Rosenberg and Ralph Brody, "The Threat or Challenge of Accountability," *Social Work* 19 (May 1974), 349.

need to reiterate its commitment to the evaluation and its need for various kinds of information for policy, strategic, and tactical decision making and for maintenance of accountability with its different publics. It may also wish to involve program staff through an ad hoc or standing advisory committee to familiarize them further with the purposes of the evaluation, elicit their input and assistance in its development and execution, and help reduce the potential threats that the evaluation poses to them. Finally, top management may wish to share useful evaluation information with staff to keep them informed and to stimulate their cooperative participation in the exercise.[19]

One more factor needs to be considered in client outcome research: ethical conduct. Accuracy and integrity are paramount. Patti emphasizes that "as an effectiveness-oriented model of administration is developed, social workers also will have to be concerned with the ethical parameters of managerial behavior."[20] Otherwise many problems will ensue.

Need for Basic Research

In social work administration and practice today there is a great need for basic scientific research for two reasons in particular: (1) a need for basic data about agency services and (2) a need to ascertain the effectiveness of administration practices. In other words, objective research may indicate what is actually happening in the delivery of the agency services and the effectiveness of the administrative methods utilized. In addition, scientific research may result in pertinent knowledge of human behavior and may place more emphasis on human relationships. We still can ask many more questions than we can answer in understanding human behavior, social problems, administration, staff behavior, and the effectiveness of skills and methods in social work administration. Basic research may help provide answers.

Some agencies designate a percentage of their total budget for research, to find out exactly what the agency is accomplishing and where it is going and to gather substantive data about human behavior and social work practice. Some hire a full-time research staff to obtain this information.

SUMMARY

Program evaluation and accountability are important ingredients of the present social work scene. Accountability in social work agencies is related to cost and effectiveness of services.

Agency programming and accountability are of interest to citizens, legislators, clients, and others. Individual evaluations in staff performance have become acceptable and are utilized in a variety of ways.

[19]Ward, "Measuring Effectiveness," pp. 410–411.

[20]Rino J. Patti, "Managing for Service Effectiveness in Social Welfare Organizations," *Social Work* 32 (September-October, 1987), 380.

Specific, measurable objectives need to be developed for the evaluation of agencies and individuals to ascertain desired client outcomes.

Research efforts regarding agency services and the effectiveness of administration methods are on the increase.

QUESTIONS FOR DISCUSSION

1. Why do you think that politicians and community leaders are now asking social work administrators to be more accountable for their services than ever before?

2. Compare and contrast agency accountability and individual accountability.

3. Describe and evaluate the twelve steps in the evaluation process in this chapter.

4. What is program evaluation and why is it becoming increasingly popular?

5. Why is basic research so needed in social work administration?

6. How can the individual administrator evaluate his or her own skills and leadership abilities?

SPECIAL ACTIVITIES

1. Invite an agency administrator to meet with you and describe his or her successes and limitations in program evaluation.

2. Formulate a program for research in a hypothetical agency on the assumption that you have been awarded a grant of $30,000 to do something to improve the delivery of social services in that agency.

3. Role-play a social worker knocking on a door at a house to ask a few questions as part of a research project on attitudes toward AIDS and its treatment.

SELECTED REFERENCES

ATTKISSON, C. CLIFFORD, WILLIAM A. HARGREAVES, MARDI J. HOROWITZ, and JAMES E. SORENSEN, eds. *Evaluation of Human Services Programs.* New York: Academic Press, 1978.
BRAGER, GEORGE, AND STEPHEN HOLLOWAY. "Assessing Prospects for Organizational Change: The Uses of Force Field Analysis." *Administration in Social Work* 16, Nos. 3/4 (1992), 15–28.
CAPUTO, RICHARD K. "Managing Information Systems: An Ethical Framework and Information Needs Matrix." *Administration in Social Work* 15, No. 4 (1991), 53–64.
DOUECK, HOWARD J., and ANN BONDANZA. "Training Social Work Staff to Evaluate Practice: A Pre/Post/Then Comparison." *Administration in Social Work* 14, No. 1 (1990), 119–133.
ELKIN, ROBERT. "Paying the Piper and Calling the Tune: Accountability in the Human Services." *Administration in Social Work* 9 (Summer 1985), 1–13.

GRASSO, ANTHONY J., and IRWIN EPSTEIN. "Toward a Developmental Approach to Program Evaluation." *Administration in Social Work* 16, Nos. 3/4 (1992), 187–203.

HUDSON, WALTER W. "Measuring Clinical Outcomes and Their Use for Managers." *Administration in Social Work* 11 (Fall/Winter 1987), 59–71.

KETTNER, PETER M., and LAWRENCE L. MARTIN. "Performance, Accountability, and Purchase of Service Contracting." *Administration in Social Work* 17, No. 1 (1993), 61–79.

MCNEECE, C. AARON, DIANA M. DINITTO, and PETER J. JOHNSON. "The Utility of Evaluation Research for Administrative Decision-Making." *Administration in Social Work* 7 (Fall/Winter 1983), 77–87.

MILLAR, KENNETH I. "Performance Appraisal of Professional Social Workers." *Administration in Social Work* 14, No. 1 (1990), 65–85.

MUTSCHLER, ELIZABETH, and RAM A. CNAAN. "Success and Failure of Computerized Information Systems: Two Case Studies in Human Service Agencies." *Administration in Social Work* 9 (Spring 1985), 67–79.

PATTI, RINO J. "Managing for Service Effectiveness in Social Welfare Organizations," *Social Work* 32 (September-October 1987), 377–381.

PECORA, PETER J., and JEFF HUNTER. "Performance Appraisal in Child Welfare: Comparing the MBO and BARS Methods." *Administration in Social Work* 12, No. 1 (1988), 55–71.

ROCK, BARRY D. "Goal and Outcome in Social Work Practice." *Social Work* 32 (September-October 1987), 393–398.

SARRI, ROSEMARY C., and CATHERINE M. SARRI. "Organizational and Community Change Through Participatory Action Research." *Administration in Social Work* 16, Nos. 3/4 (1992), 99–122.

8

Organization
for Services

Two prominent business people visited a public welfare department in an eastern city whose director held a social work degree. On their way back to the car, one turned to the other and observed, "I think that social work agencies should have businesspeople as their directors and we should put all social work administrators out in the field. This way, we would have better-organized agencies. Social workers don't know anything about organized management." What is the reality?

Most social work educators and practitioners claim that well-qualified, trained social work administrators are needed to organize and direct the activities of social service agencies. They are charged to establish and maintain effective agency organization and to help in its functioning.

Organization refers to the structure of an agency and how it functions. It includes staff at various levels, committee arrangements, board structure, chain of command, and other factors related to agency framework. Organizing is the social process of bringing an agency structure into being and changing it to keep it up to date and effective.

DEFINITIONS

Organizing, one of the traditional processes in administration, involves the action required to bring an agency into being, structurally and functionally. Organization has two major meanings: (1) the structure of an agency and (2) the process of being or becoming organized. In this chapter, we shall consider both meanings and focus on how they apply to the delivery of social services.

Barnard suggests that an organization comes into being when persons are able to communicate with one another and are willing to act to reach a common goal. He concludes that the elements of an organization are, therefore, communication, willingness to serve, and a common purpose.[1] A symbolic representation of organization and disorganization is shown in Figure 8–1. Efficiency and effectiveness of movement in the two patterns offer significant contrasts.

Formal and Informal Organization

Both formal and informal organization are needed for effective administration in the delivery of social services. Without organization, chaos would result, and efficiency, effectiveness, and morale would decrease.

Formal organization is the recognizable structure of an agency, with a director, an assistant director, supervisors, and practitioners. It includes appointed and elected committees and board-administration-staff arrangements. It encompasses the framework of staff relationships. Informal organization refers to arrangements and operations outside of the observed, regular, charted, and planned structure of the agency; it includes the arrangements "underneath the table" and at the "coffee hour."

Horizontal and Vertical Organization

Another organizational component is vertical and horizontal structure and coordination. The vertical arrangement includes the hierarchy from top to

FIGURE 8–1.   Order in Organization. From Roger Conant, *Drugs: Facts for Decisions*, rev. ed. (Syracuse, NY: New Readers Press, 1976), pp. 11–12.

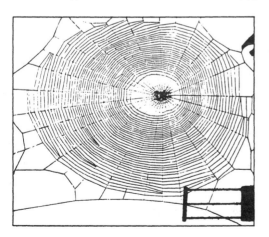 

[1]Chester I. Barnard, "Formal Organizations," in Harry A. Schatz, ed., *Social Work Administration: A Resource Book* (New York: Council on Social Work Education, 1970), p. 92.

bottom or bottom to top. Horizontal organization concerns a particular level within the structural hierarchy that goes sideways and involves numerous workers in a variety of ways.

Any social work agency is divided into departments, and there are various levels of authority and function. On the horizontal plane, an agency is departmentalized, so groups of allied services and functions enable the staff to work together and allow the specialization of services. For example, a state department of social services may be organized into the following divisions, each with equal status: corrections, family services, aging, health, mental health, and minority services.

One area of change in social service agencies is the alteration of organizational structures. Periodically, state social service agencies review their structures and try to make them more efficient and effective. "Little Hoover commissions" are common in state government and are authorized to study existing organizational structures and make improvements. In one state in the West, reorganization of the state government has moved the health and mental-health departments together and apart twice in less than ten years. Budget evaluations are now influencing agencies to develop unified services.

Vertical division of authority and responsibility becomes necessary after horizontal divisions have been made. A large number of workers cannot all report to one director or supervisor. There must be division and subdivision from top to bottom to provide lines of authority, reporting, supervision, and services. In a typical social work agency, this vertical alignment includes a director at the top, followed by assistant director(s), supervisor(s), and practitioners.

BUREAUCRACY AND ORGANIZATION

Max Weber, a prominent German sociologist in the early twentieth century, extensively discussed formal organization, particularly as it relates to bureaucracy. Social workers differ in their evaluation of his positions, but his ideas are highly respected. His main proposals follow:

> Experience tends universally to show that the thoroughly purely bureaucratic type of organization—that is the monocratic variety of bureaucracy—is, from a purely technical point of view, capable of attaining the highest degree of efficiency and is in this sense formally the most rational known means of carrying out imperative control over human beings. It is superior to any other form in precision, in stability, in the stringency of its disciplines, and in its reliability. It thus makes possible a particularly high degree of calculability of results for the heads of the organization and for those acting in relation to it. It is finally superior both in intensive efficiency and in the scope of its operations, and is formally capable of application to all kinds of administrative tasks.
>
> The development of the modern form of the organization of corporate groups in all fields is nothing less than identical with the development and continued spread of bureaucratic administration. This is true of church and of state, of

armies, political parties, economic enterprises, organizations to promote all kinds of causes, private associations, clubs, and many others. Its development is, to take the most striking case, the most crucial phenomenon of the modern Western state. . . . The whole pattern of everyday life is cut to fit this framework. For bureaucratic administration is, other things being equal, always, from a formal, technical, point of view, the most rational type. For the needs of mass administration today, it is completely indispensable. The choice is only that between bureaucracy and dilettantism in the field of administration.[2]

Stein suggests that both strengths and weaknesses are inherent in bureaucratic structure and function. On the positive side are (1) economy and efficiency, contributed by rational division of labor and pooling of expertise; (2) stability and permanence; (3) role security, with specific, designated job expectations; (4) relative job security, with fringe benefits, in-service training programs, and retirement programs; and (5) impersonality of policies, which helps to minimize subjective elements in the determination of policies and to maximize the establishment of objective and impersonal criteria. This tends to bring to the consumer "the organization's goods or services . . . democratization through uniform applicability of criteria, as long as the consumer meets the established criteria." For the personnel of the organization, impersonality of policies "make[s] for relatively objective criteria for evaluation, promotions, sick leave, vacations, and so on."[3]

The inherent weaknesses, according to Stein, can be considered in relation to personnel, the consumer, management, and the community. Two limitations in personnel are ritualism and the possibility of mediocrity and overconformity. In regard to the consumer, "the very impersonality of criteria . . . can make it difficult for the individual to be properly served and leave the organization incapable of meeting crisis situations or emergencies." In relation to management, there are dangers of "ritualistic, unimaginative, and overly formalized behavior." From the vantage point of the community, bureaucracies tend to be "self-protective, and it is difficult for the outside community . . . to gain access to the organization or affect its structure."[4]

Several writers have been critical of bureaucracy and the subservience of the individual to the organization. Whyte, in his challenging *The Organization Man*, claims that society has made us more or less puppets within a highly organized pattern. He strongly opposes bureaucracy and conformity, and he questions personality testing.[5]

There is extensive literature on the conflict between professional autonomy and bureaucratic controls. Finch, from a detailed examination of the lit-

---

[2]Max Weber, *Theory of Social and Economic Organization*, trans. A. M. Henderson and Talcott Parsons (New York: Oxford University Press, 1947), p. 337. Copyright © 1947; renewed 1975 by Talcott Parsons.

[3]Herman D. Stein, "Administrative Implications of Bureaucratic Theory," *Social Work* 6 (July 1961), 14–16.

[4]Ibid., pp. 15–16.

[5]William H. Whyte, Jr., *The Organization Man* (New York: Simon & Schuster, 1956).

erature, concludes that the "trend is toward further intrusions on worker autonomy" and that "social worker effectiveness is likely to decline as a result—unless workers increase their ability to recognize and remove organizational impediments to service delivery."[6] He concludes that

> although adept in the role of practitioner or "helper," social workers too often lack skills needed to fill organizational roles in ways supportive of their service ideal. . . . Filling an organizational role in a way that is personally satisfying may well require a more sophisticated and accomplished knowledge of organizational dynamics than many social workers presently possess.[7]

Kurzman reports that bureaucratic rules and regulations are deplored by virtually all social welfare administrators:

> The creative worker and administrator may turn to administrative theory in order to understand this organizational reality, and will seek to work imaginatively within the boundaries that are posed. Mere condemnation of rules and regulations is a little like cursing the darkness, rather than lighting a candle: After the cathartic effect has worn off, no light has been shed on the problem.[8]

However, there are some real advantages, particularly for clients, of the bureaucratic process. Bureaucratic structures and operations do tend to promote equity of treatment, produce a certain uniformity of product or treatment of people, give some protection from indiscriminate actions by employees, and ensure that clients obtain the services the agency is supposed to be offering.

Many administrators advocate that social workers take a greater part in the bureaucratic pattern, in particular, participation in actions that will improve the delivery of services. Pawlak, recognizing that bureaucratic structures often present obstacles to effective services, suggests that the "clinician would benefit the organization and its clients—as well as his own position—if he would learn certain tactics for tinkering with organizational structures, rules, and policies." One such tactic, which Pawlak says is much ignored, is the "white paper" or "position paper," which can be used to advantage in many situations to bring about appropriate changes.[9]

Gruber, who studied innovation and organization, concluded that there is a "large body of literature that points out an inverse relationship between innovation or adaptability and the degree of bureaucratization owing to such factors as rigid authority structures, excessive formalization, procedural preoccupations, and inadequate communication processes."[10] It is evident that

[6]Wilbur A. Finch, Jr., "Social Workers Versus Bureaucracy," *Social Work* 21 (September 1976), 370.

[7]Ibid., p. 375.

[8]Paul A. Kurzman, "Rules and Regulations in Large-Scale Organizations: A Theoretical Approach to the Problem," *Administration in Social Work* 1 (Winter 1977), 429.

[9]Edward J. Pawlak, "Organizational Tinkering," *Social Work* 21 (September 1976), 379.

[10]Murray Gruber, "Innovation and Organization: A Polyorganizational Approach," *Administration in Social Work* 1 (Spring 1977), 27.

social workers need to learn more about organizational patterns and how to improve their effectiveness.

The desire to change and improve organization, particularly in government and large private agencies, is almost universal among social workers, and various means have been developed to bring about desired changes. Resnick suggests an effective strategy, called Changing the Organization From Within (COFW).[11] This strategy has been developed and applied mainly in the last two decades. It involves a series of activities carried out by lower- or middle-echelon staff to modify or change organizational conditions, policies, programs, or procedures, with the ultimate goal of improving the delivery of social services to clients.

Changes take the form of analytical or interactional tasks. There are three analytical tasks: "(a) goal determination—what the change shall be; (b) resistance assessment—who and what may be potential obstacles to this change; and (c) strategy selection—which guidelines or strategies may be utilized to achieve the change goal." The two major interactional tasks are "(a) developing the action system, and (b) meeting with the administrators for decision making."[12]

York and Henley, recognizing that *bureaucracy* is a much maligned word in modern human service dialogue, sent a questionnaire to 200 members of the North Carolina Chapter of NASW in 1983. From their random sample in this rural area, they concluded that the respondents are basically satisfied with the level of bureaucracy in their organizations and the results of the study "should encourage a more balanced view of the bureaucratic model among educators and practitioners alike. In particular, greater emphasis should be placed upon such features as specialization and credentials in the discussion of bureaucracy and more attention should be paid to the positive side of each of the features of this model."[13]

STRUCTURAL FACTORS IN ORGANIZATION

Organization provides a structure for people working together toward common goals. It is particularly important in social work agencies. Poor organization is worse than no organization at all. If a basketball team were not well organized, chaos would result, and the ball would rarely drop through the hoop. In the military, if there were not careful organization, the results would be catastrophic. In social work, effective organization invites effective delivery of social services.

[11]Herman Resnick, "Tasks in Changing the Organization From Within (COFW)," *Administration in Social Work* 2 (Spring 1978), 30–43.

[12]Ibid., p. 43.

[13]Reginald O. York and H. Carl Henley, "Perceptions of Bureaucracy," *Administration in Social Work* 10 (Spring 1986), 12.

William G. Scott suggested four factors that form the basic pillars for classic organizational theory: (1) the division of labor, (2) the scalar and functional processes, (3) structure, and (4) the span of control.[14] Fulmer adds a fifth, size and complexity, and concludes that "these factors make up business organization as we know it."[15]

Division of Labor

Division of labor involves specialization related to specific jobs. In a sugar factory this might be filling and emptying the measuring tank. In social work it might be assigning staff to work with individuals, groups, or the community, or with specific problems such as drugs, alcoholism, or AIDS.

Division of labor has been in operation for a long time. In tenth-century England the textile industry was divided into small units for spinning, weaving, dyeing, and printing textiles.[16] Today's assembly line is an extreme example of the specialized division of labor. With it have come many problems, including monotony on the job and the alienation of people from their work. Many efforts have been made to combat these problems through job rotation, job enlargement, and the like. Involving workers in decision making has been introduced in many businesses and agencies as a positive response.

In recent years in social work, there have been two major thrusts, which in one sense are contrary to each other. On the one hand, one movement has been toward more specialization in services; for example, a worker specializes in dealing with older persons, drug abusers, or unwed mothers. On the other hand, many agencies, such as comprehensive mental-health centers, assign cases and work with clients on a shared basis, relegating professional identity and training to the background and endeavoring to use the staff person who can help the most rather than dividing staff by professional affiliation.

Scalar and Functional Processes

Scalar processes, or ladderlike aspects of organization, include the chain of command, delegation of authority, and unity of command. The basic premise is that there is a chain of command that includes a hierarchy from top to bottom related to power, authority, decision making, and delegation of responsibility. It means that there is a pattern in any agency, all staff interwoven into a unique group, with one person at the top with final authority and responsibility. The pattern varies and may be weak or strong, depending on the skills and abilities of those who make up the network.

---

[14]William G. Scott, "Organization Theory: An Overview and an Appraisal," *Journal of Academy of Management* 4 (April 1961), 9–26.

[15]Robert M. Fulmer, *The New Management*, 2nd ed. (New York: Macmillan, 1978), p. 122.

[16]Ibid.

No one person can do all that is required in any agency, so authority and responsibility must be delegated. This is difficult and challenging. Some leaders underdelegate; others overdelegate, which causes less efficient delivery of social services.

Koontz and O'Donnell have selected several personal attitudes and abilities that are important for the sound delegation of authority: (1) *receptiveness*—gives other people's ideas a chance; (2) *willingness to let go*—gives subordinates the right to make decisions; (3) *willingness to let others make mistakes*—avoids harping on shortcomings or hovering over subordinates; (4) *willingness to trust subordinates*—maintains confidence in them and their abilities; and (5) *willingness to establish and use broad controls*—uses basic goals and policies in judging subordinates.[17]

Structure

Organizational structure involves the actual arrangements and levels of an organization in regard to power, authority, responsibilities, and mechanisms for carrying out its functions or practices. In a given agency, departments relate to policies and functions. Departmentalization in social agencies varies considerably. Usually agency functions are divided into the (1) business or management component and (2) services to be delivered. Within each of these are a few or many subdepartments, depending on the size and complexity of the agency. The important factor is that the organizational framework fits the particular agency, and the leaders and staff feel it is optimally effective.

Organizational charts may help to clarify and bring about the efficient operation of the agency staff, but caution is needed in their use. They tend to oversimplify and inadequately present real relationships. Stieglitz suggests that "the organization chart, like milk, may be dated but not fresh. For it is increasingly understood that no organization chart is 100% current. Rather, the criticism is that even the most current chart is utterly inadequate as a diagram of the organization."[18]

Matrix organization is a development that is utilized in reorganizing some human services delivery systems. Ryan and Washington describe this pattern and concept as follows:

> The term matrix organization is derived from the existence of two managerial subsystems arrayed in an interlocking form. This arrangement is implemented in most human services organizations with two groups of managers, one of

[17]Harold Koontz and Cyril O'Donnell, *Management*, 6th ed. (New York: McGraw-Hill, 1976), pp. 382–383.
[18]Harold Stieglitz, "What's Not on the Organizational Chart," in Harry A. Schatz, ed., *Social Work Administration: A Resource Book* (New York: Council on Social Work Education, 1970), p. 258.

which is responsible for service delivery while the other is responsible for lateral integration and coordination among service groupings, including the linking of clients to services through such functions as brokerage and mediation. Many organizations define the latter functions as "case management."[19]

Tropman describes the "flat" chart of organizational structure, a wide triangle with a long base and a short distance to the top of the angle. He also mentions the hierarchical organization that often appears as a peaked triangle with a small base and a long distance to the top of the angle. He suggests a new dynamic approach, "the organizational circle,"[20] which strives for

FIGURE 8-2. **The Organizational Circle.** From John E. Tropman, "The Organizational Circle: A New Approach to Drawing an Organizational Chart," *Administration in Social Work* 13, No. 1 (1989), 41. © By The Haworth Press, Inc. All rights reserved. Reprinted with permission. For copies of the complete work, contact Marianne Arnold at The Haworth Document Delivery Service (Telephone 1-800-3-HAWORTH; 10 Alice Street, Binghamton, N.Y. 13904). For other questions concerning rights and permissions contact Wanda Latour at the above address.

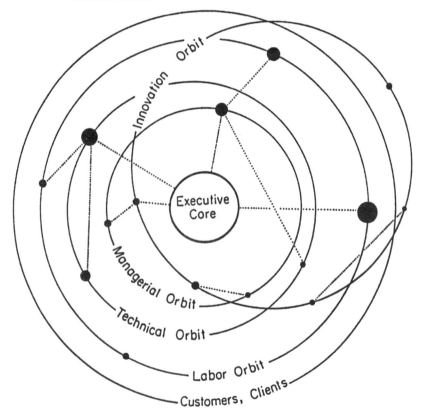

[19]Robert M. Ryan and Robert O. Washington, "New Patterns for Organizing Human Services," *Administration in Social Work* 1 (Fall 1977), 302.

[20]John E. Tropman, "The Organizational Circle: A New Approach to Drawing an Organizational Chart," *Administration in Social Work* 13, No. 1 (1989), 39.

unity, togetherness, and synchrony (see Figure 8–2). Tropman claims that the circle has several advantages over the triangle: It makes the executive core the center of the organization rather than above it; it reduces the dominance of the hierarchy in other ways; it emphasizes the possibilities of change; it allows different orbits or shapes, suggesting different subunit patterns and different relationships to the center; its orbit concept has an open flavor; and it allows the center to establish cross-orbital relationships with peripheral units that need direct attention from the center.[21]

Another current structural pattern that is becoming popular is decentralized authority. Obviously, this means a sharing of responsibilities among administrators and staff. It means working together, which is conducive to effectiveness, creativity, and morale. According to Schmid, "Research findings support studies that indicate a positive relationship between decentralized structure and service effectiveness. That is to say, the higher the degree of decentralization, the greater organizational effectiveness."[22]

Span of Control

Span of control concerns the number of subordinates under an administrator and their attached relationships. Authorities in the field of management differ on what the span should be; many have advocated that ordinarily there should not be more than five or six persons reporting to an administrator. Others have suggested that the number should depend on the kind of agency or business and the production or services to be performed. It is clear, however, that as the span is lengthened, the number of relationships between and among staff magnifies rapidly. Fulmer reports that with six subordinates, there is the likelihood of 222 relationships. If this number is increased to twelve, the number goes up to 24,708.[23]

In social work, there is commonly one supervisor for about every six or seven line workers, or fewer in small agencies. Again, there are differences of opinion about the best ratio; probably the most important factor is whether leaders and workers feel comfortable with the pattern they adopt.

A popular alternative today to the traditional organizational pattern is the *team* concept of service delivery, namely, a team leader and team members. This flattens the bottom of the bureaucratic pyramid and strengthens group impact in affecting change from the bottom. This model is used frequently in public child welfare and in the delivery of social services in a variety of other agencies. Its positive essence is that several persons working together can be more effective than one individual at the helm.

Brieland, Briggs, and Leuenberger define the social work team as any "grouping of social welfare personnel which has mutual responsibility for

[21]Ibid., pp. 40–42.
[22]Hillel Schmid, "Relationships Between Decentralized Authority and Other Structural Properties in Human Service Organizations: Implications for Service Effectiveness," *Administration in Social Work* 16, No. 1 (1992), 36.
[23]Fulmer, *New Management*, p. 221.

providing appropriate social services to a common clientele."[24] Its members may have various kinds and levels of training in social work and sometimes in other occupations and professions, or they may be nonprofessional workers. An MSW worker usually leads the team and assumes ultimate responsibility for treatment of and service to the client. The leader makes assignments to the team members based on clients' needs and the abilities of the various team members to meet these needs. The number of team members may vary from a partnership of two or as many as ten or more. Usually a team has four to eight members. In the team approach, the recipient may be served by more than one member. The client's social service needs are divided to ensure that each team member works at meeting only one or a few of the client's needs. Thus, a client often does not relate only to one worker but to several. However, clients may have face-to-face contact with only one team member, while the others are providing services behind the scenes.

HUMAN FACTORS IN ORGANIZATION

Theorists disagree on the importance of organizational patterns. Some claim that the organization is all-important; others suggest that human factors and relationships are equally important and must be given full consideration in the administration of an agency.

John Gardner, former secretary of the Department of Health, Education, and Welfare (HEW), stressed the importance of keeping organizations dynamic, alive, and renewed. He emphasized rules for organizational renewal that are relevant for all kinds of organizations, including, for example, U.S. Steel, a university, the U.S. navy, a government agency, or a local bank. Gardner highlights these rules as follows:

1. . . . The organization must have an effective program for the recruitment and development of talent. People are the ultimate source of renewal. . . .
2. . . . The organization capable of continuous renewal . . . must be a hospitable environment for the individual. Organizations that have killed the spark of individuality in their members will have greatly diminished their capacity for change. . . .
3. . . . The organization must have built-in provisions for self-criticism. It must have an atmosphere in which uncomfortable questions can be asked. . . .
4. . . . The organization that seeks continuous renewal [requires] fluidity of internal structure. Obviously, no complex modern organization can exist without the structural arrangements of division, branches, departments, and so forth. I'm not one of those who imagine that the modern world can get away from specialization. . . . In this connection, I always recall a Marx Brothers movie in which Groucho played a shyster lawyer. When a client commented on the dozens of flies buzzing around his broken-down office, Groucho said, "We have

[24]Donald Brieland, Thomas Briggs, and Paul Leuenberger, *The Team Model of Social Work Practice* (Syracuse, NY: Syracuse University School of Social Work, 1973), pp. 4–5.

a working agreement with them. They don't practice law and we don't climb the walls." . . . Most organizations have a structure that was designed to solve problems that no longer exist.

5. . . . The organization must have an adequate system of internal communication. . . .

6. The organization must have some means of combating the process by which men become prisoners of their procedures. . . .

7. The organization capable of continuous renewal will have found some means of combating the vested interests that grow up in every human institution. . . .

8. . . . The organization capable of continuous renewal is interested in what it is going to become and not what it has been. . . .

9. [The ninth rule] is obvious but difficult. An organization runs on motivation, on conviction, on morale. Men have to believe that it really makes a difference whether they do well or badly.[25]

The Peter Principle

The organizing process needs to be related to the promotion of staff in a realistic manner. The Peter Principle states that employees often tend to be promoted and rise to the highest level of their incompetency; that is, many staff members who are first-rate caseworkers are moved up the hierarchical ladder to become second-rate administrators.[26] In the organizational pattern and in its functioning, it is particularly important for promotions and changes in the administrative framework to relate to the competencies and needs of staff members as well as to the needs of the agency.

INFORMAL ORGANIZATION

That informal organization is powerful in the social service administration system is illustrated by this statement: "Coffee-cupping is often more significant than the conference table." Informal organization includes activities that go on behind the scenes, "underneath the table," at social activities, or away from the office. It is influential in many ways. In the musical *Mr. Roberts*, navy Seaman Second-class Roberts was more powerful in many ways than the captain of the ship. The men would come to him to talk and to obtain guidance on an informal basis. Similarly in agencies, informal organization is often more powerful than the formal structure. In most agencies there are key individuals in the lower levels of formal administration who hold and maintain considerable power over both policies and operations.

Informal organization is sometimes described as the invisible government. It does not show on the charts or on the blackboard but is powerful in

[25]John W. Gardner, "How to Prevent Organizational Dry-rot," *Harper's Magazine* 231 (October 1965), 20–26.

[26]Lawrence Peter and Raymond Hull, *The Peter Principle: Why Things Go Wrong* (New York: William Morrow, 1969).

actuality. Informal organization, if supportive, can strengthen formal administration; if hostile, it can undermine it.

Blau conducted an empirical study of the processes of organizational development by examining departmental daily operations and interpersonal relations of government officials in a state employment agency and a federal agency of law enforcement. He ascertained that the workers consulted much more often with one another than with their supervisors. Their informal interactions were routine and significant. Their numerous reasons for consulting with coworkers included anxiety over asking for advice from a supervisor, which might indicate stupidity and affect one's rating; the need to obtain guidance and advice without exposing one's difficulties; and a way to save time. Moreover, asking a coworker for assistance was considered less threatening than asking a supervisor, and such consultation served social as well as psychological and informational functions.[27]

Positive Uses of Informal Organization

Informal organization can be effective and positive in many ways. Political scientist J. D. Williams suggests three valuable uses of informal organization: as a communication channel, to maintain cohesiveness, and to boost the self-esteem of staff.[28]

Informal organization can act as a communication channel. Ideas and feelings discussed at the lunch hour are often channeled to an administrator of an agency and may be acted on. It has been said that at Fort Hall Indian Reservation, the "moccasin telegraphy" is the fastest and most powerful kind of communication. Sometimes the administration shares an idea with a staff member, intending it to be discussed informally at a coffee break or elsewhere with other staff members. This is a way of testing an idea—a kind of trial balloon.

As a way of maintaining cohesiveness, effective administrators identify the kingpins in the informal arena and work with them, communicate with them, and obtain their suggestions and recommendations. They recognize that if they enlist the informal leaders on their side concerning an issue, there is an excellent chance that the entire staff will support them. Unity, integration, and togetherness inhere in using informal organization in a positive manner.

Every staff member hungers for recognition and approval. Each values self-esteem and strives for self-actualization. The supervisor may interact

[27]Peter M. Blau, *The Dynamics of Bureaucracy*, rev. ed. (Chicago: University of Chicago Press, 1963), pp. 121–143.

[28]J. D. Williams, *Public Administration: The People's Business* (Boston: Little, Brown, 1980), pp. 96–99.

with line workers and supply psychological "vitamins," particularly as part of the informal organization. The director may talk to the leaders in the informal organization and give them recognition and status.

In addition, esteem and praise may come from coworkers and others who are participating in the informal process. Much psychological power is inherent in this kind of sharing. Informal organization is so significant that after talking with informal leaders, directors may be able to say to the total staff that "our decision" is such and such. Staff members are likely to feel safe because they know the key practitioners are on their side.

Handling Differences

Sometimes discrepancies in behavior between formal and informal organization arise and difficult problems surface. What, then, might or should be done?

According to Williams, there are four ways of handling significant differences, each of which relates to dissident staff members: (1) remove the cause of alienation, (2) woo them, (3) put them in office, or (4) transfer or dismiss them.[29] Often differences can be handled by removing the cause of the trouble. For example, a worker may complain about not being able to get into the office before or after regular working hours. Supplying a key may be the answer. A second approach is to woo the informal leaders so their thinking is more consonant with that of supervisors in the formal organization. This can be done by visiting, discussing, and interacting on a one-to-one basis or in a small group.

Often people who have points of view that are in opposition to the administration shift their stance when they are asked to take positions of responsibility in the formal organization. One caseworker had been openly critical of administrative policies and operations in an adoption agency. When asked to assume the role of a supervisor, her opinions began to change. After she had been in this position for three months, her administrative stance was almost the opposite of what it had been when she was a caseworker.

A fourth possibility is to fire the informal leader who will not respond to interaction for the best interests of the agency. This should be done on an individual basis, and not hastily. An agency often loses out when staff members are fired unless careful consideration has been given to alternatives. When a person has been working for an agency for some time, a considerable investment has been made by the agency, and firing such a worker is not practical unless an agreement cannot be reached. In a society that emphasizes personal rights and privileges, care must always be taken to protect the agency so that a person who is being terminated will not sue for damages or redress.

[29]Ibid., p. 96.

ROLES OF SOCIAL WORKERS

Pruger identifies three roles social workers perform in an organization. The first role is that of a helper, which social workers are trained to do. The second is an organizational role, such as that assumed by a director, intake worker, or supervisor; competence for these roles can be learned in various ways. The third role, that of a bureaucrat, is nearly totally neglected in social work education, practice, and research. However, it is here that social workers are "required to negotiate the stresses, opportunities, and constraints that permeate organizational life," regardless of the position in the organization.[30]

Pruger suggests that social workers can maintain their "vitality of action and independence of thought" and strengthen services in a bureaucracy by using the following tactics:

1. Understand legitimate authority and organizational enforcement, realizing that there is much latitude for discretion and innovation within regulations.
2. Conserve energy by not expecting abundant rewards or recognition from the organization and by not building resentment at the "paraphernalia of bureaucracy" such as collecting statistics, completing forms, and so on.
3. Acquire a competence needed by the organization, for example, in budgeting or proposal writing.
4. Don't yield unnecessarily to the requirements of administrative convenience.[31]

IMPROVING AGENCY ORGANIZATION

Efficiency and effectiveness are two major objectives of social welfare agencies in the provision of social services. Savas suggests that many techniques can be used to advantage in managing social welfare organizations. Some are highly quantitative and sophisticated; others are readily learned and more easily understood.

1. *Systems analysis.* "As a fundamental method for analyzing problems, systems analysis has no peer." It is nonquantitative and includes the following eleven steps: (a) recognize the problem; (b) identify needs; (c) establish objectives; (d) specify constraints; (e) generate alternative solutions to the problem; (f) formulate criteria for selecting the best alternative; (g) select the best alternative solution; (h) implement the solution on a pilot scale; (i) evaluate the results; (j) obtain feedback and modify the solution; (k) implement the final solution on a full scale.
2. *Means/ends analysis.* This is the "tree of alternatives" approach. It involves establishing an end for an objective and then identifying alternative means of achieving each end.

---

[30]Robert Pruger, "The Good Bureaucrat," *Social Work* 18 (July 1973), 26–27.
[31]Ibid., pp. 28–31.

3. *Decision analysis.* This includes a whole array of tools and techniques involving operations research and management science, including the use of mathematical models, cost-benefit analysis, cost effectiveness, and other models.[32]

Lippitt and Schmidt list correct and incorrect ways of handling critical issues related to organizational crises, which are summarized in Table 8–1.

Social work theorists are studying and developing various approaches to understanding organizational behavior and performance. For example,

TABLE 8–1.   Results of Handling Organizational Crises

CRITICAL ISSUE	RESULT IF THE ISSUE IS RESOLVED	
	CORRECTLY	INCORRECTLY
Creation	New organizational system comes into being and begins operating	Idea remains abstract. The organization is undercapitalized and cannot adequately develop and expose product or service
Survival	Organization accepts realities, learns from experience, becomes viable	Organization fails to adjust to realities of its environment and either dies or remains marginal—demanding continuing sacrifice
Stability	Organization develops efficiency and strength, but retains flexibility to change	Organization overextends itself and returns to survival stage, or establishes stabilizing patterns which block future flexibility
Pride and reputation	Organization's reputation reinforces efforts to improve quality of goods and service	Organization places more effort on image-creation than on quality product, or it builds an image which misrepresents its true capability
Uniqueness and adaptability	Organization changes to take fuller advantage of its unique capability and provides growth opportunities for its personnel	Organization develops too narrow a specialty to ensure secure future, fails to discover its uniqueness and spreads its efforts into inappropriate areas, or develops a paternalistic stance which inhibits growth
Contribution	Organization gains public respect and appreciation for itself as an institution contributing to society	Organization may be accused of "public be damned" and similar attitudes; or accused of using stockholder funds irresponsibly

Source: Gordon L. Lippitt and Warren H. Schmidt, "Crisis in a Developing Organization," *Harvard Business Review* 45 (November-December 1967), 109. Reprinted by permission of *The Harvard Business Review*. Copyright © 1967 by the President and Fellows of Harvard College; all rights reserved.

[32]E. S. Savas, "Organizational Strategy, Performance, and Management Technology," *Administration in Social Work* 1 (Summer 1977), 158–159.

Olmstead's ideas include the following theories of organization: structural, group, individual decision, and systems theories.[33]

Resnick emphasizes the importance of effecting internal change and suggests three patterns that might be used advantageously. The first is characterized by a catalyst who convenes an action system whose members are, or seem to be, concerned about an immediate problem in their organization. The second pattern involves a change agent, or catalyst, who recruits and selects organizational members known to be dissatisfied with the organization's functioning to form an action system to work for improvement. The third mode concerns a catalyst who pulls an action group together because of its members' interest in some innovation that they feel would benefit the agency. Resnick concludes, "All the patterns, although having advantages and disadvantages, are seen as effective ways of introducing and achieving organizational change from within."[34]

Gummer presents three models of organizational behavior: the rational model, the natural-system model, and the power-politics model. These are not mutually exclusive but may all be utilized by social work administrators. The rational model stresses the maximization of rationality and the reduction of uncertainty. The natural-system model encompasses subsystem goals, informal structure, management of internal conflict, and maintenance of the character of the system. The power-politics model views the organization as primarily a political arena, with various interest groups competing for control of organizational resources.[35]

According to Patti, there "seems to be no clear alternatives to the infusion of systems management perspectives and technology into social welfare. This approach is riding a crest of popularity compounded of the status borrowed from other fields of endeavor, its own salesmanship and soaring rhetoric, and the public's desperate quest for solutions to the 'welfare problem.'" He recommends social program managers to "have substantial grounding in the cluster of technologies that we have lumped together under the phrase 'systems management.'"[36]

Another approach that is being used currently to improve organizational patterns and social services is participatory action research. Sarri and

[33]Joseph A. Olmstead, "Organizational Factors in the Performance of Social Welfare and Rehabilitation for Workers," in Simon Slavin, ed., Social Administration (New York: Haworth Press and Council on Social Work Education, 1978), pp. 92–108.

[34]Herman Resnick, "Effecting Internal Change in Human Service Organizations," Social Casework 58 (November 1977), 553.

[35]Burton Gummer, "Organization Theory for Social Administration," in Felice Davidson Perlmutter and Simon Slavin, eds., Leadership in Social Administration (Philadelphia: Temple University Press, 1980), pp. 22–49.

[36]Rino Patti, "The New Scientific Management: Systems Management for Social Welfare," in Simon Slavin, ed., Social Administration: The Management of the Social Services, 2nd ed., Vol. II, Managing Finances, Personnel, and Information in Human Services (New York: Haworth Press, 1985), pp. 195–196.

Sarri report the use of this method in a poor Bolivian village and in an impoverished area of Detroit to overcome the resistance of individuals, organizations, and communities in adopting new ideas and service practices. The actions included the following: incorporating the active participation of community members affected by the problems, combining research and intervention strategies, building local skills and leadership to sustain the change, and facilitating the development of cooperative working relationships between social agencies and community residents. Sarri and Sarri conclude that participatory action research "is an effective tool to facilitate organizational innovation and community development."[37]

AN ORGANIZATION CASE

Many of the principles, processes, and skills inherent in social work organization are presented in the following case.

DEVELOPING A SEXUAL ABUSE TREATMENT PROGRAM

The need for a sexual abuse treatment program was presented to an agency manager by central administration. His agency had been selected to develop and implement this new program. A social worker was assigned by the manager to be the program coordinator, with full responsibility for the program.

Because of the need to include continuous agency-community coordination, an important factor for success was the development of community trust in the ability of the agency to provide a credible treatment program.

The program coordinator began the assignment by assessing, with the manager, the agency's mission and goals, staff structure and experience, present organization of services, purpose of the program in providing client-specialized services, and an effective way to establish agency-community relations.

Following is an overview of the critical steps taken by the program coordinator to initiate the program.

Research and Consultation. The program coordinator contacted agency managers presently operating similar programs in the community and consulted with managers, program coordinators, and therapists. He also reviewed and observed community programs. One of the most valuable learning experiences for the program coordinator was serving six months as a volunteer therapist in another community program. More formal specialized education was provided through university classes and workshops. Ultimately, to personally contribute and evaluate the effectiveness of the new program, the program coordinator also served as a therapist, providing individual, group, and family therapy.

[37]Rosemary C. Sarri and Catherine M. Sarri, "Organizational and Community Change Through Participatory Action Research," *Administration in Social Work* 16, Nos. 3/4 (1992), 119.

Planning. A treatment program was designed that primarily followed the successful pattern of existing community programs, with appropriate modification to comply with the agency's own uniqueness and function. A proposal was submitted to the administration and approved.

Organization. Agency staff training was conducted by the program coordinator, assisted by community resource experts, to prepare full-time and contracting staff to provide the professional services. An additional benefit was building positive multidisciplinary public relations, generating support for the agency's new treatment program and staff.

Referral and Finances. Referral procedures and financial planning were programmed through existing agency policies and procedures utilizing established practices.

Coordination. To maintain continued positive agency-community coordination and relations, the program coordinator became involved in state and local task-force committees and other committees related to the purposes of the treatment program.

Operation and Evaluation. As the program was implemented, cases were staffed by regular therapists to coordinate and evaluate the program's effectiveness. The program has been evaluated at regular time periods by agency administration and staff to refine the program and ensure a professionally sound service that meets the needs of clients, agency, and community.

Summary. A program coordinator was given a professional challenge by an agency manager. This challenge required learning the therapeutic subject from the perspective of a professional social worker and organizing, developing, implementing, and supervising an effective treatment program. This agency program has continued successfully for several years, receiving recognition in the community as one of three sexual abuse treatment programs.

SUMMARY

Organization in social work and the organizing process are essential ingredients in the delivery of social services. Vertical and horizontal coordination are vital to agency organization.

Max Weber was an ardent advocate of bureaucracy. Today bureaucracy is common in government and other large agencies, and valid arguments exist for and against it. It is agreed that social workers can utilize its resources better than they have in the past.

Four pillars of organization are division of labor, scalar and functional processes, structure, and span of control. In the operation of an agency, power and creativity inhere in both formal and informal organization.

Ordinarily, social work administrators do not have more than six or seven persons working directly under them. This keeps relationships to a minimum and provides maximum effectiveness.

Study and evaluation of social work organization, including theory and practice, are beginning to blossom and augur well for improving social services.

QUESTIONS FOR DISCUSSION

1. Define, describe, compare, and contrast formal and informal organization.
2. Give examples of horizontal and vertical organization.
3. Who was Max Weber and to what extent have his contributions influenced social work organization?
4. What is meant by "span of control"? Illustrate its importance in effective organization.
5. Describe the four ways for handling differences in formal and informal organization presented by J. D. Williams.
6. What suggestions do you have for improving organization in social work agencies?
7. What are the advantages and disadvantages of "pyramid" and "circle" organizational patterns in human service agencies?

SPECIAL ACTIVITIES

1. Role-play two situations to show differences between formal and informal organization.
2. Read Weiner's article and discuss your impressions of it with other students, either in or out of class.
3. Interview a teacher of administration in a school of business or a business executive in your community about his or her personal experiences with organizational problems.

SELECTED REFERENCES

ABRAMSON, JULIE S. "Orienting Social Work Employees in Interdisciplinary Settings: Shaping Professional and Organizational Perspectives." *Social Work* 38 (March 1993), 152–157.

BARGAL, DAVID, and HILLEL SCHMID. "Organizational Change and Development in Human Service Organizations: A Prefatory Essay." *Administration in Social Work* 16, Nos. 3/4 (1992), 1–11.

DAFT, RICHARD L., and RICHARD M. STEERS. *Organization: A Micro/Macro Approach*. Glenview, IL: Scott Foresman, 1986.

FLYNN, MARILYN L. "Using Computer-assisted Instruction to Increase Organizational Effectiveness." *Administration in Social Work* 14, No. 1 (1990), 103–118.

JOSEPH, M. VINCENTIA. "The Ethics of Organizations: Shifting Values and Ethical Dilemmas." *Administration in Social Work* 7 (Fall/Winter 1983), 47–57.

PATTI, RINO J. *Social Welfare Administration: Managing Social Programs in a Developmental Context.* Englewood Cliffs, NJ: Prentice Hall, 1983.

SARRI, ROSEMARY C., and CATHERINE M. SARRI. "Organizational and Community Change Through Participatory Action Research." *Administration in Social Work* 16, Nos. 3/4 (1992), 99–122.

SCHMID, HILLEL. "Relationships Between Decentralized Authority and Other Structural Properties in Human Service Organizations: Implications for Service Effectiveness." *Administration in Social Work* 16, No. 1 (1992), 25–38.

TUREM, S. JERRY. "Social Work Administration and Modern Management Technology." *Administration in Social Work* 10 (Fall 1986), 15–24.

WEINER, MYRON E. "Trans-Organizational Management: The New Frontier for Social Work Administrators." *Administration in Social Work* 14, No. 4 (1990), 11–27.

9

Committee and Board Operation

In a city of 200,000, the mayor invited twenty-five citizens to meet with his representative in charge of city planning to discuss recreational facilities and needs in the eastern part of the city. Letters went out with his official signature. The people invited represented a cross section of the population in that area, including professionals, laborers, and housewives. The meeting was called for 10:00 A.M.; no indication of its length was given.

The mayor's representative talked with enthusiasm about the recreational needs in that part of the city and indicated appreciation of those who had come to participate in the committee's deliberations. Twenty-five invitations had been sent, and twenty-one citizens responded to the call.

The mayor's representative presented in a clear, concise manner the desire of the administration to get ideas and suggestions from local citizens for improving recreational facilities. The meeting was opened for discussion, allowing for questions and comments. No one left the meeting for the first forty-five minutes, but then the participants started to leave. By 11:15, more than half the group had excused themselves. By 11:30, there were eight members left. At the end of the meeting, shortly after the clock struck 12:00, four people were present. The two basic questions that were being considered and about which the mayor's representative had hoped to obtain a decision had not been covered.

How effective was this meeting? The answer, of course, is obvious.

No agency is a one-person show. Administrators need the assistance of others. Group action and community support are needed for agencies that supply social services. Directors cannot and should not do everything alone. They must try to obtain the support of staff and members of the community in developing policies and translating them into effective social services.

Fulmer writes that "it has been cynically estimated that one third of all the people in the early morning traffic are headed for a committee meeting" and then states that "almost everyone has chuckled bitterly over the observation that 'A camel is a horse put together by a committee.' We know that there is some truth in the allegation that the best way to kill an idea is to appoint a committee."[1]

Green suggests that there are many kinds of committees, including "high-level committees, low-level committees, technical committees, task forces, working groups, one-man committees, program committees, community fund committees and eleemosynary committees generally, anniversary luncheon committees, committees *ad hoc*, and committees *ad infinitim*."[2]

Edson, in a jocular mood, suggests that the "committee process is notoriously susceptible to manipulation" and that "a Real Pro develops ploys to insure that meetings run exactly as he or she intends." She lists the following as tested and proved techniques for combating dictatorship or influencing committee action: reasoning, outshouting, filibustering, threatening, ganging up, putting to shame, and ostracizing.[3]

In formal organization, committees are extremely important. They provide an opportunity for the staff to contribute to efficient, effective operations. There are two kinds of committees, regularly established, or standing, and ad hoc, or task, committees. Standing committees are organized to take care of routine functions of an agency. Examples might be finance, personnel, or public relations committees. Ad hoc committees are created to handle specific tasks, problems, and operations and are disbanded when their charges have been fulfilled. An example of such a committee might be one established in a family agency to formulate legislative proposals for licensing marriage counselors.

Committee action can strengthen an agency or weaken or even destroy it. Within an effective framework of operation, committees can lessen the work of administrators and strengthen total agency services.

How the administrator and the committees get along with each other is very important. They can support and augment each other's contributions, or they can weaken or even destroy them. Administrators need to be careful to select a compatible group in establishing committees. Once a committee is established, the administrator should be willing to give full support to its operation. Committee members need to realize that they may

[1]Robert M. Fulmer, *The New Management*, 4th ed. (New York: Macmillan, 1988), p. 234.

[2]Estill I. Green, "The Nature and Use of Committees," in Harry A. Schatz, ed., *Social Work Administration* (New York: Council on Social Work Education, 1970), p. 182.

[3]Jean Brown Edson, "How to Survive on a Committee," *Social Work* 22 (May 1977), 224.

have significant responsibilities, but the ultimate authority rests with the administrator at the top. If a disagreement develops between a committee and its administrator, every attempt should be made to compromise and adjust differences, but if differences still persist, it is recognized that the agency director holds the final power. This is essential because the administrator is responsible to a board, commissioners, or some other governing body and needs to be in control when meeting with those who have ultimate authority.

COMMITTEE OPERATIONS

Several important factors in the operation of committees in a social service agency can either make or break their effectiveness and, ultimately, the services of the agency.

Size

The size of a committee depends somewhat on its objectives and functions. Having too many people on a committee may complicate the discussions and take too much time. Many experts in administrative organization maintain that to deal effectively with specific tasks, committees should be small, with only three or four members. For objectives and functions of a broader nature, committees may be enlarged to ten, fifteen, or even twenty or more to allow for adequate representation and full discussion.

In one graduate school of social work, two different patterns for the curriculum committee were practiced, each for a period of three years. The first involved a committee of ten, representing different sequences and areas of interest. This representation had advantages in allowing for all points of view, but often the committee members endeavored to further their own interests or departments when decisions were made. The second pattern was to elect three members at large from the entire school, asking them to try to represent the whole school rather than their own particular sequence or method. Over a period of three years, this smaller committee worked much more effectively and efficiently and represented the school as a whole rather than specialized interests.

The larger the committee, the more difficult it is to set a meeting time and to get full participation of its members. The smaller the committee, the easier it is to find an appropriate meeting time, and usually the percentage of attendance is higher. In a small working committee of three or four, the members usually feel committed and involved and participate actively. Even the choice of a meeting place is relevant to the size of the committee.

The basic question is whether a committee should be large to allow for representation or small enough to provide an opportunity for intensive, integrated work. Either pattern may be justified, depending on specific goals.

Composition

The makeup of a committee is significant for successful operation. Composition should be related to the functions to be performed. Competent staff members who are capable of contributing to the deliberations of the committee are needed. People invited to serve on a committee should have an interest in its objectives and functions. This is not always possible, but it renders the committee more effective. Sometimes individuals need to serve on committees even though they do not have a particular interest in its operations. They are asked to serve because they can help give an overall perspective, which benefits the total operation of the agency.

It is hoped that those who serve on a committee will be committed to expending the time and energy needed for its operation. Again, this rule cannot be absolute, but if committee members are dedicated to the objectives of the committee, they are likely to be more effective. Forcing staff members to serve on a committee against their wishes usually backfires.

Representation must be taken into consideration. It might be related to the specialized practice of the workers, length of service, training and background, community activities, gender, age, or other factors. It is never possible to get 100 percent representation of differentials, so the final alignment is always an approximation of the full range. However, to "load" the committee with people from particular interest groups tends to doom or complicate committee action.

Committee composition needs to include minority representation. Most social service agencies employ minority staff members and call on them to represent racial and cultural differences.

Time Dynamics

Effective committee operation necessitates understanding the value of committee members' time and its dynamics. Both are relevant and should be considered and reconsidered often.

Ordinarily, a stopping time should be planned for a committee meeting. Too many meetings have only a starting time and often go on too long, infringing on the personal time of committee members. Leaders who understand the value of time and who plan to stop at a certain hour usually accomplish more than those who make a meeting open-ended. Many times committee meetings go downhill if they are extended unnecessarily. Most people prefer to work hard within the time specified so that they can proceed to other meetings or activities.

If a two-hour meeting has been arranged, and at the end of the two hours decisions and plans have not been made, it is a simple matter to call another meeting. If meetings are well planned, their purposes can ordinarily be achieved in the time allotted. Occasionally an emergency may necessitate extending the committee's deliberations.

Effective committee members recognize that time is a powerful dynamic in human relationships. Certain developments occur at the beginning of a meeting, and certain actions take place at the end. Often committee members will squander time during the meeting and then bring up important matters in the last few minutes. The approaching end of a meeting tends to force consideration of crucial issues and decisions.

A helpful tool for the efficient use of time is a well-prepared agenda that has been sent to members in advance. This gives members the opportunity to prepare for the meeting. It also gives order to the conduct and operation of the committee. An agenda should not be absolute and inflexible but can be a significant guide and promote efficiency and effectiveness. An agenda should give enough detail to clarify what is going to be considered. An additional helpful tool is to estimate the amount of time needed for each item, with the understanding, of course, that the time is flexible. Another time-saver is to mail the minutes of the committee meeting in advance so that members will have a chance to read them before they meet. This facilitates making corrections or suggestions at the meeting as well as helping with preparation for committee participation.

Responsibilities and Authority

Committee members need to understand what their specific responsibilities are and what authority they possess. Some committees are strictly advisory; others are planning or decision-making bodies. The administrator needs to clarify for the committee, either by meeting with the committee or through its leader, its tasks, responsibilities, and authority.

The more specific the interpretation of the tasks and objectives to be performed, the more likely the success of the committee's operations. It is important for a committee to have a timetable, particularly for finishing a given task.

Some administrators assign responsibilities to committees and then fail to give them the authority to carry them out. This not only handicaps the committee; it also hinders the morale of individual members and reduces committee effectiveness. The members say, "Well, why should we spend our time working, when what we say won't make any difference anyway?" Ordinarily, it is helpful for a committee to have the responsibilities and degree of authority spelled out in writing. This helps administrators to clarify what they are asking the committee to do and gives specific guidelines that can be used by the members.

It is generally advisable for a committee to keep minutes. These indicate how the committee is proceeding and can be motivational and informational.

Again, minutes should be prepared and distributed to members so they can read them before the next session.

Leadership

Committee leaders may be appointed by the administration or chosen by the group, either by consensus vote or by volunteering. When a chairperson is appointed, the administrator needs to take into consideration the person's interests, commitments, and abilities and whether or not that person will spend the necessary time on the assignment. Also important is the compatibility of leaders and committee members for trust, communication, and a willingness to make compromises and to be flexible.

When committee members choose their own leader, it is usually by nomination and vote, which is customarily done openly but may be accomplished by secret ballot. In informal committees, a request may be made for someone to volunteer to lead the group. This procedure has advantages and disadvantages. People might volunteer out of sincere dedication or because they are eager for power or have certain goals other than those of the committee or agency.

Green suggests that responsibilities of committee members include advance preparation, regularity of attendance, punctuality, and intelligent participation. Responsibilities of committee chairpersons include advance planning, using businesslike procedures, high degree of participation, and familiarity with published materials that pertain to the committee's work.[4]

Trust

For effective committee operation, there needs to be a feeling of trust between and among committee members and their leader. Members of a committee must be willing to practice some of the most fundamental social work principles—for example, acceptance, respect of the individual, and the right of individuals to make decisions and choices. Acceptance means accepting people as they are, not trying to make them over in accordance with one's own standards and values. It involves an open understanding of others and a respect for their values and goals, whether they are similar to or different from one's own.

Basic trust is conducive to the successful operation of a committee because it opens the door for each member to talk freely and helps to accomplish committee tasks. If distrust is present—and it sometimes is—committee relationships are destroyed; the group is fragmented; and careful and effective consideration of questions, plans, and decisions is blocked.

[4]Green, "Committees," pp. 188–189.

Flexibility

Effective committee operation requires a flexible and conciliatory attitude among its members.

Members recognize that even when decisions have been made, new evidence or further discussion may make it necessary to reverse them. The possibility of change should be a constant companion of current developments.

Flexibility means that all members of the committee strive to further what they think is right but are willing to give in when necessary for the welfare of the group or agency. Group consensus is more important than individual commitment or opinion.

Even the manner in which opinions and ideas are presented can be helpful or can block committee operations. A person who is adamant and rigid may cause trouble. Committee members who have firm convictions but who introduce their remarks with such words as "It seems to me," or "This is one possibility" are more likely to facilitate the group process than block or hamper it.

Consensus

Sooner or later, a consensus must be reached on plans and tasks of the committee. This can be done formally or informally. Traditionally, a committee's formal decisions are made by taking a vote, either by secret ballot or openly. Small committees tend to vote verbally rather than in writing. Usually this is an indication of a basic trust among the members. Before a decision is made, it is best if all members have had the opportunity to present their views. They will then feel secure that the decision is justified.

Informal consensus can be arrived at through open discussion and some indication that the majority has a certain opinion or favors a particular decision. A sensitive chairperson is usually aware of this kind of consensus and may merely need to say, "It seems from our discussion that we are in agreement about such and such." He or she could then ask if anybody has a different opinion. If so, further discussion is probably needed.

ADVANTAGES OF COMMITTEES

Committees have many advantages and contributions to make as well as numerous disadvantages and limitations. Bedeian summarizes some of the key advantages as follows:

1. Committee decisions are likely to be accepted by their members. This makes implementation much easier.

2. Committees composed of affected work group representatives can identify potential coordination problems.
3. Committees diffuse power. Some decisions are too significant (and complex) to be decided by a single person.
4. Committees that are purposefully constituted can bring divergent experiences and training to bear on a single issue.
5. Committees can rapidly disseminate information.
6. Committees can help to train new managers.
7. Committees can avoid placing all the blame on one person for an unpopular decision.[5]

A committee may be used for educational purposes as well as for study, diagnosis, decision making, and implementation. A new member of a staff can learn much about an agency through active membership on one or more committees. Since a committee looks at problems, policies, and procedures, it is a natural place for learning about agency policies and services.

DISADVANTAGES OF COMMITTEES

Committees have many limitations. They are often costly in time and money. Getting bogged down in long committee meetings or getting together too often is common in social service agencies. Many committees are slow to act, which may hamper needed action. Sometimes compromises hinder the decision-making process and its effectiveness. Again, special interests and prejudices of committee members may cause real difficulties.

Green reports numerous shortcomings of committees, which include the following:

1. Inferiority of decisions
   a. Compromise
   b. Domination
   c. Unqualified members
   d. Lack of continuity
   e. Inadequate motivation
   f. Haste
2. Impotency of decisions
   a. Intermittency
   b. Executive instrumentalities lacking
3. Wastefulness
4. Depreciation of line organization[6]

[5]Arthur G. Bedeian, *Management*, 3rd ed. (Fort Worth, TX: Dryden Press, 1993), p. 515.
[6]Green, "Committees," p. 185.

AGENCY BOARDS

Since social service agencies serve their communities, boards of citizens are usually organized for guiding an agency's destiny. These boards are needed for several reasons: to allow for feedback from the community, to provide guidance to the agency about community needs and how to satisfy them, and to help in other ways that can improve efficiency and effectiveness.

Both private and public agencies have boards to assist with the formulation of their objectives, policies, and services. Constitutions and charters of agencies, created with board assistance, are relevant and important for the success of an agency.

Functions of the Administrative Board

Trecker suggests that the functions of the administrative board can be summed up as follows:

1. To establish the legal or corporate existence of the agency whether it be under the auspices of government or voluntary efforts;
2. To take responsibility for formulating general objectives, policies, and programs;
3. To inspire community confidence in the program because of the competence and dedication of the board members as active trustees of the agency;
4. To assume responsibility for the provision of adequate finances and to be accountable for the expenditure of funds;
5. To provide conditions of work, personnel policies, and staff. The board is particularly responsible for the selection and evaluation of the administrator;
6. To understand and interpret the work of the agency to the community;
7. To study, know, and interpret general community needs to the agency staff;
8. To relate the services of the agency to the work of other agencies and to concentrate upon the improvement of community conditions;
9. To conduct periodic evaluations of agency operations with a view toward improving and strengthening the amount and quality of work that is done;
10. To improve the continuity of experienced leadership so that major staff changes will not weaken the agency.[7]

Schmidt, a practicing administrator, proposed nine responsibilities of a board:

1. *Attaining the goals or purposes of the agency.* The board makes certain that the established goals are being pursued and advises when the goals need changing because of changed conditions.

---

[7]Harleigh B. Trecker, *Social Work Administration, Principles and Practices* (New York: Association Press, 1971), p. 109.

2. *Creating the structure.* The board of directors has the responsibility of ensuring of that the agency's legal structure is proper and that it continues to remain so under all state and federal laws.
3. *Providing the necessary facilities.*
4. *Employing the executive.* The board selects the executive, fixes the compensation, establishes the duties, delegates the necessary authority to administer the work of the agency, and relieves him or her of duties if necessary.
5. *Fixing the policies.* It is the duty of the board to prescribe the services to be provided as well as the basic policies for the administration of these services.
6. *Setting the budget and providing the finances.* The obligation rests on the governing board to set the budget and thereby establish services.
7. *Checking the operation.* The board must check the operations periodically to see that they are proceeding successfully. The trustees of an agency are accountable to the public for their stewardship. They must know that the services are provided as they have directed.
8. *Interpreting the services.* The board can act as a buffer between the staff and the public and can promote effective public relations.
9. *Participating in community planning.* The board has a duty to participate in community efforts to plan and raise funds for health and welfare operations.[8]

According to Stein, to ensure professional respect and "to strengthen our voices, we must have support, ideas, effective communication, and, above all, assumption of genuine responsibility by those who serve as trustees for the common good—even if we have to spur them to assume this responsibility. To those hundreds of board members who meet these expectations, we owe a great debt, whether or not they and we always see eye to eye."[9]

Social work administrators generally appreciate the support and assistance that a capable board of directors may provide. Levin shares his conviction about the values of a strong board as follows:

That an active, "in control" board makes for strong administration, that is, for a strong executive.
That a knowledgeable board asks crucial questions about the agency's conscience and professional wisdom—and relays informed responses to the community for community support.
That a representative board speaks for the community and rightfully comments on its behalf.
That a strong board assures the executive of a concerned and involved, yet independent, lay group worth talking to—"a window on the world."[10]

[8]William D. Schmidt, *The Executive and the Board in Social Welfare* (Cleveland: Howard Allen, 1959), pp. 40–50.
[9]Herman D. Stein, "Board, Executive, and Staff," in Simon Slavin, ed., *Social Administration: The Management of the Social Services*, 2nd ed., Vol. I, *An Introduction to Human Services Management* (New York: Haworth Press, 1985), p. 203.
[10]Herman Levin, "The Board-Executive Relationship Revisited," in Simon Slavin, ed., *Social Administration: The Management of the Social Services*, 2nd ed., Vol. I, *An Introduction to Human Services Management* (New York: Haworth Press, 1985), p. 210.

Selection of Board Members

The process of selecting board members is particularly important. If it is accomplished on a hit-or-miss basis or favors vested interests, difficulties may ensue. Several factors are important in the selection of board members, whether they are appointed or elected. They should be persons who have a sincere interest in the agency and who are committed to furthering its services.

Representation is particularly important. People from various groups, cultures, and geographic areas should be selected so that a cross section of relevant publics served is obtained. Representatives from minorities should be on the board, as well as both men and women. It is best if people who have had some experience on a board and know about the agency and its services are included along with those who have little or no past board experience.

The abilities of the individuals selected are significant. This does not mean that they have to be experts or professionals, but they should have the ability to think clearly and understand community and agency needs. These will stand them in good stead as board members. Most social agency boards are constituted of both professional and lay members. Those selected should be willing to take the time to participate fully on the board. People who talk a lot but do little or nothing for the agency should be avoided.

The Administrator and the Board

The relationship between the executive and the board members is unique, and there must be two-way communication and action for services to be effective. Levy suggests that the executive needs to play a variety of roles in working with the board, the main ones being

1. Role of helper
2. Role of clarifier
3. Role of mediator
4. Role of mobilizer[11]

Kramer notes several factors that may disturb or enhance the balance of power between board members and the executive. Some key variables that influence the extent to which the board or the executive would predominate in the policy-making process are the following:

1. The organizational structure of the agency; its size, complexity, and degree of bureaucracy.

[11]Charles S. Levy, "The Executive and the Agency Board," *Journal of the Jewish Communal Service* 38 (Spring 1962), 234–248.

2. The character of the agency's services or program, whether they are technical or highly professionalized in content or conceived as residual or institutional in nature.
3. The type of policy issue, e.g., programmatic, housekeeping, professional, ideological, or fiscal.
4. Aspects of the board member's status and relationship to the agency such as the duration of his membership, degree of financial responsibility and contributions, role as a consumer of agency services, or participant in its program; the number of his other organizational affiliations and his social status in the community.
5. The executive's professional status and duration of employment.[12]

Kramer concludes that "the executive exerts a greater influence than the board member in the policy process to the extent that these variables are maximized."[13]

Board Operations

Mitton suggests that boards are charged with the general stewardship of agencies. He includes the following committees that help to provide for the delivery of services: finance, service appraisal, personnel, management audit, policy review, nominating, and affirmative action. In addition, usually there is an executive committee, which acts in the absence of the board or between board meetings.[14]

Citizen participation in governance of social work agencies has increased considerably. In 1970 the American Public Welfare Association conducted a survey of local public welfare boards and committees to investigate the amount of participation of citizens in agencies, particularly among low-income persons and recipients of services. A sample of 750 local departments, drawn from a list of 2,800 eligible agencies, was used. A questionnaire was sent to each administrator in the sample, and 458 replies were received, a response rate of 60 percent. A board was defined as a group of people who set policy, and a committee as a group of people who give advice to an agency.

One striking fact shown in this study is that nearly a quarter (24 percent) of the agencies reported they had neither a public welfare board nor an advisory committee, although a fifth (19 percent) reported having both. More than a third (36 percent) reported having a board only, and a fifth (20 percent)

[12]Ralph M. Kramer, "Ideology, Status, and Power in Board-Executive Relationships," *Social Work* 10 (October 1965), 114.

[13]Ibid.

[14]Daryl G. Mitton, "Utilizing the Board of Trustees: A Unique Structural Design," in Simon Slavin, ed., *Social Administration: The Management of the Social Services* (New York: Haworth Press and Council on Social Work Education, 1978), p. 120.

reported having a committee only.[15] Some highlights of the differences between boards and committees that emerged from this study are the following:

1. Boards are less likely to meet if the administrator is not present.
2. Boards are less likely to be served by staff members.
3. Boards are smaller than committees.
4. Boards are less likely to have recipient representation and participation by poor persons.
5. Boards are more likely to have an effect on agency services and more likely to be innovative and improve agency operations.
6. Boards make policy; committees make recommendations.[16]

A current development is the use of educational programs for new board members. It is common for social work agencies to provide training for new members. These programs are formulated to help board members

1. Through orientation and interpretation, gain a sound understanding of the goals, resources, and services of the agency
2. Use their diverse abilities and backgrounds to become effective, participating members, contributing to the best interests of the agency in the delivery of its social services
3. Gain understanding and skills so they can assist with public relations and interpretation of the agency to the community

SUMMARY

The effective operation of committees is fundamental to the administrative process in the delivery of social services. Those selecting committees should be concerned with size, composition, and representation. Ordinarily the most effective work is done by small committees of three to five members. It is advisable for committees to set stopping times as well as starting times for their meetings. Committee members need to know what their responsibilities are and how much authority they have. Trust and flexibility are essential for effective participation of committee members.

Boards are important aspects of social service agencies and usually help in successful administration. In the selection of board members, the following factors are relevant: interest, commitment, representativeness, gender,

[15]Edward J. O'Donnell and Ott M. Reid, "Citizen Participation on Public Welfare Boards and Committees," in Simon Slavin, ed., *Social Administration: The Management of the Social Services* (New York: Haworth Press and Council on Social Work Education, 1978), pp. 134–148.

[16]Ibid., pp. 146–147.

ability, and willingness to take time to serve effectively. Board members should be able to trust one another and be flexible, as well as willing to devote the time and energy required to make significant contributions to the agency.

QUESTIONS FOR DISCUSSION

1. Why are committees so important in the operation of social welfare agencies?

2. Discuss the significance of the size of committees in relation to their tasks.

3. What are the advantages of having a stopping time for committee meetings as well as a starting time?

4. What are the advantages and disadvantages if a committee chooses its own chairperson?

5. Do you think that boards should be eliminated in social welfare agencies? Why or why not?

6. Describe some of the values of having an effective board in a family service agency.

7. What factors should be taken into consideration in the selection of board members for a county welfare department?

SPECIAL ACTIVITIES

1. Using an agenda, role-play for seven minutes a meeting of a seven-member budget committee in a mental-health center; then do it again without an agenda. Evaluate what occurred.

2. Invite an agency administrator from your community to talk about the assets and liabilities of committee organization and operation.

3. Have a panel of five discuss this topic: Boards should have representation from different social and cultural groups.

SELECTED REFERENCES

BEDEIAN, ARTHUR G. *Management*, 3rd ed., pp. 515–518. Fort Worth, TX: Dryden Press, 1993.
EDSON, JEAN BROWN. "How to Survive on a Committee." *Social Work* 22 (May 1977), 224–226.
GREEN, ESTILL I. "The Nature and Use of Committees." in Harry A. Schatz, ed., *Social Work Administration: A Resource Book*, pp. 181–189. New York: Council on Social Work Education, 1970.
KRAMER, RALPH M. "Toward a Contingency Model of Board-Executive Relations." *Administration in Social Work* 9 (Fall 1985), 15–33.

LEVIN, HERMAN. "The Board-Executive Relationship Revisited." In Simon Slavin, ed., *Social Administration: The Management of the Social Services*, 2nd ed. Vol. I, *An Introduction to Human Services Management*, pp. 205–211. New York: Haworth Press, 1985.

O'CONNELL, BRIAN. *The Board Member's Book*. New York: Foundation Center, 1985.

O'DONNELL, EDWARD J., and OTT M. REID. "Citizen Participation on Public Welfare Boards and Committees." In Simon Slavin, ed., *Social Administration: The Management of the Social Services*, pp. 134–148. New York: Haworth Press and Council on Social Work Education, 1978.

STEIN, HERMAN D. "Board, Executive, and Staff." In Simon Slavin, ed., *Social Administration: The Management of the Social Services*, 2nd ed. Vol. I, *An Introduction to Human Services Management*, pp. 191–204. New York: Haworth Press, 1985.

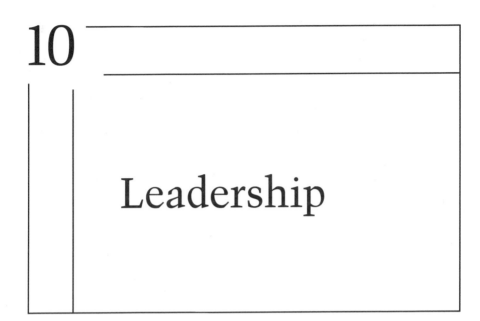

10

Leadership

A group of Boy Scouts was on a hike. They were nearing the top of a small hill, their scoutmaster lagging about 100 yards behind. He paused for a moment to rest and chat with a farmer. He remarked, "Up ahead you can see a group of Boy Scouts." Then he added, "And I am their leader."

Leadership may be defined as both a position and an ability. As a *position*, it means that a person is responsible for the control of certain situations and is in a directing or guiding position. A leader may be at the head of an organization, agency, or activity. Leadership *ability* refers to the capacity or skill to influence relationships with others so that they will follow the path taken by the leader. Leadership involves the ability to bring about a desired change or action from or with others. It implies a kind of movement that invites others to follow in their thinking, feeling, or actions. A leader encourages people to act to benefit themselves and others.

Bedeian suggests that "effective leadership is essential to business, government, military, the arts, and all the other institutions that influence the way we live, work, and play. From a managerial perspective, *leadership* is the process of influencing others toward the accomplishment of goals."[1]

The need for creative leadership is paramount in social work today, although it has always been important. Pioneering leaders in the nineteenth and twentieth centuries set the stage for the development of social work as a profession. Innovative social work leaders are needed to help political, government, religious, and community leaders to understand more about people and their social relationships, their social problems and needs, and how they can be helped to function better in interactional situations.

[1]Arthur G. Bedeian, *Management*, 3rd ed. (Forth Worth, TX: Dryden Press, 1993), p. 470.

WHY BE A SOCIAL WORK LEADER?

Various attempts have been made to ascertain why many social workers gravitate to administrative positions in social service agencies. The following factors appear to be significant:

Prestige and status. All people hunger for recognition and importance. Being an administrator or executive in a social service agency or a school of social work offers this kind of fulfillment.

Higher salaries. Although there are exceptions, administrators are usually paid more than caseworkers or others in practice. In an age of inflation, this factor is especially important for many.

Desire to achieve. A basic human drive is to want to act, to accomplish. Leadership roles offer ample opportunities for action.

Desire to change and improve policies and services. Administration is where changes are made where the action takes place.

Reach for power. Many social workers want to be in on the plans and decisions that affect the delivery of social services. Power may be used positively as well as negatively, and many social workers want to be a part of the positive process, particularly in delivering services and in improving society. French and Raven describe five kinds of power that can be exercised in leadership and administrative roles:

1. *Reward power* is based on the ability to give rewards for accomplishments. The strength of the power increases with the magnitude of the rewards. Social work staff might be rewarded by salary increases, promotions, or commendations for work well done.
2. *Coercive power* is based on workers' fear that they may be punished if they fail to conform to the request or direction of the superior. Such power stems from individuals' expectation of punishment if they do not do as their administrators suggest or if they oppose their decisions or opinions.
3. *Legitimate power* relates to norms and values. It stems from internalized values, so that workers agree that workers agree that a leader has a right to influence them and they have an obligation to accept it. Cultural values constitute one common basis for legitimate power.
4. *Referent power* has its base in the identification of the worker with the leader. Workers can be influenced because they admire and respect the leader.
5. *Expert power* varies with the extent of the knowledge or perceptiveness that the worker attributes to the leader. It also involves accepting advice from or guidelines set by a superior. In such instances, workers trust their leaders and believe they are telling the truth.[2]

Stepping-stone. Some social workers reach executive positions with the aim of climbing up the community ladder. Some want to shift to education or research, and leadership experience is conducive to moving in those directions.

---

[2]John R. P. French, Jr., and Bertram Raven, "The Bases of Social Power," in Dorwin Cartwright and Alvin Zander, eds., *Group Dynamics*, 3rd ed. (New York: Harper & Row, 1968), pp. 262–268. Copyright © 1968 by Dorwin Cartwright and Alvin Zander. Reprinted by permission of Harper & Row, Publishers, Inc.

Opportunity for creativity. W. I. Thomas observed that one of the "four wishes" he believed all humankind shared was the wish for new experiences. Leadership in social work provides opportunities for creativity in methods and procedures, in trying to help people with personal problems, and in making worthwhile changes in communities. For example, the fields of prevention and enrichment are developing in ways that offer almost unlimited challenges to social work leaders.

Neurotic needs. Numerous studies show that some leaders move into their positions to fulfill the need to be controlling, overbearing, or even sadistic or masochistic at times.

Service, giving of self. Most mature executives in social work genuinely want to give of themselves, to use their abilities to help others. Why not? In fact, most practitioners feel this is the most significant factor in successful leadership in social work. Mature, effective social work leaders want to do all they can to help others.

LEADERSHIP ACTIVITIES

Leadership roles relate to the actual work that administrators perform in social welfare agencies. Patti reported a study based on interviews with ninety managers selected to represent several administrative levels in public, quasi-public, and voluntary agencies in the state of Washington. The objective was to develop an empirically grounded understanding of the tasks and functions that characterize management practice in social welfare that might be of value in planning content in educational programs for administrators. The mean hours spent in various activities are reported in Table 10–1.

TABLE 10-1. Mean Hours Spent in Each Activity by Managers

ACTIVITY	MEAN HOURS
Planning	3.9
Information processing	6.2
Controlling	5.4
Coordinating	3.8
Evaluating	1.5
Negotiating	.8
Representing	1.8
Staffing	.9
Supervising	6.7
Supplying	.3
Extracurricular	1.9
Direct practice	4.1
Budgeting	1.0

Source: Rino J. Patti, "Patterns of Management Activity in Social Welfare Agencies," in Simon Slavin, ed., *Social Administration: The Management of the Social Services,* 2nd ed., Vol. I, *An Introduction to Human Services Management* (New York: Haworth Press, 1985), p. 28.

It is evident that social work administrators assume many different leadership roles and participate in a variety of activities. Most of their efforts involve managing the agency and interacting with staff members. Some, in smaller agencies, participate in direct practice with clients. Some administrators are involved in research projects, whereas others perform minimally or not at all in this area. Finally, agency contacts and public relations consume a considerable amount of time for most social work administrators.

Social work leaders often shift positions of leadership. Political changes in public agencies and voluntary changes in private agencies bring in new faces and alter leadership positions. Personal and professional factors cause considerable movement from one agency or organization to another, whether social work leaders are involved in regular practice or in the educational system. This process is illustrated by the large turnover of deans in schools of social work. Otis and Caragonne indicate that in 1976–1977 there were approximately twenty-seven vacancies in the eighty-five graduate social work programs. They also report that for the years 1975–1977, the vacancy rate in schools of social work was approximately 33 percent. During the same time the vacancy rate was only 15 percent in colleges of law, 15 percent in schools of nursing, and 4 percent in colleges of medicine. They concluded from their study that seven major sources of pressure affected those who resigned and those who continued to serve: fund-raising activities, faculty, inability to pursue one's own professional goals, insufficient time and/or administrative support for responsibilities of the position, university-system administration, personal concerns, and students.[3]

THEORIES OF LEADERSHIP

Numerous authors have propounded theories about leadership. Fulmer suggests that such leadership theories can be grouped into three main categories: trait theories, behavioral theories, and situational theories.[4]

Various writers have stressed the importance of personality traits as they relate to leadership. Some have suggested that physical traits, including good looks, are particularly significant; others have emphasized mental traits. For example, Ralph Stogdill observed that leadership ability is related to the capacity for judgment and the verbal facility of the leader. Edwin E. Ghiselli concluded from his studies that intelligence is particularly significant. The importance of personality traits and combinations of them in developing leadership has been stressed by many. Dynamic, colorful presidents like

[3]Jack Otis and Penelope Caragonne, "Factors in the Resignation of Graduate School of Social Work Deans: 1975–77," *Journal of Education for Social Work* 15 (Spring 1979), 59.

[4]Robert M. Fulmer, *The New Management*, 2nd ed. (New York: Macmillan, 1978), p. 312; also see 4th ed., 1988, pp. 299–321.

Franklin D. Roosevelt, John F. Kennedy, and Ronald Reagan illustrate the influence of charisma in leadership roles.

Fulmer gives the following examples of behavioral theories of leadership:

1. The benevolent-autocracy theory describes an all-powerful ruler who listens considerately to the staff's opinions and then makes his or her own decision. Robert N. McMurry advocated this approach, which is basically antidemocratic.

2. The continuum theory, closely related to the benevolent-autocratic theory, suggests that types of leaders can be charted along a continuum. At one end is the total authoritarian, and at the other, the laissez-faire leader. Rensis Likert and his associates conducted statistical studies into the behavioral style of management leadership and concluded that those that were more employee-centered (laissez-faire) rather than job-centered were the most effective.[5]

Blake and Mouton developed a well-known "managerial grid" theory, which depicts how the concern for production and the concern for people are related. The grid shows a range of possible interactions between these two concerns. The horizontal axis shows concern for production, and the vertical axis indicates concern for people. Each is expressed on a nine-point scale, in which the number 1 represents minimum concern and the number 9 maximum concern. Blake and Mouton conclude that the "manner in which these two concerns are linked together by a manager defines how he uses hierarchy."[6]

Blake, Mouton, Tomaino, and Gutierrez formulated a social work grid that depicts a concern for problem solving on the horizontal plane and concern for the client as a person on the vertical axis. The 1.1 low spot in this grid is "take-it-or-leave-it-oriented," described by "I place agency expectations before the client and it is up to him or her to decide whether the problem will be solved." The 9.9 high rating is "mutual-problem-solving-oriented," with the description "I consult with my client so we can work on mutual goals designed to solve the problem."[7]

The third category includes situational theories. This approach suggests that leadership is related not only to the leader's and the group's personality but also to the situations. This type of theory is illustrated by Fred E. Fidler, whose focus on adaptive situational leadership style includes the following dimensions, summarized by Fulmer:

(1) *Leader-member* relations refers to the degree of confidence the subordinates have in the leader. It also entails the loyalty shown for and the attractiveness of

[5]Ibid., pp. 314–316.

[6]Robert R. Blake and Jane Srygley Mouton, *The Managerial Grid* (Houston: Gulf Publishing, 1964), pp. 9–11; Robert R. Blake and Jane S. Mouton, *The New Managerial Grid* (Houston: Gulf Publishing, 1978), p. 11.

[7]Robert R. Blake, Jane S. Mouton, Louis Tomaino, and Sharon Gutierrez, *The Social Work Grid* (Springfield, IL: Charles C. Thomas, 1979), p. 6.

the leader; *(2) Task structure* refers to the degree to which the followers' jobs are routine as opposed to being ill structured and undefined, and *(3) Position power* refers to the power inherent in the leadership position. It includes the rewards and punishments that are typically associated with the position, the leader's official authority (based on his ranking in the managerial hierarchy), and the support that the leader receives from his superiors and the overall organization.[8]

Carlisle suggests that the division of leadership into autocratic, democratic, and laissez-faire categories has numerous political meanings, both obvious and subtle. To avoid value connotations, he substitutes the use of the terms *directive, participative,* and *free rein.* He suggests that the free-rein style has limited uses and that the directive and participative styles are commonly used.[9] Table 10–2 summarizes the characteristics of each of these patterns.

Kotin and Sharaf suggest two main leadership styles that describe the executive's professional behavior, "the characteristic way in which he functions as an executive, how he structures his role, and how he influences the roles and functioning of others in the organization. It is, for the most part,

TABLE 10–2. Conditions Associated with Different Leadership Styles

CONDITION	DIRECTIVE STYLE	PARTICIPATIVE STYLE	FREE-REIN STYLE
Focus	Leader-centered	Group-centered	Individual-centered
Decisions	Leader makes most decisions	Subordinates involved in decisions	Subordinates make decisions
Independence	Little freedom of action permitted	Fosters some independence	Almost complete independence
Communication	One-way communication	Two-way communication	Free, open communication
Power	Uses power and discipline	Tries to persuade, not force	Reliance on self-control
Subordinates' feelings	Little concern for subordinates' feelings	Subordinates' feelings are considered	Subordinates' feelings predominate
Orientation	Task-centered	People- and group-centered	Individual accomplishment
Leader's role	Provide direction	Group involvement	Provide support resources
Psychological results	Obedience and dependency	Cooperation and participation	Independence and individual performance

Source: Howard M. Carlisle, *Management Essentials: Concepts for Productivity and Innovation,* 2nd ed. Chicago: Science Research Associates, 1987, p. 475.

[8]Fulmer, *New Management,* p. 321.

[9]Howard M. Carlisle, *Management Essentials: Concepts for Productivity and Innovation,* 2nd ed. (Chicago: Science Research Associates, 1987), p. 475.

unrelated to policy; it is not *what* he does, but *how* he does it." The two styles are the *tight* and the *loose* administration patterns. A tight administrative style relates to the military model, with emphasis on hierarchical authority and communication. A tight style implies

(1) clear-cut delegation of authority and responsibility; (2) an orderly and hierarchical chain of command through which communication flows upward and downward, without skipping levels; (3) a reliance on formal communications—for example, regular meetings, reports, printed forms; (4) formal expression of power—for example, hearings, written notification of promotions and dismissals; (5) reliance on explicit, written rules, or, in their absence, on tradition.

The second style, a loose administrative pattern, is characterized by flexibility, with fluid lines of authority and communication. It implies

(1) absence, in many areas, of clearly designated authority and responsibility; (2) considerable tolerance of role ambiguity and role diffusion; (3) frequent bypassing of chain of command, both in communication and authority; (4) informal communications; (5) informal exercise of power; (6) relatively little reliance on rules and tradition.[10]

Tannenbaum and Schmidt proposed a continuum for leadership that has received wide attention. They suggest that there are many variations of roles and relationships between boss-centered and subordinate-centered leadership (see Figure 10–1).

FIGURE 10-1. Continuum of Leadership Behavior. From Robert Tannenbaum and Warren H. Schmidt, "How to Choose a Leadership Pattern," *Harvard Business Review* 36 (March-April 1958), 96. Copyright © 1958 by the President and Fellows of Harvard College. All rights reserved.

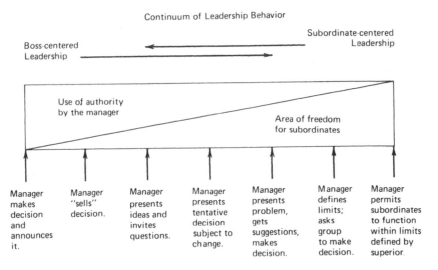

[10]Joel Kotin and Myron R. Sharaf, "Management Succession and Administrative Style," in Simon Slavin, ed., *Social Administration: The Management of the Social Services*, 2nd ed., Vol. I, *An Introduction to Human Services Management* (New York: Haworth Press, 1985), pp. 173–174.

Zaleznik suggests that leaders feel two main kinds of inner conflict: status anxiety and competition anxiety. Status anxiety refers to negative feelings of those at or near the top in their organizational world. Competition anxiety refers to feelings generated while moving to the top. Zaleznik gives the following guidelines for resolving and managing inner conflicts:

1. *The necessity of acknowledging and accepting the diversity of motivations.* Leaders must realize that people have a variety of negative as well as positive feelings.
2. *The necessity of establishing a firm sense of identity.* It is necessary to know who one is and who one is not.
3. *The necessity of maintaining constancy and continuity in response.* Leaders should be consistent in how they represent and present themselves to others.
4. *The necessity of becoming selective in activities and relationships.* One must be highly selective, setting priorities and being able to say no to the less important activities.
5. *The necessity of learning to communicate.* It is particularly important to be aware of one's own reactions to make one's opinions and attitudes known without wasteful delay.
6. *The necessity of living within a cyclical life pattern.* One must create a rhythm that allows for various activities during the day.[11]

A POSITIVE SOCIAL WORK PROGRAM

Social work draws on theories, knowledge, and skills about leadership from many disciplines. A body of knowledge and theory germane to social work leadership has developed in which workers, board members, and other leaders ask these questions: What makes leaders capable in social work? How do they perform? What do they do? What do they avoid?

The following dichotomies concern attributes significant for effective administration in social work.

Trust Versus Mistrust

Trust engenders trust; mistrust engenders mistrust. Most social workers put trust near the top of the list for leaders and leadership. When trust exists on both sides, morale is usually strong. When mistrust permeates an agency, morale deteriorates.

Effective leaders, whether in social work education or practice, are those who genuinely accept and trust those with whom they work; even more important, they live and act accordingly. They consistently let their staff members know that they accept them and believe their abilities are adequate to accomplish their tasks. When they give staff members an assignment, they confidently assume it will be completed.

[11]Abraham Zaleznik, "The Human Dilemmas of Leadership," in Harry A. Schatz, ed., *Social Work Administration: A Resource Book* (New York: Council on Social Work Education, 1970), pp. 228–234.

One example of mistrust involves the director of a public welfare agency who "talked out of both corners of his mouth." He would continually tell those on his staff that he cared about them, that they were competent, and that he knew they would carry out the responsibilities he gave them. Yet behind their backs he would take over their responsibilities and undercut them at nearly every turn. The staff members, of course, strongly resented this behavior, and their work suffered accordingly. When difficulties arose, he would say, "Come to my office, and let's talk about it." But few would go because they knew he did not really trust them.

Building Versus Destruction

Administrators can either help to build staff morale or they can help to destroy it. The administrator may be operating on a conscious or an unconscious level. Effective administrators consciously endeavor to build their staff members' morale. They compliment them when appropriate, show appreciation for their achievements, and let them know how important they are. Everybody hungers for recognition, approval, and appreciation. Mature, effective administrators supply these emotional ingredients daily. One outstanding example involves a director of a family service agency. She had a daily personal goal to say something constructive to each person she met. Of course, she did this on a genuine basis or it would have backfired. She didn't meet her goal every time, but she came close to it.

In contrast, there are administrators who consciously disagree and sometimes psychologically bully staff members. Some administrators say one thing and do another. What they do, of course, is much more important than what they say. Sometimes these slights are unconscious. The administrator says, "I care about my staff. Come see me if you have questions or problems. My door is always open." But when workers do come in, the leader belittles or degrades them so they will not voluntarily come back again.

It was said of President Harry S Truman that in dealing with people, he would always ask, "Who will be hurt by this decision?" He also claimed that the capacity to lead was "the ability to get people to do what they don't want to do, and like it."

Support Versus Abandonment

Competent administrative leaders put psychological arms around their staff members, to tell them they are on the same team. This does not mean they agree with everything workers say and do—in fact, at times they may need to disagree, even strongly—but it does mean that when staff members have been asked to do something and have done their best, the administrators support them. If workers are taken to task by someone outside the agency, the administrator is on their side, helping them to work through criticisms and questions that may have been raised. Competent administrators do not desert their staffs. Some leaders give responsibilities to staff members and then, if they make a mistake, undermine them.

Professional leaders use various techniques for manifesting support. One outstanding leader would come to each staff member periodically and ask two questions: (1) What do you really want to do in this agency? and (2) How can I help you achieve this goal? These two questions were meaningful to the workers; they knew that their leader was interested in them and would support them.

Consistency Versus Inconsistency

Effective leaders are ordinarily consistent; that is, when they say something, they follow through with appropriate action. They do not send conflicting messages at different times. When they make an assignment or a suggestion to a staff member, they back it up with genuinely supportive behavior.

One mark of a poor leader is consistent inconsistency. If a leader is frequently inconsistent, he or she will soon be looking for another job because staff members and agencies will not tolerate such behavior for long. There are two main types of inconsistency in leadership: (1) saying one thing in the morning and then contradicting oneself in the afternoon or the next day; (2) telling one staff member one thing about agency policy and practice and another staff member the opposite. Both procedures damage morale and impair the delivery of social services.

Caring Versus Coldness

Many studies conducted by psychiatrists, psychologists, and social workers show that one of people's basic needs, if not their most basic need, is to care for or to be cared about. The administrative process provides an emotional climate in which these ingredients are particularly important. When they are lacking or are minimal, difficulties may ensue.

Caring involves feelings. If these feelings are positive, if a worker has the sense that a supervisor really cares, it makes a great difference. Even more important is the leader who *acts* in a caring way: being interested, doing things *for* and *with* staff members, and facilitating what they would like to or need to do. Taking time to help a staff member is particularly important. Leaders who hold themselves aloof or are cold in their relationships with the staff build a roadblock that is difficult to cross and often damaging. People do not put their hands on a block of ice to warm them. Workers will not expect affection when they have known only frozen glances and cold actions.

The essence of caring and loving is *giving*. The most effective leaders are those who give of themselves and their time. This does not mean that they should give all of themselves or all of their time. They still require privacy and need not share all their thoughts and feelings. It does mean that often during the day, competent, outstanding leaders give their staffs, directly and indirectly, the feeling that they care.

LEADERSHIP SKILLS

Important attributes for effective leadership in social work practice follow.

Persistence

Capable leaders are thoughtful, plan well, make appropriate proposals, and carry through decisions and plans. They will not accept a negative answer the first time a proposal is considered, especially if they feel that the matter under consideration is important.

Indecisive administrators usually do not last very long. An administrator needs courage, conviction, and confidence to achieve desired results. All kinds of examples show that such action pays huge dividends. A director of a neighborhood house who felt, along with his staff, that a new building would be highly advantageous was told on four different occasions that it was impossible for such a building to be approved. After each rejection, he went back to the drawing board, thought and planned some more, and engineered a new approach. On the fifth try, he and his staff were successful in getting general plans for a new building approved.

The leader who has been told by the board that there is no way to increase the budget should not be idle. If the agency's needs are bona fide, additional possibilities for obtaining funds will be researched, and the administrator will come back again and again, if necessary, to ensure that the agency provides the best possible services to the community.

Time Management

As discussed in Chapter 9, the effective leader in an agency is one who appreciates the value of time, understands its dynamics, and is able to utilize it to facilitate the use of staff members' abilities. Competent leaders respect the value not only of their own time but also that of others. For example, many social work meetings go on for too long and then disintegrate. Ordinarily, a closing time should be set for meetings.

Effective leaders plan the total operations of their agency so that the time of each worker is utilized for the best delivery of agency services. Good leaders use their own time wisely. They plan their work efficiently and then carry it out as expeditiously as possible. Each morning, they formulate goals for the day, list them in order of priority, and then carry them out.

Time management receives considerable emphasis in social work administration. For example, Alan Lakein, international authority on time management, published a popular book, *How to Get Control of Your Time and*

Your Life.[12] He also helped with the production of a related film used extensively in social work educational endeavors and in the business world. It contains seven main suggestions for improving the use of time: listing specific goals; making a daily "do it list"; setting priorities, A (highest), B (next), and C (lowest); starting with A's not C's; figuring out the best use of one's time right now; handling each piece of paper only once; and doing it now. Also, a publication by Charles Hobbs describes the Time Power System, which "helps you do the thing that needs to be done when it needs to be done in the way it needs to be done whether you like it or not." This integrated system is built on three key concepts: (1) time management is the act of controlling events; (2) congruity represents balance, harmony, and appropriateness among the events in one's life; and (3) concentration of power is the ability to focus on and accomplish one's most vital priorities.[13]

Compromise

Capable leaders realize that they do not have all the answers. Even when they feel strongly about an issue, they are open-minded and willing to listen to the other side. Effective leaders are willing to make concessions when they realize they are wrong or have inadequate information. If they disagree with their staff, they may be willing to make compromises, knowing that everyone's welfare is involved. They recognize that what they think is right is not necessarily best for the agency, and their concern is to maintain good relations with staff members and further the agency's goals.

Simons observes that conflicting demands are often placed on administrators in human service organizations and that the ability for them "to use persuasion in their efforts toward improving service effectiveness for clients is a critical skill." He suggests the following significant principles for constructing persuasive communications: emphasize advantages; be comprehensive; show compatibility of values; cite proven results; allow for trials; refer to influential others; avoid high-pressure tactics; and minimize threats to security, status, or esteem.[14]

A Soft Touch

Leaders should allow each worker as much freedom as possible within the framework of the goals, needs, and policies of the agency. Ordinarily, leaders do not battle with the staff but try to provide opportunities; they work with staff members rather than dictate to them. Even the words leaders use are important. Competent administrators rarely say, "I'm right," "You're wrong,"

[12]Alan Lakein, *How to Get Control of Your Time and Your Life* (New York: New American Library, 1973).

[13]Charles R. Hobbs, *Time Power* (New York: Harper & Row, 1987), pp. 2–3.

[14]Ronald L. Simons, "Generic Social Work Skills in Social Administration: The Example of Persuasion," *Administration in Social Work* 11 (Fall/Winter 1987), 250.

"I'll show you," or "I'll prove it to you." Rather, they commonly use some of the following phrases: "I'm not certain about this; what do you think?" "I haven't made up my mind; what is your opinion?" "What do you think the best answer is?" "My tentative thinking is. . . ." "I'm often wrong, but I'm learning." Or they may ask, "Could this be the best answer?" or "I wonder about this position."

Again, there may be a considerable difference between what is best for an agency and what seems right for the leader. When they differ, the position that is best for the agency should take precedence.

Creativity

Creativity calls for thinking and acting in an original manner. Creativity is not the exclusive property of a gifted few but should be an attribute of leaders of social work agencies. Leaders should spend time—periodically, daily, or weekly—contemplating and planning new, effective ways of improving agency services.

Effective leaders also provide time and opportunity, and give encouragement to all staff workers to do likewise, individually and in groups. Inactivity and stagnation should not be allowed. Individuals and groups in an agency need to get together to consider where they are now, where they want to be, and how they might get there. Frequent consideration of an agency's current achievements and future goals is essential to the leadership process.

AN EXAMPLE OF LEADERSHIP

The following case presents pertinent principles and creative actions of social work leaders along with organizational changes in services.

CREATIVE LEADERSHIP AND ORGANIZATION FOR SERVICES

Background. In a private, nonprofit social service agency providing shelter and comprehensive social services to the homeless population, a change in leadership occurred after four years of operation. The executive director, who had opened in the capital of a state a facility with a capacity for 400 to 500 individuals daily, resigned to take another assignment. He had been very effective in nurturing the organization, providing advocacy for the homeless population, developing needed services including transitional housing, developing resources to support the agency's rapid expansion, and generally providing excellent leadership.

During this time, the agency faced annual budget crises, which resulted in last-minute appeals to the community for emergency funding. A new executive director was appointed and charged by the board of directors not to expand programs, to begin divesting housing units the agency owned or leased, and to continue the comprehensive service delivery system. After a thorough self-assessment, it became apparent to the agency that many residents were not being connected with a caseworker and a self-sufficiency plan in a timely manner or at all. Another budget shortfall of 10 percent of the total operating budget developed, and drastic action was required.

Action. The executive director appointed a staff committee to examine the feedback from interviews conducted as part of the self-assessment and data collected about the population being served and to examine the service delivery system and determine the most effective and efficient means of providing services. At the same time, seventeen of eighty-two regular staff positions were eliminated, resulting in the dismissal of twelve employees. Additional money was raised, as had been done in the past, to cover the pending deficit.

As a result of the staff committee's action and with the support and encouragement of the executive director and the board of directors, a new organizational structure and service delivery process was developed. Instead of operating three separate, self-contained shelters for single men, single women, and families with children, the day-to-day operation of the shelters was placed under the direction of a single manager. Similarly, the case management services for all three populations were placed under the direction and leadership of a single supervisor. Another unit was established to handle the coordination of resources needed by homeless residents to become self-reliant, and a staff development and training position was established to implement a comprehensive training program.

The advantages of the new organizational structure were many. First, shelter operations became more efficient because front-line staff could be used in all three shelters, filling in when someone was ill or on leave. Policies concerning treatment of residents and expectations of residents were standardized for consistency across all three shelters. For example, all shelter residents were expected to complete a work detail to help maintain the facility. Previously, this policy had varied from shelter to shelter and, in some instances, had not been enforced.

With the case management services centralized, a new assessment process was implemented that provided a comprehensive social service assessment for every new resident within one working day of entering the shelter. A case manager was then assigned, based on the assessment process, within a week. In the past, some residents had waited as long as thirty days just to see a case manager. In addition, case aide positions were established to work with some of the residents who needed only information and referral services or less intensive intervention to make their way back to independent living.

The total number of employees in the agency was reduced from eighty-two full-time equivalent positions to 71.5 for the next fiscal year. On this basis, the annual budget was reduced nearly 5 percent, while at the same time the agency provided an across-the-board raise for all staff members and implemented a small retirement benefit and a cafeteria plan of other benefits.

Analysis. Leadership, the ability to move people in new directions, was critical to get this agency to look at its operation and make fairly drastic changes to improve services to the residents and at the same time increase efficiency and reduce costs. The change in executive directors was an impetus for the self-analysis. An individual who is not personally invested in a particular way of

doing business and who sees things from a fresh perspective has the opportunity to help individuals and organizations look at themselves and make
changes to address specific concerns and improve service outcomes.

The structure and organization of the service delivery system can enhance an
agency's capacity to provide effective, cost-efficient services and to improve
the utilization of scarce resources.

MINORITIES AND LEADERSHIP

Leadership from minorities had been minimal in social work agencies at one
time. The first National Conference on the Role of Minorities in Urban
Management and Related Fields was held in June 1973, in Washington, D.C.
Herbert suggests the significance of this conference:

> (1) It was the first organized national meeting of non-elected minority public
> administrators and educators held to discuss the problems, education, respon-
> sibilities, and needs of minority public sector professionals; (2) it represented a
> symbolic acknowledgement that the quest of minority groups for more respon-
> sive government must, and does now include a sophisticated concentration on
> the political and administrative affairs of government; and (3) its theme sug-
> gested, quite appropriately, that minority administrators do have an important
> and unique role to play in the public management field, which they must accept
> if the plight of minority (if not all) people in America is to be improved.[15]

Although there has been a conscious effort to give equal employment
opportunities to everyone through affirmative action since about 1960, many
inequities remain. Perlmutter and Alexander reported in 1977 that data available about the position of minorities in social agency staffing patterns are so
meager that it is difficult to arrive at firm conclusions regarding trends or realities. Yet they observed that "minorities are underrepresented as professional
staff, both in educational and agency settings."[16]

Scurfield made a survey of 285 social work administrators in a variety
of agencies in the Los Angeles area. He observed that Spanish-surnamed
administrators were the only ethnic group to be substantially underrepresented among the administrators (4.6 percent) in comparison to their percentage among the total population of Los Angeles county (15.5 percent).
Anglos and Asian-Americans were slightly overrepresented among the
administrators.[17]

[15]Adam W. Herbert, "The Minority Administrator: Problems, Prospects, and Challenges,"
in Simon Slavin, ed., *Social Administration: The Management of the Social Services*, 2nd ed., Vol. I,
An Introduction to Human Services Management (New York: Haworth Press, 1985), pp. 212–213.

[16]Felice Davidson Perlmutter and Leslie B. Alexander, "Racism and Sexism in Social Work
Practice: An Empirical View," *Administration in Social Work* 1 (Winter 1977), 438.

[17]Raymond Monsour Scurfield, "Social Work Administrators, Their Educational Preparation, Value Orientation, Role Transition, and Satisfaction," *Administration in Social Work* 4
(Summer 1980), 50.

Herbert describes the following dilemmas facing minority leaders in social work agencies:

> Governmental role expectations of minority administrators do not necessarily coincide with the minority administrator's own perceptions, goals, or expectations.
> Unresponsive public policies put minority administrators in extremely tenuous positions vis-a-vis the agency, himself/herself, and the community of which he/she is a part.
> Frequently the minority administrator is put into flack-catching positions without the capacity to make meaningful decisions, but is expected to accept the responsibilities of programmatic failures and "keep the natives calm."
> Advancement within the governmental system is generally a function of adherence to established organizational norms; one of these norms historically has been that one need not be concerned about the needs or priorities of minority communities.
> Informal pay and promotional quotas still seem to exist for minority administrators; moreover, it is assumed that they can only fill certain types of positions, usually related to social service delivery or to communication with other minority group members.
> Minority communities sometimes expect much more of the minority administrator than he/she can provide; and in most cases demand a far faster response to their demands than these administrators have developed the capacity to deliver.
> Agencies seem to search for the "super" minority administrator; and even these are frequently hired as show pieces. In other cases there has been evidence of agencies hiring individuals who clearly would be unable to do a job with the intent of showing that an effort was made but "they just can't do this kind of work."[18]

A follow-up study by Biggerstaff of students majoring in administration in eight schools of social work showed that most of them found positions in administration. A sample of administration graduates from 1970 through January 1977 resulted in 146 responses; 53 percent were male, and 82 percent were Caucasian. The other ethnic groups were represented as follows: Native American, 4; Asian-American, 1; black, 11; Chicano, 4; and "other," 5.[19]

Bush made a study of fifteen black and fifteen Chicano top-level administrators that included both men and women. The findings indicate that these leaders perceived themselves as being required to have greater job-entrance capabilities than their Anglo peers, received less organizational support, had less intrinsic authority, had limited channels for communication, and had limited opportunities for upward movement. As a result of this study, Bush suggests two major goals: (1) to sensitize minority administrators to the subtleties and meaning of their experience and (2) to sensitize potential minority

[18]Herbert, "Minority Administrator," pp. 222–223.
[19]Marilyn A. Biggerstaff, "Preparation of Administrators in Social Welfare: A Follow-up Study of Administration Concentration Graduates," *Administration in Social Work* 2 (Fall 1978), 360–361.

administrators to recognize the problems and prepare themselves for the unique tasks they will face as administrators.[20]

Arguello, from a literature review, concluded that there is sufficient information to concede that the rise of minority administrators to top management positions continues to be blocked by "numerous barriers attributable to their ethnicity. Many of these barriers are invisibly rooted in long-held attitudes and beliefs about the inferiority of minority group members. Many are residual vestiges of the overt oppression to which minority groups were exposed. Most of these barriers have yet to be addressed in the mainstream of organization and management education."[21]

Although many more minority social work administrators have now been hired, there is a long way to go. Herbert's position reflects the attitude of most social workers: "For almost two centuries, minority groups have been systematically excluded from making inputs into the administrative processes of government as both decision makers and policy implementors. In the final analysis, it is now the responsibility of governmental leaders generally to expand opportunities for the perspectives of minority administrators to be articulated and acted upon."[22]

WOMEN AND LEADERSHIP

Traditionally men have held the top positions of leadership in agencies, although some women have asserted their abilities and assumed executive roles. Today most heads of social work agencies are men, although the situation is changing. In middle management, particularly for supervisors, the situation is somewhat different, as many women are employed.

Weaver made a study of gender as a determinant of job satisfaction and found few significant differences. He suggested that this finding might be explained because women tend to give subjectively positive evaluations to objectively negative situations. For example, "Perhaps the strongest evidence for this interpretation is from a cross-sectional study of the U.S. labor force. . . . in which 95 percent of female workers were discriminated against in pay, but only 8 percent perceived any discrimination."[23]

Data from two surveys of members of the National Association of Social Workers (NASW), one including all members in 1971–1972 and the other of members entering the association in 1973 through 1975 (mostly new graduates), reflected higher percentages of men in administration, although social

[20]James A. Bush, "The Minority Administrator: Implications for Social Work Education, *Journal of Education for Social Work* 13 (Winter 1977), 15–22.

[21]David F. Arguello, "Minorities in Administration: A Review of Ethnicity's Influence in Management," *Administration in Social Work* 8 (Fall 1984), 26.

[22]Herbert, "Minority Administrator," p. 223.

[23]Charles N. Weaver, "Sex Differences in the Determinants of Job Satisfaction," *Academy of Management Journal* 21 (June 1978), 273.

work is regarded as a woman's profession by many and most social workers are women. In the 1971–1972 survey, 37 percent of the men and only 18 percent of the women listed administration as their primary work; in the later survey, 11 percent of the men and 5 percent of the women indicated they were in administration.

Salary information from the 1971–1972 survey showed that women receive less compensation than men for their services. Although 39 percent of the men reported an income of $16,000 or more, only 20 percent of the single women were in the same salary range. More than 50 percent of the currently married women earned less than $12,000 a year, compared to 36 percent of the single women and 18 percent of the men.[24]

In 1983 a questionnaire was mailed to a random sample of 200 NASW members in North Carolina. The results showed that gender was a better predictor of salary than education, position, or job experience. "When these three variables were controlled, males were found to earn an average of $5,645 more per year than females."[25]

A mail survey of 3,145 human service workers in four county welfare departments in disparate areas of the United States, showed lower salaries for women and fewer women in managerial positions. McNeely reported that 11.8 percent of all males occupied managerial positions, whereas only 4.8 percent of females were so employed. Findings indicated that upper-echelon males (middle-aged) earned significantly more than upper-echelon females (middle-aged), $29,236 and $25,723 respectively.[26]

Scurfield surveyed 285 social work administrators in a variety of agencies in the Los Angeles area. He found that the typical social work administrator was about forty-five years old, white, and a former clinician. Two-thirds of the administrators had performed in primarily clinical roles for at least four years, and only 9 percent had never performed in clinical roles. Respondents were equally likely to be male or female and to work in a publicly or privately funded setting employing fewer than 100 or more than 500 persons. Scurfield reported that 46 percent of the respondents were females, yet they were substantially underrepresented (only 38 percent) among top-level administrators; furthermore, this underrepresentation was "even more striking when one considers that over 60 percent of all MSW graduates from U.S. schools of social work in the past three decades have been females."[27]

Perlmutter and Alexander observe that women have not fared well in reaching administrative positions. In spite of the reality that the social service

[24]David Fanshel, "Status Differentials: Men and Women in Social Work," *Social Work* 21 (November 1976), 448–454.

[25]Reginald O. York, H. Carl Henley, and Dorothy N. Gamble, "Sexual Discrimination in Social Work: Is It Salary or Advancement?" *Social Work* 32 (July–August 1987), 336.

[26]R. L. McNeely, "Gender, Job Satisfaction, Earnings, and Other Characteristics of Human Service Workers During and After Midlife," *Administration in Social Work* 13, No. 2 (1989), 105–111.

[27]Scurfield, "Social Work Administrators," pp. 49–50.

work force is predominantly female (63 percent), a study by the Committee on Women's Issues of the National Association of Social Workers found that "women comprise a very small percentage of the decision-making body in social work. . . . of the 868 agencies surveyed, 141, or 16 percent, were directed by women in 1976."[28]

It is clearly apparent that women social workers do not receive their share of administrative appointments in business and industry or in most social work settings. Also, they are more apt to receive sexual harassment on the job. Maypole reports that in a cross-sectional survey of 50 percent of the members of the Iowa chapter of the National Association of Social Workers, 27 percent of the women and men surveyed reported sexual harassment at work. A gender differential indicated that over one-third of the women and only one-seventh of the men surveyed were so victimized.[29]

Jayaratne and Chess reported data collected from members of NASW as part of a national survey on work stress and strain. The members were working full time, had MSW degrees, and identified themselves as administrators or as caseworkers. Although males made up only 35.6 percent of the total sample, 52.8 percent of the administrators were male. In contrast, 74.1 percent of the caseworkers were female.[30]

Ozawa explains the cultural dilemma that exists for women:

There seems to be a cultural schizophrenia in the United States which places women in a no-win situation. In an achievement-oriented society like ours, women are encouraged to succeed in their work but not to the extent they lose their femininity. If they fail in their work, they are not meeting their own standards of performance; if they succeed in it, they may not be living up to societal expectations regarding the role of women.[31]

Hanlan observes that "social work administration is generally perceived as a male role within a female profession" and discusses some problems and variables in social work administration. She indicates that the meager data available show that males are favored and that changes should be made to give equal opportunity for males and females to assume leadership positions. She suggests that the stereotypic habits and thinking need to be altered, and the following may be helpful: (1) firmly and unequivocally reject the notion that male administrative enclaves ought to be protected; (2) there should be specific training of women for managerial positions; and (3) thought should be given to the possibilities of differing career patterns and

[28]Perlmutter and Alexander, "Racism and Sexism," p. 440.
[29]Donald E. Maypole, "Sexual Harassment of Social Workers at Work: Injustice Within?" *Social Work* 31 (January-February 1986), 32.
[30]Srinika Jayaratne and Wayne A. Chess, "Job Satisfaction: A Comparison of Caseworkers and Administrators," *Social Work* 31 (March-April 1986), 144.
[31]Martha N. Ozawa, "Women and Work," *Social Work* 21 (November 1976), 458.

their applicability to managerial and administrative positions, to allow for differing backgrounds and preparation of women.[32]

Curlee and Raymond indicate that males in social agencies often find it difficult to relate to female administrators and resort to casting them into previously learned, traditional family roles, sexual roles, and rival roles. It is apparent that male social workers engage in sex-role stereotyping and consequent behaviors in relation to their female colleagues. The sexist family roles are illustrated by the roles of "daughter," "mother," or "homemaker/hostess." Sex roles include "the tease" and "the lover." Rival roles are illustrated by "the rookie" and "the dumb broad."

These authors suggest several ways in which females might improve their work situation. First, they should look at their own attitudes and beliefs about sex roles and try to understand them. Second, they should deal honestly and openly with role casting when it occurs. Third, female executives should keep their work in proper perspective. And finally, the development of women's groups and caucuses within social service agencies may be helpful in dealing with questionable practices.

Curlee and Raymond recommend that males in social agencies should first become aware of sex-role stereotypes and should try to determine how they may be affecting their relationships with female administrators. Second, they can refuse to get caught up in sexist discussions and joking. Third, they can deal with their female executives in an androgynous manner, relating to them as professional administrators. Finally, when sexist issues or problems arise, they should recognize them and deal with them openly and candidly.[33]

Martin and Chernesky list five main strategies for women's advancement. Each has produced successes, but each has also been limited in its capacity to bring lasting, fundamental change.

1. Individual change—alterations in dress, skills, credentials, styles, or outlook
2. Affirmative action—organizations or groups working to bring about change
3. Organizational reform—changing the work patterns to utilize the full talents of employees
4. Occupational/job integration—working on equalization of job status and earnings
5. Comparable worth—being paid equally for work that is comparable rather than equal to men's work.[34]

---

[32]Mary S. Hanlan, "Women in Social Work Administration: Current Role Strains," *Administration in Social Work* 1 (Fall 1977), 259–265.

[33]Mary B. Curlee and Frank B. Raymond, "The Female Administrator: Who Is She?" *Administration in Social Work* 2 (Fall 1978), 307–318.

[34]Patricia Yancey Martin and Roslyn H. Chernesky, "Women's Prospects for Leadership in Social Welfare: A Political Economy Perspective," *Administration in Social Work* 13, Nos. 3/4 (1989), 128–134.

Martin and Chernesky conclude that

> white and black women (and black men) are disadvantaged in social welfare organizations, in comparison to white men. While this is no surprise, it indicates that efforts to improve women's prospects for leadership will need to take race/ethnicity into account. A political economy perspective suggests that women in social welfare will have to cooperate with activists of many persuasions to improve their prospects. It also suggests that fundamental change can be accomplished only by political struggles that challenge the political economy and ideology of status quo arrangements.[35]

Healy, Havens, and Chin report that a course entitled Women in Social Welfare Administration was begun in 1978 in one school of social work in response to increased awareness of discrimination against women in the profession. In a follow-up study they sent questionnaires to ninety former students who had taken the class and received forty-eight responses. Findings included the following: 66.77 percent indicated that the course helped motivate them to pursue an administrative position, and 89.6 percent stated that women need special preparation for management roles.[36] Other findings made the authors conclude that "discrimination against women persists in social agencies. It manifests itself blatantly in hiring practices, in promotional opportunities, and in salaries." Then they added, "Based on the study results, we recommend that content on women's issues in administration be addressed both in required administration concentration courses and in a separate elective for students wanting more emphasis."[37]

VALUES AND LEADERSHIP

McMurry observes that conflicts in human values are important factors in leadership and management problems. He suggests that "while it is commonly recognized that values differ widely from person to person and from culture to culture, their influence on people's thinking, acting, and behavior tends to be seriously underestimated." Of course, these same ideas are applicable to social work practice.

> Of all problems in the entire field of value judgments in industry, the greatest one probably is to convince top management of some simple truths. Its members are often accustomed to believing that their standards are infallible and should prevail. Great progress can be made if they can be led to see that:

[35]Ibid., p. 138.
[36]Lynne M. Healy, Catherine M. Havens, and Alice Chin, "Preparing Women for Human Service Administration: Building on Experience," *Administration in Social Work* 14, No. 2 (1990), 83–84.
[37]Ibid., p. 91.

1. Their points of view are not the only ones.
2. Most issues are not absolutely black or white but do have some gray areas.
3. They personally do not enjoy a monopoly of the truth.
4. Because someone espouses a system of values which differs from theirs, he is not necessarily ignorant, stupid, or disloyal.[38]

Most leaders in social work practice and education today have arrived in these positions as a result of experience on the job and have not received specific training for their leadership positions. As mentioned earlier, a majority of schools of social work are preparing administrators and leaders for such positions by offering curricula in administrative knowledge, engendering leadership attitudes, and acquiring leadership skills. There is a real need to increase this effort to meet the demand for leaders in both social work practice and education.

A critical need exists for training social work administrators for executive positions within social service agencies. It is not enough to move from clinical practice into a leadership role. Also, some professionals from other disciplines seeking administrative positions in social welfare agencies and organizations are offered such work because they have up-to-date training in managerial skills and program evaluation. Social work schools need to augment their offerings to provide more training for administrative leadership.

SUMMARY

Effective leadership is needed in social work more than ever before. It can make a significant difference in the delivery of an agency's social services.

Key leadership dichotomies are trust versus mistrust, building versus destroying, support versus abandonment, consistency versus inconsistency, and caring versus coldness.

Important leadership qualities include (1) persistence, (2) effective use of time, (3) ability to compromise, (4) the soft touch, and (5) creativity.

Traditionally, minorities and women social workers have not been given their share of administrative positions and leadership opportunities. Although the situation is changing, there is still a considerable distance to go. More training and opportunities for leadership are needed for both groups.

Leadership training needs to be improved in schools of social work so that graduates may become effective leaders in social work practice and in the communities in which they live.

---

[38]Robert N. McMurry, "Conflicts in Human Values," in Harry A. Schatz, *Social Work Administration: A Resource Book* (New York: Council on Social Work Education, 1970), p. 278.

QUESTIONS FOR DISCUSSION

1. Why is the study of leadership so important for the profession of social work?

2. What are some of the rewards and challenges in being a social work leader?

3. Select the theory of leadership that you think makes the most sense from among the theories presented in this book and describe it briefly.

4. Describe and evaluate one of the dichotomies mentioned in the discussion of a positive social work program.

5. How important is creativity for agency leaders? Illustrate your opinion.

6. What are some ways in which minorities may gain better representation as managers and leaders in social work agencies?

7. What suggestions do you have for improving the salaries and the number of women in leadership positions?

8. Would you favor a separate class on women in social work administration? Why or why not?

SPECIAL ACTIVITIES

1. Sponsor a debate in your class, with three debaters on each side, to consider the following statement: Strong leadership is the most important need of the social work profession today.

2. Interview a successful social work leader in one of your community agencies and gain a list of attributes and skills that are particularly important in this role.

3. Have a panel discussion on this challenging theme: how to raise the level of salaries and increase the number of administrative positions for women in social work.

SELECTED REFERENCES

BEDEIAN, ARTHUR G. "Effective Leadership." *Management;* 3rd ed., pp. 469–495. Fort Worth, TX: Dryden Press, 1993.

CHERNESKY, ROSLYN H. "The Sex Dimension of Organizational Processes: Its Impact on Women Managers." In Simon Slavin, ed., *Social Administration: The Management of the Social Services,* 2nd ed. Vol. I, *An Introduction to Human Services Management,* pp. 225–236. (New York: Haworth Press, 1985).

HAGEN, JAN L. "Women, Work, and Welfare: Is There a Role for Social Work?" *Social Work* 37 (January 1992), 9–14.

HART, AILEEN. "Training Social Administrators for Leadership in the Coming Decades." *Administration in Social Work* 12 No. 3, 1988, 1–11.

HASENFELD, YEHESKEL, ed. "Administrative Leadership in the Social Services: The Next Challenge." *Administration in Social Work* 13, Nos. 3/4 (1989), 1–269.
HAYNES, KAREN S. *Women Managers in Human Services.* New York: Springer, 1989.
HEALY, LYNNE M., CATHERINE M. HAVENS, and ALICE CHIN. "Preparing Women for Human Service Administration: Building on Experience." *Administration in Social Work* 14, No. 2 (1990), 79–94.
KRAVETZ, DIANE, and CAROL D. AUSTIN. "Women's Issues in Social Service Administration: The Views and Experiences of Women Administrators," *Administration in Social Work* 8 (Winter 1984), 25–38.
SCHWARTZ, FELICE N. "Management Women and the New Facts of Life." *Harvard Business Review* 67 (January–February, 1989), 65–76.
SIMONS, RONALD L. "Generic Social Work Skills in Social Administration: The Example of Persuasion." *Administration in Social Work* 11 (Fall/Winter 1987), 241–253.
WEIL, MARIE. "Preparing Women for Administration: A Self-Directed Learning Model." *Administration in Social Work* 7 (Fall/Winter 1983), 117–131.
WEINER, MYRON E. "Managing People for Enhanced Performance." *Administration in Social Work* 11 (Fall/Winter 1987), 147–149.

11

The Nature of Dynamic Teamship

Jan and Martha, caseworkers in a family service counseling center in a large metropolitan area, helped clients with marital problems as well as with family conflicts. They often ate lunch together and occasionally discussed some of their cases. Outside of the agency, Jan kept her work to herself. Martha was prone to tell some of her friends about confidential matters and occasionally was caustically critical of the agency director.

Martha's outside comments caused considerable trouble, and before long she was released from her position. Instead of helping the agency in the community, she had hurt it. Her part in the total agency administration was destructive; Jan's was constructive.

How important are individual workers in the administrative process?

Considerable emphasis has been placed on the importance of leadership in the administration process. However, teamship, or lack of it, is also vital. Teamship means teamwork plus the ability to work effectively in a joint endeavor. *The New Twentieth Century Webster's Dictionary* states that teamwork is "joint action by a group of people, in which each person subordinates his individual interests and opinions to the unity and efficiency of the group; co-ordinated effort."

In their best-seller *The One Minute Manager*, Blanchard and Johnson stress the importance of people in the total management process. They suggest that capable administrators need to take a minute out of their day and look into the faces of the people they manage, "to realize that they are our most important resource." Their streamlined philosophy and guidelines involve three one-minute actions: goal setting, praising, and reprimands, ending with positive reinforcement.[1]

The ability of staff members to work together effectively is part of teamship. A total team effort in social work practice, involving leaders and workers, is particularly significant since social work involves people, their relationships and their feelings. Competent leadership and supportive team-work can make a major difference in the services offered. The contributions of individual staff members to an agency can equal more than the sum of their efforts. They can be synergistic, with joint efforts and combined actions enhancing the significance of individual efforts. Staff members working coop-eratively together can bring results that surpass in quantity and quality the mere addition of the contributions of each. When they do not work together, the results may be negative or diminished. As in football, cooperative, uni-fied action brings the team's efforts and forces together; individual competi-tion, inaction, or showing off by players may do the opposite.

A classic example of the power of working together is seen in the World Series of Mule Team Competition, which was held in 1885 in Chicago. The winning team of mules pulled 9,000 pounds, and the second-place winners slightly less. The two teams were hitched together, and it was found that they could pull a load of 30,000 pounds. People are not so different; their pooled resources can be greater than any individual's.[2]

Whitehouse describes eighteen characteristics of teamwork. Of these, the following are especially significant in agency operation: opportunity for communication and communing, freedom of discussion, consensuality of decisions, and good personal relations among members.[3]

In discussing the dynamics of teamwork in the agency, community, and neighborhood, Kramer suggests that it may be helpful to conceive of team-work as a continuum with seven stages:

(1) Acquaintance, (2) exchange of information (communication), (3) consulta-tion, (4) referrals, (5) planning and co-ordination, (6) concurrent co-operative service, (7) joint operating responsibility.
  As can be seen, these co-operative relationships increase in intensity and com-plexity as we proceed from (1) to (7). Individually and in combination, it is sug-gested, these seven relationships are the referents of the term "teamwork."[4]

---

[1]Kenneth Blanchard and Spencer Johnson, *The One Minute Manager* (New York: William Morrow, 1982), pp. 34, 38, 53.

[2]Robert M. Fulmer, *The New Management*, 2nd ed. (New York: Macmillan, 1978), p. 239.

[3]Frederick A. Whitehouse, "Professional Teamwork," *The Social Welfare Forum, 1957* (New York: Columbia University Press, 1957), p. 157.

[4]Ralph M. Kramer, "Dynamics of Teamwork in the Agency, Community, and Neighbor-hood," in Beulah Roberts Compton and Burt Galaway, *Social Work Processes* (Homewood, IL: Dorsey Press, 1975), p. 456.

Teamship is one part of administration that, along with leadership, can vitalize an agency and bring about desired results. Leadership and teamship, understood and practiced, can make significant differences in the delivery of social services. This chapter includes consideration of teamship qualities, processes, and problems, based on the premise that administration involves all staff members and how they interact with one another.

CHARACTERISTICS OF TEAMWORK

Participation of All Levels of Staff

Experts in administration believe that all staff members contribute to the administrative process—either positively or negatively, and sometimes in both ways. Every staff member, from director to caseworker to secretary, plays a part in agency operations. This principle is recognized in both social work education and practice.

As schools of social work were organized at the turn of the nineteenth century in New York, Chicago, Boston, and other eastern cities, some effort was made to understand the processes and procedures of administration. By 1944 administration was included as one of the basic eight courses required of all students, based on the premise that all students need to know about administration since they will become a part of it, whether as executives, supervisors, or line workers. The 1962 policy statement of the Council on Social Work Education opened the door for administration as an enabling method to accompany casework, group work, and community organization. The 1969 curriculum statement, more generic in nature, provided for different options and programs, which made it possible for administration to be offered as a "concentration." This pattern allowed selected students to concentrate on the study of administration but also made it possible for all students to gain some knowledge of, and acquire beginning skills in, the administrative process. The 1992 curriculum policy statement reaffirmed the concentration pattern, which allows students interested in positions in social work administration to pursue an appropriate class and practicum program.

To have sound social work practice, all workers need to have a basic knowledge of administration because today all staff members are usually involved in the operation of an agency. Most staffs practice democratic participation, and workers have some say in making decisions and determining agency policies. All workers have a part to play, either positive or negative, in the development of agency morale by being supportive or overcritical of the leaders and other staff members.

Workers at different levels have ideas about agency policies and procedures. Many may be helpful to the welfare of the agency. Schatz states, "A wise and competent administrator continually turns to his staff members at all levels and in various areas of competency for information and for various viewpoints. He places facts and opinions before him, weighing one factor against another, and ultimately makes a decision which is partially based on fact and partially based on a value system."[5]

Attributes of Agency Workers

What are some of the characteristics of agency workers that are important to the administrative process, morale, and services? Several of the major factors considered next are significant for all workers in an agency.

Demonstrated Competency and Commitment. Competent social workers help build an agency and strengthen the administrative setup by their performance. An incompetent worker can weaken an agency and cause many difficulties.

Each worker should be committed, one who is willing to put his or her "heart, hand, and head" into the job. A competent social worker, at any level, puts in a day's work for a day's pay, and usually more if needed. Those who try to get by with a minimum of effort are destructive. As staff workers fulfill their obligations, the agency benefits and the delivery of social services is enhanced.

Loyalty to Other Staff and Administration Members and the Agency. Loyalty means that staff members do not criticize their leaders or coworkers outside the agency but rather do it appropriately within its confines. If a difference exists, the worker takes it directly to the leader and does not discuss it behind that person's back. Many agencies and administrators have been damaged by staff members who belittled their executives outside of the agency.

Loyalty means showing an interest in and caring about leaders and coworkers. Everyone needs support and approbation. Genuinely loyal workers will, on appropriate occasions, tell their leaders and other staff members their feelings, when they are positive as well as when they are negative. Leaders often report that as they go up the ladder of authority, they are gradually cut off from other staff members, and the higher they go, the more lonely the position becomes. Workers on the firing line can help build up their leaders and coworkers and enhance morale in the whole agency.

Workers can show their loyalty through integrity and honesty, not by spreading half-truths or untruths within and outside the agency. Workers can

---

[5]Harry A. Schatz, ed., *Social Work Administration: A Resource Book* (New York: Council on Social Work Education, 1970), p. 285.

stand up for their leaders if others are overly critical or attack their comments or plans.

Loyal workers maintain a basic trust in their leaders, recognizing that leaders cannot tell them everything. It is assumed that the leader will do what is best for the workers as well as for the agency. Workers trust their leaders, believing that the leaders will tell them what they can and will withhold only personal, special, or confidential matters.

Confidentiality.   Confidentiality is important in different relationships: executive to worker, worker to worker, and worker to client. Each is meaningful in the total administrative process. Maintaining confidences of the client is, of course, paramount in sound practice. Also, maintaining the confidentiality of worker to worker and worker to administrator is essential. If a worker breaches a confidence, a crack in agency morale may appear.

Workers should not tell everything they learn or know in an agency to other workers; certainly this information should never leak outside the walls of the agency. Yet this sometimes happens, to the detriment of client, worker, and agency.

Team workers should keep to themselves data and materials given to them by an administrator. If this trust is broken, difficulties may arise. In other words, to state it positively, at all levels workers owe it to themselves, the agency, clients, and administrators, as well as to the community, to keep confidential matters confidential. This is part of the Code of Ethics and a professional trust. Yet too many workers break it.

Sensitivity to One Another's Needs.   Administrators are often advised to learn the needs of those with whom they work. It is equally important for team workers to do so.

Caseworkers, group workers, and others on the social service line need to listen for signals from their leaders and coworkers to become aware of their needs, and then they should do everything possible to help fulfill those needs. An effective agency team involves a symbiotic relationship in which leaders and followers are sensitive and responsive to one another's needs.

Social workers can and should commend their administrators and coworkers when appropriate. They should also indicate appreciation for a job well done or for something that a leader may have done specifically for a worker. Sincere appreciation and commendation can do much to enhance human relationships and build an agency team.

Realistic Acceptance of Administrators and Other Staff.   Professional social workers are usually accepting of clients, yet some fail to accept their leaders or coworkers. Accepting administrators and coworkers means understanding that no one is perfect, that everyone makes mistakes, and that being overly critical only hurts individuals and the agency. Some workers expect their supervisors to be perfect, and when they find they are not, are disappointed and critical. Others are demanding of their colleagues and have unrealistic expectations of them.

To be accepting, one must be realistic, trying to understand and get along with others. It does not mean that one should not offer criticisms or suggestions for change. One can and should, but such matters should be important and handled aboveboard.

Team members also need to be accepting of one another. Subtly and sometimes not so subtly, staff members may berate or question associates. Few situations tend to be more destructive than those in which staff members are overly critical of fellow workers. This is true whether it involves individuals' personalities, handling of cases, or both. Again, positively stated, when team members can live with one another as they are, recognizing limitations as well as strengths, a positive bond develops, tending to keep morale high and delivery of services effective.

Creativity. Creativity means searching for and finding new ideas, goals, plans, methods, or procedures. The creativity of a staff member may focus on individual interests or assignments, on those of colleagues with whom he or she is working in close association, or on the agency as a whole. Successful team members endeavor to consider innovations for all three, particularly for themselves and for the agency. Many important suggestions are made and new procedures stem from innovative acts of staff who are far removed from top echelons. And why not? The administrative process not only allows this kind of activity but also invites it and thrives on it.

Creativity sometimes occurs almost by accident. It is important for people to keep their eyes and ears open so that they can be receptive to innovation and change. However, most creativity involves hard work. Thomas Edison failed many times before he invented the incandescent lamp. When someone called him a genius, he gave his famous reply: "Genius is two percent inspiration and ninety-eight percent perspiration." Social workers may fail, time after time, in trying to develop a better method of solving a social or personal problem, yet at some point a breakthrough may be made. This means that social workers need to spend time and energy purposefully, trying to originate and develop new ways of helping others.

Some workers spend a minimum of two hours a week, about fifteen minutes a day, in meditative thought and experimentation, trying to invent or create something new and worthwhile. Working together in small groups can often be creative. Also, small committees may open doors to creativity.

TEAMWORK PROCESSES

The teamwork process includes five major subprocesses: communication, compromise, cooperation, coordination, and consummation. Each is essential and will be discussed briefly.

Communication

Teamwork begins with communication (see Chapter 13) among staff members. This means sharing ideas and feelings. It involves listening, rather than just hearing. It means interacting and reflecting back ideas, even mirrorlike at times. It has both verbal and nonverbal components. It takes place whenever two or more persons interact, directly or indirectly.

Line workers need to let their superiors know what they think and feel about agency policies, goals, procedures, and services. This may be done by informal meetings with an administrator, in groups, or in written form. Memos, letters, reports, and other written documents can let the head office know how others feel. Many times both face-to-face conferences and written memos are needed to convey and affirm ideas or suggestions to be considered by those at the helm. Communication should be honest and related to issues rather than to persons.

Compromise

When two or more people have communicated with each other, the next process is to accept the plans or work out a compromise if differences exist. Two people may agree on a solution to a problem and proceed together with it. If they disagree, they must compromise, which is a dynamic process. Every person thinks and feels differently from every other person. This means that differences, both minor and major, are bound to arise. Staff workers need to be willing to look at differences and make compromises to resolve dilemmas when they exist. This requires flexibility, sensitivity, and a willingness to change.

Some workers attack others or their administrators, drawing battle lines for personal confrontation. Battle lines usually deepen differences and block or weaken solutions to problems. Workers may win a battle but lose the cause. Often compromises can bring results that are far better than those that would have been accomplished by either of the parties alone.

When differences in basic values exist, all involved must respect the others and do everything possible to understand and solve the problem. If agreement cannot be reached, it may be necessary to get outside assistance to work out what is best for the agency. Sometimes the person at the top has to make the final decision. If that decision is contrary to the one desired by the workers, they can either accept it or work to change or modify it. Experience shows that most differences can be worked out, *when* and *if* workers are willing to try. In solving conflicts, negotiation is fast becoming an important process in the administration of an agency.

Occasionally a director or other high-level administrator is incompetent and should be removed. Team members may need to work together to bring about a change in leadership. This is always difficult, but it can and should be accomplished. Team members can work together, bolstering one another, to cause an incompetent leader to resign or to change positions.

Cooperation

Cooperation is a major social process that brings about change. It is needed not only for and with top executives but also for the entire staff, from line workers to department heads to top administrators. Cooperation is the process of two or more people working together, helping each other. Lack of cooperation, or a minimum of it, may reduce or destroy an agency's effectiveness. Participative management, a current popular administrative method, calls for a good deal of cooperation. Otherwise it is ineffective.

Cooperation involves doing one's own work efficiently and effectively and making successful contributions to the agency as a whole. This means that workers understand the policies and goals of the agency and attempt to carry them out by making their particular contributions. If they fail to do their part, the agency's effectiveness is reduced.

The worker's next challenge is to work with associates and administrators, in committees and other groups, to facilitate total agency services. When workers are supportive, creative, and industrious in regard to the agency's roles and services, the overall effect is positive. When a line worker stalls, objects, criticizes, or hurts others, the agency suffers. As staff members interact and perform their services, they may do any of the following: (1) help one another, (2) remain neutral, or (3) block or depreciate one another. The essence of cooperation is giving, not getting; helping, not hurting.

Cooperation involves a commitment of time and energy. Sometimes one must come to work early or stay late—one must be flexible and willing to adapt to the schedule of others. Some staff members are "too busy" to meet with others and do their share. A competent, effective staff member is willing and eager not only to do his or her share but also to do it, if necessary, at times that are convenient for others.

One of the enemies of teamwork is competition among staff. Instead of working together, cooperatively sharing knowledge and abilities, some staff members work individually, to reach their own goals and achieve recognition. Subtly or blatantly, some practitioners block other staff members and reduce the effectiveness of an operation. Such workers want to be prima donnas, reaching for status and power, rather than helping others to succeed for the betterment of the agency.

Game theorists suggest that competition in games and in agency operations may be put into three categories: "(1) the maximizer, who is interested only in his own payoff; (2) the rivalist, who is interested only in defeating his partner and is not concerned with the result of the game itself; and (3) the cooperator, who is interested in helping both himself and his partner."[6]

Coordination

Coordination in an agency requires the involvement of all staff members at all levels. In this process, different persons and parts of an agency tie in with one another, so that efficiency and effectiveness are nurtured through sound organization.

Coordination requires a clearly defined organization, with roles and responsibilities specified and functions clearly delineated. It means that the staff is divided and subdivided into working units, tied together but with specific individual responsibilities. Ordinarily individual organizational units are arranged so that no one person has more than six or seven others to supervise, which increases efficiency and effectiveness.

The organization of most social work agencies includes an executive, one or more assistant directors (depending on agency size), department or division heads, supervisors, and line workers. When staff members are aware of the lines of authority and respond appropriately, the agency benefits. If one or more of the workers pulls off the road and tries to proceed alone, trouble may ensue.

Coordination means that the strands of an agency are intertwined in organization and practice so that the agency's strengths come to the fore and friction and difficulties are minimized.

Consummation

Teamwork involves not only starting activities and projects with others but also completing them. Many programs fall short because services or activities are not completed or are put off indefinitely. Bringing services or activities to a conclusion is a major part of the teamwork process. Getting the runner to third base doesn't count unless one takes the next step—moving to home plate.

[6]Beulah Roberts Compton and Burt Galaway, *Social Work Processes* (Homewood, IL: Dorsey Press, 1975), p. 447.

INTERPROFESSIONAL TEAMWORK

Teamwork is important not only within an agency but also on an interprofessional or interagency level. Current social work is replete with services involving workers from various professions or agencies working together. Whitehouse, in his classic article "Teamwork—A Democracy of Professions," defined teamwork as a

> close, cooperative, democratic, multiprofessional union devoted to a common purpose—the best treatment for the fundamental need of the individual. Its members work thru a combined and integrated diagnosis; flexible, dynamic planning; proper timing and sequence of treatment; and balance in action. It is an organismic group distinct in its parts yet acting as a unit, i.e., no important action is taken by members of one profession without the consent of the group. Just as the individual acts as an interrelated whole, and not as a sum of his characteristics, so must the professions act, think, interpret, and contribute toward a diagnosis which is the product of all, and a treatment plan which is dynamic to accommodate the changes which a dynamic human organism is constantly making.[7]

Social work often joins with the professions of psychiatry, psychology, nursing, and others to help persons, families, and communities with social problems and/or social functioning. When representatives from these groups cooperate and coordinate their skills and knowledge, their services may be effective. When they compete or conflict with one another, trouble often ensues. The same qualities and processes mentioned earlier are also applicable to this kind of network. An encouraging trend is the coming together of these different professions, not only to provide treatment services but also for research, education, prevention, and enrichment.

SUMMARY

All levels of staff need to participate in the administrative process in a positive manner. Attributes of effective agency workers include the following:

Is competent
Is loyal
Maintains confidentiality
Is sensitive to the needs of all workers
Realistically accepts administrators and coworkers
Is creative

[7]Frederick A. Whitehouse, "Teamwork—A Democracy of Professions," *Exceptional Children* 18 (November 1951), 46.

Team processes germane to effective administration include these:

Cooperation
Coordination
Communication
Compromise
Consummation

As administrators and agency workers team together and reveal their ideas and feelings, the morale and effectiveness of an agency may be enhanced. Some of the best suggestions for improving administration in an agency come from ordinary workers. Participative management is gaining momentum in social service agencies and in the delivery of social services.

QUESTIONS FOR DISCUSSION

1. Compare, contrast, and illustrate *leadership* and *teamship*.

2. Discuss the implications of the statement "All levels of staff participate in administration."

3. What attributes, in your opinion, are especially important for workers as members of the agency team?

4. Describe and evaluate the significance of five teamwork processes.

5. Give an example of interprofessional teamwork and describe its importance in providing effective social services.

6. Describe the relevance of loyalty to and acceptance of fellow workers in a social work agency.

SPECIAL ACTIVITIES

1. Role-play a situation to illustrate how a secretary may make a significant contribution to the administrative process in an agency.

2. Write a brief report on one of the five teamwork processes and read it to your class.

3. Invite a social work agency manager to talk to your class on the importance of loyalty between a manager and staff members.

SELECTED REFERENCES

BEDEIAN, ARTHUR G. *Management*, 3rd ed., pp. 325–329, 515–517. Fort Worth, TX: Dryden Press, 1993.
BRIELAND, DONALD, THOMAS L. BRIGGS, and PAUL LEUENBERGER. *The Team Model of Social Work Practice*. Syracuse, NY: Syracuse University School of Social Work, 1973.

BRILL, NAOMI I. *Teamwork: Working Together in the Human Services.* Philadelphia: J. B. Lippincott, 1976.

EDWARDS, RICHARD L., and JOHN A. YANKEY, eds. *Skills for Effective Human Services Management.* Silver Spring, MD: NASW Press, 1991.

EZELL, MARK, DAVID MENEFEE, and RINO J. PATTI. "Managerial Leadership and Service Quality: Toward a Model of Social Work Administration." *Administration in Social Work* 13, Nos. 3/4 (1989), 73–98.

FALLON, KENNETH P., JR. "Participatory Management: An Alternative in Human Service Delivery Systems." In Simon Slavin, ed., *Social Administration: The Management of the Social Services,* 2nd ed. Vol. I, *An Introduction to Human Services Management,* pp. 251–259. New York: Haworth Press, 1985.

HASENFELD, YEHESKEL, ed. "Administrative Leadership in the Social Services: The Next Challenge." *Administration in Social Work* 13, Nos. 3/4 (1989), 1–269.

LONSDALE, SUSAN, ADRIAN WEBB, and THOMAS L. BRIGGS, eds. *Teamwork in the Personal Social Services and Health Care.* London: Personal Social Services Council, 1980.

PATTI, RINO J. *Social Welfare Administration: Managing Social Programs in a Developmental Context.* Englewood Cliffs, NJ: Prentice Hall, 1983.

PECORA, PETER J., and MICHAEL J. AUSTIN. *Managing Human Services Personnel.* Newbury Park, CA: Sage Publications, 1987.

POPPLE, PHILIP R. "Negotiation: A Critical Skill for Social Work Administrators." *Administration in Social Work* 8 (Summer 1984), 1–11.

RESNICK, HERMAN, and RINO J. PATTI, eds. *Change from Within: Humanizing Social Welfare Organizations.* Philadelphia: Temple University Press, 1980.

WEATHERLEY, RICHARD A. "Participatory Management in Public Welfare: What Are the Prospects?" *Administration in Social Work* 7 (Spring 1983), 39–49.

12

Motivation and Job Satisfaction

Dr. S. was hired as the director of a county public welfare department with a staff of fourteen social workers. He came to this position with excellent training and four years of casework and administrative practice. He brought a sincere desire to do everything possible to provide optimal services for clients in need.

He met with each staff member and was sensitive to their backgrounds, training, and professional competencies. He was aware of their needs and capabilities. After he had been in this administrative position for six months, he remarked to a professional colleague, "I can't believe how different workers are. Each makes a contribution, but some are highly productive, whereas others seem lazy or indifferent. I have two caseworkers with similar training and experience who are as different as night and day. One does twice the work of the other, really. Worker A not only accomplishes more but also enjoys work more, gains basic satisfaction from the services she provides, and projects a positive image of a social worker. Worker B is mopish; she avoids her share of cases and does a poor job with those she handles. She is negative much of the time and is always watching the clock."

Why was the performance of these two workers so different, when their backgrounds, training, and capabilities were almost identical? Why do some social workers gain more satisfaction from practice than others? What motivational factors are significant in social work?

Motivation is fascinating to study. Administrators, agencies, and practitioners differ in part because of motivational factors or their lack. Motivation is a major factor in administering social services. Why do some staff members work with enthusiasm and verve and others move at a snail's pace, seemingly caring little about their work or their clients? What makes the difference in performance of workers in practice? For many years management has shown an interest in motivation, particularly because of its relationship to production and profit making. Social work is just beginning to focus on motivation and job satisfaction, trying to find out what is significant and effective and what is not. Why do some workers, and not others, have high morale and act efficiently? This chapter considers some of the main motivation theories and developments and how they relate to social work.

THEORIES OF MOTIVATION

Classical Theory

Frederick W. Taylor, in 1911, recognized the importance of motivation in business and management and proposed several ideas that have made basic contributions to the classical theory. From his studies, he concluded that if an ambitious person were paid the same amount for his or her work as a person who was indifferent or lazy and produced less, sooner or later the ambitious or energetic person would slow down and be less productive. Consequently, he advocated giving rewards that would be appreciated by an energetic person and would bring about higher levels of production.[1]

Taylor brought into operation two significant factors: the stopwatch and the piecework bonus-pay system. He used the stopwatch to make careful measurements and recordings of how long a given task took, so that efficiency and effectiveness could be improved. This created expectations and standards of achievement. It also brought about clearer job descriptions and specific job requirements and goals. Taylor reduced different positions to a series of timed and tested movements. Thus, expectations for a given job developed and quotas could be set in relation to specific targets. Taylor introduced a reward system that recognized and rewarded those who produced more than was expected. In other words, he emphasized the piecework bonus system. Ambitious, capable workers were given monetary rewards for doing more than the expected work.

Classical theory was built on the basic idea that money and increased income were major motivating factors in production. Although Taylor's data and explanations have been considered carefully and respected, it is evident that money in and of itself is not the only factor that can bring about increased production and services.

[1] Frederick W. Taylor, *Scientific Management* (New York: Harper & Brothers, 1911).

Maslow's Need Theory

Abraham Maslow, in 1943, expounded his ideas about basic needs and satisfactions. His hierarchy of needs started simply, at the physiological level, then became increasingly sophisticated, proceeding through four more levels, to safety needs, to social needs and the desire for love, to the need for esteem, and finally to the need for self-actualization. Maslow noted that since individuals are different, they must be respected and treated accordingly. He suggested that the way to increase production and to motivate workers was to understand what employees' needs were and then to supply them through work opportunities. The physiological level included basic needs: food, clothing, and shelter. Self-actualization, at the other end of the spectrum, involves achievement, importance, and accomplishment.

Basically Maslow says that if workers need to be motivated in a given agency, they should be understood as individuals, their personal and group needs should be considered, and then working conditions and challenges that would fulfill their needs should be provided. In particular, they should be given opportunities to fulfill their more complicated needs, especially self-actualization, which involves ego satisfaction, individuality, independence, and achievement and, related to them, social approval and recognition.[2]

Maslow's theory about needs has been studied and evaluated by many researchers, educators, and social workers. Most studies show that his basic ideas are valid, but because behavior is so individual there are exceptions to his hierarchical five-level description. Thus it is difficult to validate Maslow's studies empirically since needs are so individual and difficult to measure.

Hofstede made a study of more than 18,000 employees from a company with offices in sixteen different countries. The workers were asked to rank their four most important work goals. The professionals ranked the need for self-actualization and esteem at the top, whereas the clerical and unskilled workers gave high priority to fulfilling social, security, and physiological needs.[3] Results of Hofstede's study are shown in Table 12–1.

Human Relations Theory

Contrasted with the importance of money and rewards and the whole gamut of individual needs is the human relations theory, which stresses the importance of people and their relationships with others. Rensis Likert, who emphasized this theory, noted that the administrator or the manager, who may well be the motivator, is a key person in work development and production.[4] His basic idea is that since the motivator is the key person, if he or

---

[2]Abraham H. Maslow, "A Theory of Human Motivation," *Psychological Review* 50 (July 1943), 370–396.

[3]Geert H. Hofstede, "The Colors of Collars," *Columbia Journal of World Business* 7 (September–October 1972), 78.

[4]Rensis Likert, *New Patterns of Management* (New York: McGraw-Hill, 1961).

TABLE 12–1. Ranking of the Four Most Important Goals for Seven Different Occupational Groups

GOALS RANKED IN NEED HIERARCHY	PROFESSIONALS (RESEARCH LABORATORIES)	PROFESSIONALS (BRANCH OFFICES)	MANAGERS	TECHNICIANS (BRANCH OFFICES)	TECHNICIANS (MANUFACTURING PLANTS)	CLERICAL WORKERS (BRANCH OFFICES)	UNSKILLED WORKERS (MANUFACTURING PLANTS)
High:							
Self-actualization and esteem needs:							
Challenge	1	2	1	3	3		
Training		1		1			
Autonomy	3	3	2				
Up-to-dateness	2	4		4			
Use of skills	4						
Middle:							
Social needs:							
Cooperation			3/4			1	
Manager			3/4		4	2	
Friendly dept.						3	
Efficient dept.						4	
Low:							
Security and physiological needs:							
Security				2	1		2
Earnings					2		3
Benefits							4
Physical conditions							1

Source: Geert H. Hofstede, "The Colors of Collars," *Columbia Journal of World Business* 7 (September–October 1972), 78.

she sends out the right number and kinds of signals, the production desired will probably be achieved. Administrators and managers are encouraged to use as many motivating factors as possible; these would include satisfying economic, security, and ego needs, as well as fulfilling curiosity and the wish to be creative.

Human relations theory says that organizational units with a high level of production are characterized by favorable attitudes of each of the members. That is, they all get along and help and motivate one another. The idea is that satisfied people working with satisfied people who like and can assist one another will motivate one another and achieve the desired level of production. This theory encompasses the widespread participation of staff members in the decision-making and planning processes. Workers feel that they are a part of the agency, are helping to control and run it, and are motivated to do their best.

Likert interprets the human relations approach further when he describes the following operating characteristics:

> The principle of supportive relationships which has been proposed for the newer theory specifies conditions that lead to a full and efficient flow of all relevant information in all directions—upward, downward, and between peers—throughout the organization. This full and open flow of useful and relevant information provides at all points in the organization accurate data to guide action, to call attention to problems as they arise, and to assure that sound decisions based on all available facts are made.
>
> The principle of supportive relationships calls for an exercise of influence comparable with the flow of information. In organizations which effectively use the newer theory, consequently, every person feels, and is correct in his feeling, that he can and does exercise influence upon the decisions and behavior of all those with whom he is in more or less regular contact. Through them he exerts at least some influence upon the entire organization.
>
> Persons in organizations operating under the newer theory, in comparison with those in most existing organizations, exercise greater influence upon what happens in the organization. This is true at every hierarchical level from nonsupervisory employees to the head of the organization. The application of the newer theory results in a greater total amount of influence being exercised throughout the organization. As a consequence, the organization can more fully mobilize and focus all its resources to accomplish its goals than can present-day organizations.[5]

Carl Rogers illustrates this same basic approach in his *client-centered counseling*, in which he emphasizes that the person who is asking for help can be best assisted by someone who will listen carefully, sympathetically, and with a caring attitude but who will reflect back to the counselee the questions, feelings, and decisions that are being faced. Basically, the idea is that counselees have the potential to solve their own problems if someone acts as a mirror, reflecting their thoughts, plans, and state of mind. In social services,

[5]Ibid., pp. 238–239.

workers need to feel they can play a major role in planning, policymaking, and other agency decisions. As they feel they belong to the organization and become an interacting member, they are motivated to participate, to provide better services.

Behavior Modification

Many learning theories concern personal counseling as well as work satisfaction. One of these is *behavior modification*, or *operant conditioning*. This psychological theory suggests that people's behavior, individually and in groups, may be affected by the expectation of rewards and punishments. Behavior may be changed through either consistent punishment or consistent rewards. The behavior-modification theory emphasizes that rewards are usually more desirable than punishment.

Psychologist B. F. Skinner led the way with theories about operant conditioning. He noted that behavior can be modified and directed by controlling the environment and outside stimuli. Internal drives and needs are important, but environmental forces are also significant. Positive reinforcement can bring about modification in behavior; negative reinforcement helps to discourage repetition of an undesired behavior.

In counseling, such items as candy and other rewards may be used to influence the behavior of children, youths, and adults. When children realize that certain actions will be rewarded, over a period of time they will be likely to change their behavior. In the work situation, the idea is basically the same. If rewards, such as increased salary and promotion, are provided and understood to relate to job performance, over a period of time these may make a difference.

Jablonsky and DeVries have summarized the following basic rules for an organization to exert maximum influence on its members through operant conditioning.

Avoid using punishment as a primary means of obtaining desired behavior.
Positively reinforce desired behavior and, when possible, ignore undesirable behavior.
Minimize the time lag between the desired response and reinforcement.
Apply positive reinforcement relatively frequently.
Ascertain the response level of each individual and use a shaping procedure to obtain a final complex response.
Ascertain contingencies that are experienced as positive and/or negative by the individual.
Specify the desired behavior in explicitly operational terms.[6]

[6]Stephen F. Jablonsky and David L. DeVries, "Operant Conditioning Principles Extrapolated to the Theory of Management," *Organization Behavior and Human Performance 7* (April 1972), 340–358.

Environmental Approach

Another approach to understanding motivation relates to the environment, particularly working conditions and climate. Performance on the job not only involves personality characteristics, training, and previous experience but also the physical, psychological, and emotional climate of the agency. In actuality, work performance and satisfaction relate to the attitudes a worker brings to a job and how he or she interacts with the working conditions.

Carlisle suggests that although motivation is related to personal factors in many ways, environmental factors are highly significant and

> consist of job assignments, pay and fringe benefits, promotional opportunities, the rules and regulations of the organization, relationships with associates, and other physical and psychological factors in the work climate. Since most of these can be modified and are the rewards that determine behavior, a supervisor will be much more effective in motivating others by concentrating on them. Too frequently the supervisor asks the question, "What is wrong with the individual?", instead of asking, "What is wrong with the work we ask the employee to perform?" Since many of us are not very motivated to wash dishes, dig trenches, or do "busy work," there is little reason to expect others to approach these tasks with enthusiasm.[7]

X and Y Theories

Douglas McGregor postulated the much-discussed X and Y theories of motivation.[8] When he introduced them in 1960, he suggested that there are two kinds of working conditions, one basically positive and the other basically negative. His theories have been questioned by those who hold that it is impossible to dichotomize working conditions, that there are many varieties and levels within any classification. Nevertheless his theories have been introduced to students at all levels of management study.

Theory X suggests that workers need considerable direction and control, centralized and authoritative, with minimal democratic participation. It states that the average human being has an inherent dislike of work and will avoid it if possible. Thus, workers need to be coerced, controlled, and threatened with punishment in order to perform. The average person has relatively little ambition, wants to be directed, and seeks security above all else.

Theory Y is the opposite of Theory X in many ways. It involves considerable participation in decision making by workers, is less centralized, and advocates minimal control and direction. Its basic premise is that physical

[7]Howard M. Carlisle, *Management Essentials: Concepts for Productivity and Innovation*, 2nd ed. (Chicago: Science Research Associates, 1987), p. 299.

[8]Douglas McGregor, *The Human Side of Enterprise* (New York: McGraw-Hill, 1960), pp. 33–57.

and mental efforts in work are as natural as play and rest, a factor that minimizes the need for external control and the threat of punishment. The average human being learns not only to accept but also to seek responsibility. The capacity for imagination, ingenuity, and creativity in solving organizational problems is widespread among workers.

Theory Z, which was introduced later, suggests that managers might use a middle approach with variations, depending on the specific administrative situation at a given moment. Although these three theories have had a considerable impact on management and evaluative studies indicate varying results on workers and production, research has not yet produced conclusive data about their significance.

Motivation-Hygiene Theory

Frederick Herzberg, called the "father of job enrichment," has become known for his motivation-hygiene theory, which suggests that a person's job must satisfy two basic human needs: to avoid pain and to achieve psychological growth and satisfaction.

This theory, based on more than fifty studies involving all types of workers, suggests that factors that satisfy workers are related to what they do. What counts is job content and psychological satisfaction. Unhappiness, in contrast, is produced by pain, causing "hygiene" problems in the work environment. Such problems include inadequate salaries, sweatshop conditions, and poor relationships with coworkers and supervisors. Herzberg says that one of the primary causes of flagging productivity is "that most jobs—in the name of efficiency—have been robbed of meaning and psychological income." He also simply suggests, "If you want a person to do a good job, give him a good job to do."[9]

Herzberg observes that many hygienic or maintenance factors are important, particularly if they are lacking in the workplace, but they do not bring basic satisfaction in work or positive motivation in and of themselves. These include company policy and administration, technical supervision, interpersonal relations with a supervisor, interpersonal relations with peers, interpersonal relations with subordinates, salary, job security, personal life, work conditions, and status. The genuine motivational factors are

1. Achievement
2. Recognition
3. Advancement
4. The work itself

[9]Frederick Herzberg, *Work and the Nature of Man* (New York: Thomas Y. Crowell, 1966); and Frederick Herzberg, *The Managerial Choice: To Be Efficient and to Be Human* (Homewood, IL: Dow Jones-Irwin, 1976), pp. 53–101.

5. The possibility of growth
6. Responsibility

Again, it is difficult to look at a specific dichotomy and expect to find all the answers. Individuals differ, and there are many degrees of hygiene and motivation. Nevertheless, Herzberg's emphasis on ego-satisfying psychological factors has not been disproved.

Preference-Expectation Theory

In 1964 Vroom advanced a theory based on the consideration of more than five hundred research investigations into motivation and work results that introduced ideas about job preferences and expectations.[10] This theory recognizes individual differences and acknowledges that the preferences and expectations of workers can influence their behavior in the production of services. The probability of performing an act is related to expectations and likely outcomes. Behavior is affected not only by preferences for particular outcomes but also by the degree to which the worker believes these outcomes to be probable.

Expectancy is defined as a "momentary belief concerning the likelihood that a particular act will be followed by a particular outcome."[11] The main feature of this model is that it views "behavior as subjectively rational and as directed toward the attainment of desired outcomes and away from aversive outcomes."[12]

This theory provides helpful ideas for understanding individual differences and their importance in motivation and work performance. Applied to social workers, it means that participatory management is particularly important and that workers' preferences ought to be considered by administrators. Also, workers need to know what results to expect from their work.

Money and Motivation

Many people claim that money is the main motivating factor of production in the business world, and some claim the same is true for the delivery of social services. Research studies do not bear this out. They show that money is important, but it is not the salient factor in motivation. Money is so relative, and attitudes toward it vary so much, that there is no set pattern regarding its motivational value.

Whyte estimates that only about 10 percent of workers on the industrial production line in the United States respond positively to a financial incentive by producing to capacity. He observes that "money incentives sometimes seem to work, in stimulating production, and sometimes show little

---

[10]Victor H. Vroom, *Work and Motivation* (New York: Wiley, 1964).

[11]Ibid., p. 17.

[12]Ibid., p. 276.

effect. . . . Even where the incentive seems to work, in most cases its success is only partial."[13] Herzberg, in his study of many groups of workers, came to the conclusion that salaries and salary increases were important as hygiene factors, fulfilling basic needs, but were not major motivating factors in work production.[14]

Japanese Management

In this world of increased international trade, Japanese management is of considerable interest. It provides for more participatory management by workers at all levels, in making decisions and otherwise. This system offers more training of workers and subsequent less turnover. There is greater security, as jobs may be for life. Also, there is considerable emphasis on achieving cooperation among employees.

Japanese management emphasizes group performance with concomitant approvals, authority, and rewards. The team concept is paramount. Employees are organized in small groups, *quality circles*, with ten to twenty members in size, which are given considerable authority and autonomy. These groups may get together several times a week and offer suggestions for improving quality and methodology in production or services. These small teams often bring job enrichment through their discussions and related activities.

COMMON FACTORS IN MOTIVATION

These brief descriptions of selected theories of motivation show that although there are numerous approaches to motivation, certain common factors seem particularly significant. Most of these are found in varying degrees in each of the theories. Following is a listing of some of the pragmatic principles and factors that relate to motivation in social work agencies.

Personal Interests

Personal interest in an agency and in the job to be performed is of prime importance in motivation and in the provision of high-quality social services. If workers are doing what they like to do, they will probably produce high-quality work as well as increase quantitative output. If they are not interested, the opposite is likely to occur.

It is possible, of course, for interests to be developed or augmented on the job. Capable administrators do whatever they can to enhance personal interests and to allow for their expression. Interests may be developed in an

[13]William F. Whyte, *Money and Motivation* (New York: Harper & Row, 1955), p. 1.
[14]Herzberg, *Managerial Choice*, pp. 69–83.

agency by sharing cases and experiences, and particularly by involving staff members in planning and decision-making processes that are significant to the agency's operation. A democratic, participatory climate is conducive to developing and enriching personal interests.

Time Management

Workers in an agency usually ask for at least two concessions in regard to time: that the administrators have respect for the use of time within the agency's framework and that workers have some time to themselves to be creative, to plan, and to improve their services.

In an agency where the value of each staff member's time, including administrators', is respected, high morale and productivity are likely. This means that administrators must set an example by using their time effectively. They structure committee operations and decision-making processes so that maximum results occur in a minimum of time. They may prepare agendas for meetings that allocate time for the consideration of goals, problems, and decisions.

It is also important for each staff member to have some time to meditate, evaluate, justify, plan, and create to the advantage of the agency.

Administrative Support

Administrators who help staff members feel they are all on the same team, working together toward common goals, help build morale as well as increase productivity. As we have frequently emphasized, trust engenders trust; support engenders support. Being supportive means not only backing workers in what they are doing, have done, or are attempting to do but also giving approval and recognition when appropriate. In staff meetings, brief statements can provide such recognition. All staff members hunger for approval and wish to find accomplishment and worth. Stimulating such feelings can result in an increased desire to work with others to build agency services.

Supporting workers means that the administrator stands behind them if they run into trouble because of a decision or an act. It does not mean that administrators approve of every action by a worker but have an understanding, accepting attitude. The administration should do everything possible to help clarify and resolve the problem, whatever it may be.

Clarity of Responsibility and Authority

When workers understand their specific responsibilities and feel they have the authority to carry them out, they have positive feelings and are motivated to do what they can to further the interests and services of the agency. Often responsibilities are so general that they have little or no meaning. The more specific and targeted the responsibilities, the more likely they are to be carried out.

Some administrators are eager to assign responsibilities but hesitate or neglect to provide authority to accompany them. This is a difficult situation for a worker and hinders the treatment process.

Approval and Appreciation

Workers always need feedback from their leaders. Competent administrators are eager to show appreciation for their workers. Approval can be verbal or written. Workers need to know if their work is satisfactory, in keeping with agency goals and services. A wise administrator gives feedback often, showing workers that their actions have been observed.

In personal interviews and staff meetings competent administrators convey to staff members appreciation for what they have done and are doing, particularly for achievements beyond the ordinary.

Opportunities for Achievement

In keeping with what has been discussed, an opportunity to do something worthwhile is extremely important for motivation and agency morale. Genuine achievement opens the door to individual and collective satisfaction. Inactivity or frivolous activity, in contrast, causes restlessness, boredom, inefficiency, and ineffectiveness.

Real work must be available in an agency so that workers do not need to pretend to be busy. People gain genuine satisfaction and positive feelings from accomplishing something worthwhile. Certainly in a social work agency this is important for morale. Motivation and satisfaction are enhanced as workers are given opportunities to help people help themselves with personal, family, and community problems.

Weiner suggests that linking worker performance (job satisfaction) with organizational performance (client outcomes) is of paramount importance in sound administration. He is aware that the process of blending worker performance and organizational performance is "a very delicate one." Yet "one can quickly present the thesis that the primary talent for managing people in human services organizations is skill in blending and linking organizational with personal/professional goals."[15] He offers an interesting figure to show dynamic relationships in this process. (Figure 12–1).

[15]Myron E. Weiner, "Managing People for Enhanced Performance," *Administration in Social Work* 11 (Fall/Winter 1987), 148.

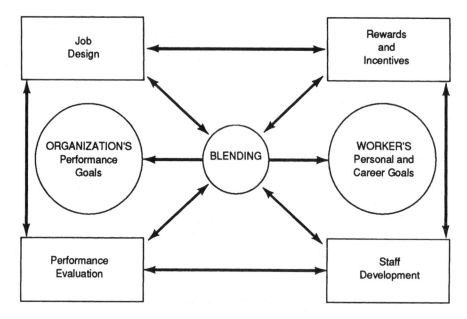

FIGURE 12-1   **Blending: The Critical People Management Skill.** Source: Myron E. Weiner, "Managing People for Enhanced Performance," *Administration in Social Work* 11 (Fall/Winter 1987), 148.

BURNOUT AND MOTIVATION

Burnout among social workers in practice is on the increase. This represents a low ebb on the motivational continuum. Studies indicate that many workers feel emotional fatigue, some at a level that makes them unable to use their professional skills adequately.

The question arises, Why burnout among social workers today? Not long ago this phenomenon was almost unknown, or at least was not openly discussed. A variety of causes seems to surface. Any one of the following, or a combination, may play a significant role in causing burnout:

1. Social workers often work with people who have emotionally laden problems that spill over into the lives of workers, whether they want them to or not. These problems are often intense, personal, and volatile. Absorbing or cushioning some of the feelings takes its toll.

2. Many social workers are given large caseloads. Numerous probation officers, for example, are assigned more than double the number of cases recommended by professionals. In addition, workers may receive a call from a client at midnight or in the early hours of the morning.

3. Some positions in social work are limited in the services performed and tend to become routine and monotonous. In some agencies, varying services and using individual abilities and skills are at a minimum.

4. Various groups, such as legislatures and citizen organizations, are increasing their demands for more accountability by social workers. No longer is a mere listing of the number of interviews sufficient to satisfy the public. More and more groups ask, What are the outcomes? Do your services make any difference in the lives of people?

Arches made a study of 275 randomly selected social workers who were practicing in Massachusetts in 1988 to better understand burnout and job satisfaction. She concluded that "as long as workers lack the autonomy they expect to use in their work with clients, they are likely to be dissatisfied and experience some degree of burnout. Workers are most satisfied when they have autonomy, are not limited by demands of funding sources, and are not stifled by bureaucracy."[16]

Role conflict has been suggested as a significant factor in burnout among social workers. Jones, in a year-long study of public child-welfare administrators, examined the effects of role conflict on their attitudes and performance. Her study reflected that the individuals had "developed specific, effective skills for responding to role conflict. Although there was a public presentation of self that indicated they were under stress and in 'impossible' situations, there was in fact an energizing resulting from the ongoing challenge of dealing with conflict."[17] She observed that her study was qualitative and exploratory and that more research is needed with other groups of workers.

Social work administrators and practitioners are making concerted efforts to reduce and prevent burnout. These vary considerably from agency to agency. Borland summarizes several strategies for combating burnout, which include the following: (1) keep lines of communication open among staff; (2) provide positive feedback to workers; (3) offer a variety of job activities; (4) develop a support system among staff members; (5) provide opportunities for workers to share their feelings with colleagues; (6) be sure administrators are supportive of staff members; (7) involve staff members in decision making.[18]

Harvey and Raider studied administrator burnout and concluded that "two points should not be considered debatable. First, administrator burnout is real; and second, to resolve the problems of social agency administration . . . it will first be necessary to recognize and resolve the problem of administrator burnout."[19]

[16]Joan Arches, "Social Structure, Burnout, and Job Satisfaction," *Social Work* 36 (May 1991), 206.

[17]Martha L. Jones, "Role Conflict: Cause of Burnout or Energizer?" *Social Work* 38 (March 1993), 136.

[18]James J. Borland, "Burnout Among Workers and Administrators," *Health and Social Work* 6 (February 1981), 73–78.

[19]Sally H. Harvey and Melvyn C. Raider, "Administrator Burnout," *Administration in Social Work* 8 (Summer 1984), 88.

Although burnout is a serious problem at times, apparently most social work administrators are basically satisfied with their roles as leaders. Jayaratne and Chess reported a study related to job satisfaction based on a national sample of social workers randomly drawn from the NASW membership. They concluded that the administrators, regardless of gender, were generally satisfied with their work and felt that they were successful at it. A fair percentage did indicate that they intended to seek new employment. The major correlate of job satisfaction for both men and women was the "challenge that the job offers."[20]

SUMMARY

Motivation is a key factor in social services. Some important theories that contribute to an understanding of motivation are Taylor's emphasis on the time-quota system and reward; Likert's focus on the importance of human relationships and the participation of staff; Maslow's definition of the hierarchy of human needs; Skinner's behavior modification and its emphasis on rewards; McGregor's X, Y, and Z theories; and Herzberg's motivational-hygiene framework.

Research studies indicate that individuals vary considerably in performance and that numerous motivational factors may be relevant. More research needs to be done into the influence of motivation on social work practice.

The following are key factors in successfully providing motivation in social work agencies:

Personal interests
Time management
Administrative support
Clear understanding of specific responsibilities, accompanied by requisite authority
Approval and appreciation shared often
Opportunities for genuine achievement

Burnout in social work practice is on the increase. More research and experimentation are needed to reduce burnout among administrators as well as other staff members.

The study of motivation reflects the vital significance of human relationships in achievement and in performance. Relationships are particularly powerful in social work practice and administration.

---

[20]Srinika Jayaratne and Wayne A. Chess, "Job Satisfaction and Turnover Among Social Work Administrators: A National Survey," *Administration in Social Work* 7 (Summer 1983), 21.

QUESTIONS FOR DISCUSSION

1. Do you agree that motivation and job satisfaction are closely related in social work practice? Justify your position.

2. Evaluate Maslow's need theory as it applies to social work practice and motivation.

3. What is your opinion of McGregor's X and Y theories in relation to motivation for effective casework in a marriage and family counseling agency?

4. How important are high salaries in bringing job satisfaction to social workers in practice?

5. Discuss the importance of opportunities for achievement in the effectiveness of the agency and the satisfaction level of its workers.

6. What suggestions would you make to reduce burnout of social workers employed in public welfare agencies?

7. What motivated you to become a social worker?

SPECIAL ACTIVITIES

1. Read the article "Eight Myths on Motivating Social Service Workers: Theory-Based Perspectives," by Jean Kantambu Latting and evaluate these myths.

2. Role-play an interview between a social worker and a client to illustrate emotional pressures that may lead to burnout.

3. Invite a psychiatrist to talk to your class on emotional stress in social work practice.

SELECTED REFERENCES

ARCHES, JOAN. "Social Structure, Burnout, and Job Satisfaction." *Social Work* 36 (May 1991), 202–206.
BARGAL, DAVID, AARON BACK, and PNINA ARIAV. "Occupational Social Work and Prolonged Job Insecurity in a Declining Organization." *Administration in Social Work* 16, No. 1 (1992), 55–67.
FULMER, ROBERT M. *The New Management*, 4th ed., pp. 277–297. New York: Macmillan, 1988.
HARVEY, SALLY H., and MELVYN C. RAIDER. "Administrator Burnout." *Administration in Social Work* 8 (Summer 1984), 81–89.
JAYARATNE, SRINIKA, and WAYNE A. CHESS. "Job Satisfaction and Turnover Among Social Work Administrators: A National Survey." *Administration in Social Work* 7 (Summer 1983), 11–22.
KETS DE VRIES, MANFRED F. R. "The Motivating Role of Envy, Forgotten Factor in Management Theory." *Administration and Society* 24 (May 1992), 41–61.
LATTING, JEAN KANTAMBU. "Eight Myths on Motivating Social Services Workers: Theory-Based Perspectives." *Administration in Social Work* 15, No. 3 (1991), 49–63.

MURPHY, JOHN W., and JOHN T. PARDECK. "Computerization and the Dehumanization of Social Services." *Administration in Social Work* 16, No. 2 (1992), 61–71.

SCHODERBEK, PETER P., and SATISH P. DESHPANDE. "Managerial Pay-Allocations in a Not-for-Profit Organization: An Empirical Analysis." *Administration in Social Work* 16, No. 2 (1992), 1–13.

SLAVIN, SIMON, ed. *Social Administration: The Management of the Social Services*, 2nd ed. Vol. II, *Managing Finances, Personnel, and Information in Human Services*. New York: Haworth Press, 1985.

ZUSSMAN, YALE E. "Learning from the Japanese: Management in a Resource-scarce World." *Organizational Dynamics*, Winter 1983, pp. 68–80.

13

Communication in Administration

Two social workers were talking about their directors. One enthusiastically commented, "I really like her because I always know what she thinks and feels. She keeps us posted day by day."

The other replied, "We really have trouble in our agency because we don't know where our boss stands or what is important to him." He then added, "He sends lots of memos, but they're slanted and vague and don't mean a thing."

Why the difference?

Various studies indicate that communication is a cardinal component of human relationships. If a husband and wife are able to communicate, the wheels of matrimony are lubricated. If friends and associates tell one another what they think and feel, they deepen their relationships. Business associates who confide in one another are usually supportive and help in production. Nearly every course in social work training gives some consideration to basic knowledge, principles, and skills used in communication, which is so needed for effective social work practice and especially for successful administration.

EFFECTIVE COMMUNICATION

Communication in social work administration is extremely important for three main reasons: (1) effectiveness, (2) efficiency, and (3) morale. For the effective delivery of services in an agency, it is imperative for staff members to be able to communicate with one another. How can sound policies be formulated if staff communication does not take place? How can meaningful decisions be made if staff members are unable to reveal their ideas, opinions, and feelings? Two-way communication is part of the democratic process and is essential for making sound decisions and determining effective policies.

Efficiency is enhanced as staff members communicate openly with one another about procedures, methods, cases, policies, goals, and even aspirations. A staff member who has learned an efficient technique for expediting or improving social services can strengthen the agency by revealing it. Staff members who have found certain procedures to be clumsy or ineffective can, again, help the agency by letting others know their findings.

The third factor, morale, is particularly significant in agency operation. If leaders and team members feel connected, they are more likely to be supportive of one another and achieve agency goals. Morale depends, in part at least, on leaders and staff telling one another what they think and why. This does not mean they will agree on everything or that team members will necessarily get their way, but it does indicate that they are cognizant of how others feel. Agency morale is built on the understanding of administrators and other staff members, who communicate and help one another in the delivery of social services.

Carlisle suggests four primary reasons why communication is considered central to the entire management process:

1. Communication is one of the two linking processes of management. It is the basis for social interaction that is fundamental to all human activity in an organization. "Interaction is to the organization what the cell is to the human body."
2. Communication is the "primary means for people to obtain and exchange information. Making decisions and functioning as a manager is dependent on the quality and quantity of information received."
3. Communication is the most time-consuming activity of a manager; the average manager spends about 70 to 90 percent of his or her time in communicating. A study by John Hinrichs indicates that first-line supervisors spend 74 percent of their time communicating, second-level supervisors 81 percent, and third-level administrators 87 percent.
4. Information and communication "represent power in organization. . . . Those who have the information relative to company goals, plans, and operations become centers of power in an organization."[1]

Zelko studied the amount of time spent in communication in the business world and concluded that approximately 10 percent was spent in writing, 15 percent in reading, 35 percent in speaking, and 40 percent in listening.[2] Oral communication plays the central role.

[1]Howard M. Carlisle, *Management Essentials: Concepts and Applications* (Chicago: Science Research Associates, Inc., 1979), p. 316. Copyright © 1979 Science Research Associates, Inc. Reproduced by permission of the publisher.

[2]Harold P. Zelko, *Art of Communicating Your Ideas* (New York: Reading Rack Service, 1968), p. 3.

Some observations can help us understand what communication is. John Powell observes, for example, "The genius of communication is the ability to be both totally honest and totally kind at the same time." Herbert Greenberg went so far as to say, "All negative behavior toward others can be understood as a way of dealing with our own negative feelings about ourselves." Sidney Hourart suggests "that no man can come to know himself except as an outcome of disclosing himself to another person."

Trecker, a pioneer administration educator, proposed six criteria of effective communication for the social work administrator:

1. The purpose of the communication must be clear and must be understood by the person making it and by the person receiving it.
2. Both spoken and written material must be as clear as possible and subject to one and only one interpretation. If it is not possible to be this precise, every effort should be made to reduce the number of exceptions or options that are left open at the point of interpretation.
3. Effective communication is a series of consistent acts. In other words, subsequent communications are consistently related to earlier communications and avoid the hazard of nullification.
4. Good communication is adequate to accomplish its purpose; it is neither too much or too little; it has a sharp focus and is selective as to content.
5. Good communication is timely in that thought is given to the timing at point of issue and the readiness on the part of the recipient.
6. In good communication, thought is given to the channels to be utilized and to the distribution, so that the right persons will receive the material. This usually requires a system which will make for not only downward and upward communication but for lateral communication as well.[3]

VERBAL AND NONVERBAL COMMUNICATION

Communication is the process of conveying ideas and feelings to another person or persons. It is a two-way process. Both verbal and nonverbal communication are important. Verbal communication refers to the spoken word—what one says and another hears. In social service agencies, verbal communication takes place in staff meetings, committee meetings, interviews, and conferences between two or more people. It also takes place in the halls, during the coffee break, and so on. Verbal communication in an agency involves messages that can be created through talking with an individual or a group. However, there are several limitations to this process, and they should be considered:

1. Verbal communication places its major emphasis on ideas and facts and may not give an accurate picture of feelings.
2. What one chooses to say may be only an approximation of the total situation, which may lead a listener in the wrong direction.

[3]Harleigh B. Trecker, *Social Work Administration: Principles and Practices* (New York: Association Press, 1971), pp. 135–136.

3. Sometimes it is difficult to get people together to discuss all that needs to be said.

Nonverbal communication, often overlooked by writers, is particularly significant, especially in social work. It is an important part of the therapy process, as well as of staff interaction. Often feelings and ideas are conveyed through nonverbal action more effectively than through verbalization. Nonverbal communication involves body action—eyes, posture, gait, speaking speed, pitch of the voice, tension of the lips, redness of the cheeks, and tears. A supervisor may say to an employee, "This means nothing to me," while his posture and demeanor affirm the opposite.

In 1956 an innovative book, *Nonverbal Communication*,[4] appeared. Its authors, a psychiatrist and a photographer, presented numerous ideas and examples of such communication. The pictures showed meaningful expressions of feeling, for example, a photo of one person placing a reassuring hand on another's shoulder.

Employees need to "listen" with their eyes if they are truly going to understand what others are saying. Carefully observing a person while communicating will help convey and receive ideas, meanings, and feelings. Employees also need to *listen* with their ears, not just to hear what is said. This means giving undivided attention to a speaker.

An example of the significance of nonverbal communication was described by Dr. Andrew S. Watson, a psychiatrist, at a training program for judges sponsored by the National Council of Juvenile Court Judges in Boulder, Colorado, in 1968. He reported that he and his colleagues had conducted considerable research into facial expressions. They had come to the conclusion that by filming a person's face for eight seconds and studying the pictures, they could develop a fairly accurate evaluation of that person's personality. In eight seconds, with 1×16 frames, 128 different photographs would be taken. It would take about eighty hours to analyze and interpret these photographs accurately. Dr. Watson indicated that he seldom puts a patient "on the couch any more," as he wishes to observe their facial expressions and body reactions.

THE COMMUNICATION PROCESS

Communication includes three processes: sharing, understanding, and clarifying. All involve two-way action between people. In social work agencies these processes are particularly significant. Sharing—the sending and receiving process—can take place in a variety of ways, either verbally, nonverbally,

---

[4]Jurgen Ruesch and Weldon Rees, *Nonverbal Communication* (Berkeley: University of California Press, 1956).

or in writing. It can and should go up and down the staff hierarchy, as well as sideways.

Understanding, the second element of communication, means that what is said and what is heard are basically the same. If a worker says one thing and the recipient "hears" something else, communication is not taking place. This commonly occurs. We often hear something that was not said or misinterpret what was. Understanding involves the attempt to listen realistically to what is said, so that the message of the sender and the message received are consonant.

The third process, clarifying, is particularly significant in bringing about effective communication. If two people are talking and one is uncertain about what has been said or what is meant, questions should be asked to clarify the issue. The aim in clarification should not be to prove that one is right or wrong but rather to understand what has been said. No one wins a battle when differences are not resolved.

Redfield describes the principal elements in the communication process as applied to public administration in Figure 13–1. Fulmer reduces the components of the communication process to a simple diagram, illustrated by Figure 13–2.

A person with an idea or feeling decides to share it with someone else. It is encoded into some form of language (written, spoken, or body) and then transmitted, unless noises block or obliterate the message. "When the message is received via the eyes, ears, or emotions of the second person, it passes to the brain, where the language is *decoded*. The resulting impressions make up the *received idea*."[5] It is to be hoped that the originating and receiving idea

FIGURE 13–1   **Elements of the Communication Process.** From Charles E. Redfield, "The Theory of Communication: Its Application to Public Administration," in Harry A. Schatz, *Social Work Administration: A Resource Book* (New York: Council on Social Work Education, 1970), p. 174. By permission of the publisher, The University of Chicago Press.

Communicator (speaker, sender, issuer)
   who

Transmits (says, sends, issues)

Messages (orders, reports, suggestions)
   to a

Communicatee (addressee, respondent, audience)
   to influence the behavior of the
   communicatee, as seen in the

Response (reply, reaction)

[5]Robert M. Fulmer, *The New Management*, 4th ed. (New York: Macmillan, 1988), p. 256.

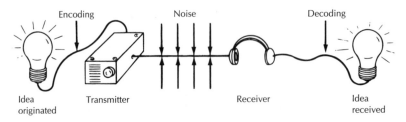

FIGURE 13-2   **The Communication Process.** From Robert M. Fulmer, *The New Management,* 4th ed. (New York: Macmillan, 1988), p. 256.

are exactly the same, although this rarely occurs. The closer their congruence, the better the communication.

Communication is a skill. The ability to communicate can be developed and improved through practice. Some people are particularly skilled communicators; others are not. In social work agencies, communication skills of administrators and team members must be developed to improve human relationships and the delivery of social services.

An educational film entitled *Avoiding Communication Breakdown* presents four problems that often develop in agencies or organizations: (1) message competition, (2) ego and status threats, (3) false expectations, and (4) too many links. Message competition involves who says what and when. An administrator may be busy and will not listen, or workers may not present their messages clearly. If the director is in a conference and a worker calls to talk, there is message competition. The director may not be able to give equal attention to the two messages and may slight one of them.

Sometimes workers feel that their ego and status are threatened by what they say. They may hesitate to speak for fear of saying the wrong thing or not saying something worthwhile. They may feel free to talk to coworkers but not to their supervisors. Often difficulties are caused by false expectations of what a message should be. Or there may be too many links; that is, a message may be handed from worker to worker and garbled along the way. When it reaches its final destination, it may be so changed that its meaning is different from, or even opposite to, what was intended originally.

In effective communication, people try to talk *with* each other rather than *to* or *at* each other. No one likes to be treated like a servant, and workers in an agency are no exception. Talking with a staff member on an equal level makes the flow of information and feelings a two-way process and facilitates communication. Dictatorship and an "I'm always right" attitude are strongly resented. Absolute opinions usually cause trouble. It is preferable to say, "It seems to me to be this way, but I'm not sure. What do you think?" Many workers hesitate to express their ideas and feelings if they are speaking to an all-knowing authoritarian.

Some workers attack or hurt one another psychologically or emotionally as they attempt to communicate. Questionable communication involves saying, for instance, "You said . . . now, don't deny it"; "You don't know what you're talking about"; "I'm right; you're absolutely wrong." Positive ways of questioning and even disagreeing include such expressions as "I'm not sure, but it seems to me . . ."; "I'm uncertain—what's your opinion?"; "I may be wrong and often am . . ."; "One possible way is . . ."; "I don't quite understand your point; help me to understand it better." The genius of communication is the art of asking, not dictating orders or bullying.

Fulmer suggests that brevity is ordinarily a desirable aspect of communication. He observes that the Gettysburg Address contains only 266 words, the Ten Commandments only 297, and yet a government order to reduce the price of cabbage required 26,911 words. "When you know what to say, it doesn't take many words to say it."[6]

Flippo and Munsinger believe that there are many ways of facilitating communication in a management operation to allow for a flow of information and feelings.

1. *The chain of command.* The flow of communication is a two-way process between superior and subordinate, with the superior having an open-door attitude.

2. *The grievance procedure.* A systematic grievance procedure is a fundamental device for communicating with those in positions of authority and allows for appeal beyond the authority of the immediate supervisor.

3. *The complaint system.* "Gripe boxes" may be established to provide for communication with the authorities while still maintaining anonymity.

4. *Counseling.* Perhaps regular supervisors or special staff counselors talk with staff members.

5. *Morale questionnaires.* This channel preserves the identity of workers yet provides comments about the firm and its management.

6. *An open-door policy.* It is particularly important for supervisors to be available when needed.

7. *Exit interview.* This may give the organization an opportunity to obtain from employees who leave some of their feelings and views of the workplace and its atmosphere.

8. *Grapevine.* This channel occurs spontaneously and often provides management with meaningful clues about staff problems.

9. *Labor union.* Both formal and informal conveyance of employees' feelings and demands may take place via this channel.

10. *The informer.* Although used at times, this channel is generally questioned by professionals.

11. *Special meetings.* These vary in kind and scope but may be used for the consideration of various policies, procedures, problems, and decisions, as well as to get employee feedback.

12. *The ombudsman.* This person attempts to represent workers when problems arise with the company and acts in a conciliatory manner to solve differences.[7]

[6]Ibid., p. 261.

[7]Edwin B. Flippo and Gary M. Munsinger, *Management*, 4th ed. (Boston: Allyn and Bacon, 1978), pp. 430–431.

Facts and Feelings

Communication in social work, whether therapeutic or administrative, encompasses both facts and feelings. An understanding of this duality is essential for effective agency administration. Facts and ideas about an agency need to be stated clearly and often so that staff members are aware of policies, problems, plans, decisions, and activities of the agency. These may be transmitted in writing, verbally, or both.

Some administrators communicate too often and say too much about agency operations. Others are too withdrawn. Staff members need to know about current developments, including anticipated changes, decisions, and problems confronting the agency. Not only should data be shared but so should attitudes, opinions, and priorities related to them, so that the staff is aware of what their leaders think and why.

In addition to facts and thoughts, feelings are particularly important in communication. These ordinarily come through with the most clarity in face-to-face relationships—an interview, a committee meeting, or a staff conference. Administrators need to convey to their staff what they really feel and also to discuss their priorities with appropriate explanations.

Length of Communication

Another important factor in administrative communication is its length. Obviously, a message should be neither too long nor too short. In verbal communication, length depends on whether an individual conference, committee session, or staff meeting is taking place. In each instance it is helpful to have at least a tentative time limit for communicating ideas and feelings. Any of these meetings can be too long or too short. Exceptions must sometimes be made, but ordinarily there should be a prearranged stopping time. On the one hand, ample time should be allocated for difficult decisions or personal problems. On the other hand, some administrators do not stop once the situation is under control and so begin to undo what they have accomplished.

Sometimes the amount of time for communication is limited. This necessitates careful preparation, making every minute count. For example, a social work administrator was invited to appear before a regional policymaking body. He was asked to prepare a presentation about a recommendation for the establishment of an organization of social workers within the region. The board was extremely busy and could only allocate two minutes for this presentation. This social worker traveled 700 miles to make his pitch. He had prepared adequately, made his point in two minutes, and secured the approval needed from the board.

In 1974 the Council on Social Work Education was invited to appear before the finance committee of the U.S. Senate to explain its services and make recommendations about funding for social work education. The council leaders were allocated fifteen minutes for their presentation and ten minutes for questions and discussion. Four social work administrators from different parts of the country participated in this presentation. Even though time was limited, the results were positive. Effective communication resulted from careful preparation.

Listening

An important part of communication, of course, is being an effective listener. Fulmer, from the management arena, suggests the following practical guidelines for listening:

1. Stop talking. You cannot listen if you are talking.
2. Put the talker at ease. Help him feel that he is free to talk.
3. Show her that you want to listen. Look and act interested. Do not read your mail while she talks. Listen to understand rather than to oppose.
4. Remove distractions. Don't doodle, tap, or shuffle papers. It might be quieter if you would shut the door.
5. Empathize with the talker. Try to put yourself in his place so that you can see his point of view.
6. Be patient. Allow plenty of time. Do not interrupt her. Don't start for the door or walk away.
7. Hold your temper. An angry person gets the wrong meaning from words.
8. Go easy on argument and criticism, which will put him on the defensive. He may clam up or get angry. Don't argue: even if you win, you lose.
9. Ask questions. This encourages her and shows you are listening. It helps to develop points further.
10. Stop talking. This is first and last because all other commandments depend on it. You just cannot do a good listening job while you are talking.[8]

According to Bedeian, failures in listening are frequent and "include not hearing what was said, hearing only part of what was said, and hearing information incorrectly." He reports that the principal reason for these limitations is "that most people talk at about 125 words a minute, whereas they listen and understand at four times that rate."[9]

Repetition

Many administrators think that they can make a statement once to staff members, verbally or in writing, and that is sufficient. Most people have short memories and are unable to recall most of what they hear and read. If information, plans, and events are important, it is essential that they be mentioned more than once. Often, staff members do not read what comes to their desks. Sometimes they do not hear what is presented in staff meetings because they

[8]Fulmer, *New Management*, p. 261.
[9]Arthur G. Bedeian, *Management*, 3rd ed. (Fort Worth, TX: Dryden Press, 1993), p. 542.

are thinking of something else. Thus, it is apparent that repetition is often necessary for effective communication.

The Five C's of Communication

Fulmer lists five C's that are particularly important for effective communication: clarity, completeness, conciseness, concreteness, and correctness.

1. *Clarity.* Ambiguity makes it possible for people to give different signals and directions, even at the same time. Messages should be simple and clear.
2. *Completeness.* An instruction that is only partially complete is difficult to follow.
3. *Conciseness.* The shorter a presentation, the better, as long as it covers the subject.
4. *Concreteness.* Communication should be on target. It should be very specific, citing names and expectations, so that no misunderstanding arises.
5. *Correctness.* If false information is reported, difficulties ensue from the outset. Accuracy is essential.[10]

LOGISTICS OF COMMUNICATION

Administrators in social work use a variety of techniques for communicating and interacting with staff members. The following are some of the more common methods.

Minutes of Meetings.   A highlighted account of the main actions and information discussed in a meeting can be effective when reported in minutes. These help to remind participants what they talked about and what actions will be performed.

Staff Meetings.   Staff meetings serve two main purposes: communication and decision making by both executives and team members. These communications can be effective given orally, but with written, concise minutes as a follow-up.

Letters and Notes.   Letters and notes can be used for congratulatory and informational purposes. Capable administrators send complimentary letters to members of their staff when they complete significant tasks or receive special recognition.

Informal Conferences.   An administrator who talks with staff members periodically can usually develop a positive relationship with them. Conferences also provide an opportunity for the worker to share ideas, questions,

---

[10]Fulmer, *New Management*, pp. 269–272.

and feelings with the administrator. Some workers request regular conferences with their superiors—once a month, for instance—to allow for direct
communication between them. Others prefer to get together only when
specific needs arise.

Newsletters.   A newsletter can be effective within an agency. Newsletters may vary in size and format, depending on the size of and services performed by the agency. Information sent periodically to the staff keeps it aware
of current developments.

Bulletin Boards.   One or two workers may be asked to maintain bulletin boards, which may be divided into formal materials and informal
announcements or other kinds of listings.

Social Activities.   Luncheons, receptions, and other recreational and
social activities may be effective in bringing about informal communication
for and with agency associates.

Suggestion Box.   A suggestion box provides confidentiality to the
worker making the suggestion yet often brings helpful recommendations.

Telephone Calls.   Sometimes a telephone call is more effective than a
personal note in giving recognition to a staff member or community leader or
expressing appreciation for some accomplishment.

The Grapevine.   In a grapevine information is received and passed on
informally. Sometimes the information is merely rumor and can be damaging. At other times, staff members pass around news and opinions that are
important to the welfare of the agency. A competent administrator recognizes
the value of this kind of communication. Sometimes an administrator inten-
tionally gives information to a staff member, anticipating that it will be passed
on informally to others.

Improving Communication

Because communication is important in administration, numerous attempts
have been made to study the process and improve its effectiveness. Weinshall
introduced the Communicogram, a method by which each participating manager records his or her telephone and face-to-face interactions with other
managers. The recordings are fed into a computer and checked with one
another to find out whether they match. Each participating manager subse-
quently receives his or her own communication results, the agreements and
disagreements about the interactions recorded, and the degree of consensus
about what has occurred in the interaction. "The personal results he receives
are compared with the averages of his own managerial group. This enables

him to draw conclusions as to his own behavior, his suitability to the requirements of his job, and what he could do about it."[11]

Conducting meetings by administrators of social work agencies is one
area in which considerable improvement is needed. Often time is wasted and
the desired results are not achieved because of the lack of leadership skills.
Whetten and Cameron observe that skills can be improved in this process,
and they suggest four crucial steps for an effective meeting: specify the purpose of the meeting, invite the right number and mix of participants, carefully
plan the meeting's content and format, and effectively manage the process of
the meeting[12] (see Figure 13–3).

SUMMARY

Communication is particularly important in social work agencies because it
relates to efficiency, effectiveness, and morale. Verbal and nonverbal communications are both significant. Feelings as well as facts and ideas need to
be shared in effective communication.

The process of communication includes sharing, understanding, and
clarifying. Time dynamics are important in effective communication.

Communication can take place in a variety of ways, both written and
verbal. Repetition is essential for effective communication. The five C's
in communication are clarity, completeness, conciseness, concreteness, and
correctness.

More emphasis is needed in social work education and practice in
improving skills in communication, both for administrators and practitioners.

QUESTIONS FOR DISCUSSION

1. Why is effective communication so important in administrative leadership?

FIGURE 13–3 **The Four P's: Steps for Planning and Managing an Effective Meeting.** Source: David A.
Whetten and Kim S. Cameron, *Developing Management Skills: Applied Commun-
ication Skills* (New York: HarperCollins College Publishers, 1993), p. 23. Reprinted by
permission.

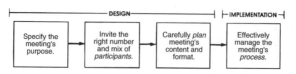

[11]Theodore D. Weinshall, *Managerial Communication: Concepts, Approaches and Techniques*
(London: Academic Press, 1979), pp. 3–4.

[12]David A. Whetten and Kim S. Cameron, *Developing Management Skills: Applied Communication Skills* (New York: HarperCollins College Publishers, 1993), p. 23.

2. Relate a positive or negative personal experience involving communication.

3. Compare and contrast the effectiveness of verbal and nonverbal communication.

4. What are the main steps in the communication process?

5. Do you agree or disagree with the statement "Feelings are often more important than facts in communicating with others."

6. Describe and illustrate the five C's of communication.

7. What are your best suggestions for improving listening abilities?

8. How do leaders who are effective conductors of meetings proceed?

SPECIAL ACTIVITIES

1. Invite a staff member from the communications department to talk to your class on practical suggestions for improving communication skills for social work administrators.

2. Demonstrate some of the problems in communication by asking six class members to take part in the following exercise: Give one person a paragraph describing an automobile accident. Then ask that person to relate, privately and verbally, the description to person 2. Have person 2 do the same with person 3, and so on. Compare the written paragraph with the sixth person's description. Discuss the results.

3. Invite two teams of three people each to debate the following statement: Messages often relate more to nonverbal actions than to verbal statements.

SELECTED REFERENCES

BASKIN, OTIS W., and CRAIG E. ARONOFF. *Interpersonal Communication in Organizations*. Santa Monica, CA: Goodyear Publishing, 1980.

BEDEIAN, ARTHUR G. "Effective Communication." *Management*, 3rd ed., pp. 523–555. Fort Worth, TX: Dryden Press, 1993.

CARLISLE, HOWARD M. *Management Essentials: Concepts for Productivity and Innovation*, 2nd ed., pp. 343–370. Chicago: Science Research Associates, 1987.

ERIKSEN, KARIN. *Communication Skills for Human Services*. Reston, VA: Reston Publishing Co., 1979.

FEIN, EDITH, and ILENE STAFF. "Measuring the Use of Time." *Administration in Social Work* 15, No. 4 (1991), 81–93.

FULMER, ROBERT M. *The New Management*, 4th ed., pp. 253–275. New York: Macmillan, 1988.

MUNSON, CARLTON E., ed. *Social Work Supervision, Classic Statements and Critical Issues*. New York: Free Press, 1979.

RESNICK, HERMAN, and RINO J. PATTI. *Change from Within: Humanizing Social Welfare Organizations*. Philadelphia: Temple University Press, 1980.

ROBERTS, KARLENE H. *Communicating in Organizations*. Chicago: Science Research Associates, 1984.

WHETTEN, DAVID A., and KIM S. CAMERON. *Developing Management Skills: Applied Communication Skills*. New York: HarperCollins College Publishers, 1993.

14

Community Relations

The state department of corrections decided to establish a halfway house for selected prisoners. Plans were made to locate it in a residential area near some businesses. Immediately, irate protests came from citizens residing in this neighborhood. They asserted, "We do not want a prison in our backyard!" "We would be afraid of becoming victims of crime!"

The director of the department called the staff together and discussed the pros and cons of the planned move. After careful consideration, it was decided to go forward but to do everything possible to explain the proposed plans in advance to the residents of that neighborhood and to all inhabitants of the city.

The administrator issued press releases to the newspapers, radio, and television. In addition, staff members interviewed several residents of the neighborhood where they planned to open the halfway house. The attitude of most of the people living in that neighborhood changed. The department of corrections was able to proceed with its plans to establish the halfway house.

Six months later, several of the residents of the neighborhood were interviewed. Most felt positively about the correctional unit in their own backyards. A few retained negative feelings and questioned the advisability and fairness of its location.

Why was the halfway house accepted by the neighborhood? Because a capable social work administrator understood the neighborhood and interpreted to its residents the need for and meaning of such a unit.

Community relations are an essential part of social work administration. In theory and practice, social workers are knowledgeable about community resources and ordinarily are capable of utilizing them. In working with individual and family problems, social workers must understand the community network—its limitations and liabilities as well as its resources. Administrators also need to be aware of local social problems and have a desire to alleviate them or prevent their occurrence. They recognize that the mission of social work is to help, whenever and wherever possible, to reduce human suffering.

Mary Richmond, a pioneer practitioner, focused on the challenge of community social work with these words, reported by Edith Abbott more than sixty years ago: "The good social worker doesn't go on mechanically helping people out of a ditch. Pretty soon she begins to find out what ought to be done to get rid of the ditch."[1]

Social work administrators spend most of their time working with their staff so that together they can provide meaningful services. Since each agency is a part of the community in which it is located, administrators also spend considerable time and effort on community activities and services—for example, preparing and presenting public relations materials and participating in meetings with other agency representatives. Competent administrators do what they can to understand the community in which they operate, its social problems and resources, and utilize their knowledge and skills to further the interests of both their agency and the total community.

BACKGROUND

By the turn of the twentieth century, social work emphasized treatment of the individual and the family, or social casework. Group work came into its own in the 1930s, with an emphasis on the group as a tool for reducing problems of individuals and families. Within the past few decades, community organization has come to the fore as an excellent method for helping disadvantaged people within their communities. Promoting effective community relations is a distinguishing characteristic of the social work profession. Competent administrators recognize the power inherent in community resources and work closely with people in key positions.

The 1962 curriculum policy statement of the Council on Social Work Education (CSWE) included community organization as one of three basic methods, along with casework and group work. The 1969 curriculum policy statement did not list specific methods but provided for concentrations. Several graduate schools of social work offer a concentration in community orga-

---

[1]Edith Abbott, "The Social Caseworker and the Enforcement of Industrial Legislation," in *Proceedings of the National Conference on Social Work, 1918* (Chicago: Rogers and Hall, 1919), p. 313.

nization. Some of these programs require two full years of graduate study. Others offer one year of generic social work and in the second year place particular emphasis on community services. The concept of community organization has been broadened somewhat in recent years to include an emphasis on the planning process. In 1980 the CSWE, in its annual statistical report, defined this area as "community organization, planning, development." A combination of concentrations was permitted by the CSWE 1992 curriculum policy statement for master's programs, which makes it possible for a combined concentration with administration and an allied area, such as community organization or social planning.

Dunham suggests that community organization is the

> conscious process of social interaction and a method of social work concerned with any or all of the following objectives: (1) the meeting of broad needs and bringing about and maintaining adjustment between needs and resources in a community or other area; (2) helping people to deal more effectively with their problems and objectives, by helping them develop, strengthen, and maintain qualities of participation, self-direction, and cooperation; (3) bringing about changes in community and group relationships and in the distribution of decision-making power.[2]

McNeil sees community organization as "the process by which people of communities, as individual citizens or as representatives of groups, join together to determine social welfare needs, plan ways of meeting them, and mobilize the necessary resources."[3]

Brager and Specht give a slightly different definition—closely allied to administration—when they state that community organization is a

> method of intervention whereby individuals, groups, and organizations engage in planned action to influence social problems. It is concerned with the enrichment, development, and/or change of social institutions, and involves two major related processes: planning (that is, identifying problem areas, diagnosing causes, and formulating solutions) and organizing (that is, developing the constituencies and devising the strategies necessary to effect action).[4]

Kettner, Daley, and Nichols define the community approach in the context of a planned change model. The three components of their model include the change process, arenas for practice, and types of interventive effort anticipated. The change process includes the following nine steps:

1. Identifying the change opportunity
2. Analyzing the change opportunity

---

[2]Arthur Dunham, *The New Community Organization* (New York: Thomas Y. Crowell, 1970), p. 4.

[3]C. F. McNeil, "Community Organization for Social Welfare," *Social Work Year Book, 1954* (New York: American Association of Social Workers, 1954), p. 121.

[4]George Brager and Harry Specht, *Community Organization* (New York: Columbia University Press, 1973), pp. 27–28.

3. Setting goals and objectives
4. Designing and structuring the change effort
5. Resource planning
6. Implementing the change effort
7. Monitoring the change effort
8. Evaluating the change effort
9. Reassessing and stabilizing the situation.[5]

From these and other definitions it is apparent that community organization may connote any one of three meanings: a field, a stage, or a method. A field of service includes such agencies as community welfare councils, United Way, and community information centers. A stage refers to a level of development and portrays it in terms of a community's past, present, and future. Community organization is one of the major methods in social work, one that utilizes the *intergroup* process in trying to understand and solve social problems. It is an ally of social work administration, and they are involved in many joint efforts.

UNDERLYING PRINCIPLES

Social work administrators need to understand the principles of community social work. McNeil describes several that are universally applicable:

1. Community organization for social welfare is concerned with people and their needs. Its objective is to enrich human life by bringing about and maintaining a progressively more effective adjustment between social welfare resources and social welfare needs.
2. The community is the primary client in community organization for social welfare. The community may be a neighborhood, city, county, state, or nation. Rapidly, too, there has emerged the international community. . . .
3. It is an axiom in community organization that the community is to be understood and accepted as it is and where it is. . . .
4. All of the people of the community are concerned in its health and welfare services. Representation of all interests and elements in the population and their full and meaningful participation are essential objectives in community organization.
5. The fact of ever-changing human needs and the reality of relationships between and among people and groups are the dynamics in the community organization process. Acceptance of the concept of purposeful change and John Dewey's philosophy of the "ever-enduring process of perfecting, maturing, refining" as goals in community organization is basic.
6. Interdependence of all threads in the social welfare fabric of organization is a fundamental truth. No single agency can usefully "live unto itself alone," but is constantly performing its functions in relation to others.

[5]Peter Kettner, John M. Daley, and Ann Weaver Nichols, *Initiating Change in Organizations and Communities* (Monterey, CA: Brooks/Cole, 1985), p. 25.

7. Community organization for social welfare as a process is a part of generic social work. . . . [6]

Ross suggests fundamental assumptions on which community social work is based:

1. Communities of people can develop the capacity to deal with their own problems.
2. People want change and are capable of making it.
3. People should participate in making, adjusting, or controlling the major changes taking place in their communities.
4. Changes in community living that are self-imposed or self-developed have a meaning and permanence that imposed changes do not have. "Man, insofar as he acts on nature to change it, changes his own nature," says Hegel.
5. A "holistic approach" can deal successfully with problems with which a "fragmented approach" cannot cope.
6. Democracy requires cooperative participation and action in the affairs of the community, and people must learn the skills that make this possible.
7. Frequently communities of people need help in organizing to deal with their needs, just as many individuals need help in coping with their own individual needs.[7]

The National Association of Social Workers has maintained a vital interest in community social work practice. Its committee on community organization summarized the purposes and specific objectives of community organization as follows:

1. Providing the community or segments of the community with the opportunity to mobilize its resources to meet social problems or prevent their onset:
    a. Providing a means for citizens to mobilize, express, and discharge efficiently their responsibility to the community.
    b. Providing an important means for the social agencies to discharge efficiently their responsibility to the community.
    c. Providing an important means for the social work profession to meet its community responsibilities.
2. Providing an important means of interaction between segments of the community:
    a. Between a variety of citizens and groups concerned with community welfare.
    b. Between specializations within the profession and between practitioners and community leadership.
    c. Between specializations and institutional forces such as the school system, the medical profession, the legal profession, etc.
    d. Between the political community and the social welfare community.

[6]McNeil, "Community Organization," p. 123.

[7]Murray G. Ross, *Community Organization, Theory, Principles and Practice*, 2nd ed. (New York: Harper & Row, 1967), pp. 86–93.

3. Providing social welfare planning service to the community through:
   a. Development of social welfare plans.
   b. Effecting these plans.
   c. Influencing social welfare policies and other public policies related or having a potential influence upon the welfare of people.
   d. Assisting in the mobilization of adequate financing, governmental and voluntary.[8]

COMMUNITY SOCIAL WORK PROCESSES

Community social work involves several processes. A knowledge of these is essential for working with other agencies in a community. The following is a brief discussion of the major processes of community social work practice.

Research

Research is an attempt to gather facts, to ascertain truth. Various kinds of research are sponsored in community agencies, including statistical studies, surveys, case studies, demonstration projects, and program evaluations. The underlying premise of research is that to act intelligently community leaders must know the basic facts about their agency and other related agencies. They need to be aware of pertinent data about their services and the people they serve.

Most community organization agencies sponsor research, and some large ones employ professionals who devote all their time to research. Administrators need to be aware of the community research that is being conducted and of information that becomes available as projects are completed and publications appear. Most administrators are committed to sponsoring research in their agencies that can benefit their own services and be of value to other agencies in the community research network. Also, administrators are now joining with other administrators in carrying out interagency research projects.

Planning

Planning is a purposeful formulation of future actions and procedures (see Chapter 4). It is used extensively in community social work. Representatives of various groups meet together, make decisions regarding social problems, and suggest solutions.

Ecklein and Lauffer define and illustrate, with case studies, many functions and roles of the community social worker, particularly as he or she becomes an effective social planner. They talk about the social planner as a

[8]Reprinted with permission from *Defining Community Organization Practice* (New York, 1962), pp. 8–9. Copyright 1964, National Association of Social Workers, Inc.

"grantsman," in which role he or she is a facilitator, helping to get money and resources for projects. Grantsmanship is considered both a political and technical art. Ecklein and Lauffer describe the social planner as a "concertmaster," who has a challenging opportunity to build and maintain support, particularly to coordinate and integrate various activities and developments related to the understanding of social problems and their solutions. They discuss the community planner as a "technician" who must have the ability to interpret a considerable amount of information and help with the mechanics and actualization of social action, including the use of the concepts and principles of management. These include Program Evaluation and Review Technique (PERT) and Program Planning and Budgeting Systems (PPBS).[9]

Coordination

Coordination is the process of working together to avoid unnecessary conflict and duplication of effort. A major process in community social work theoretically, coordination should help to avoid unnecessary duplication and to fill gaps in social services.

Coordination includes cooperation but goes much further. Individuals may cooperate with one another in negative action that does not benefit the community or may even be hurtful to it. Coordination is basically positive and calls for cooperation and additional activities. It should help to integrate various resources for improving the community, solving social problems, and enriching the daily life of the inhabitants. Interorganizational exchanges and referral networks are currently being utilized effectively to improve services and to bring more comprehensive coverage for those in need. As agency administrators share and coordinate their programs with one another, they ordinarily increase the quantity and quality of their services.

Organization

Organization is the process of establishing a structure to accomplish selected goals (see Chapter 8). In community social work, it is a method of formulating a structure to consider community needs and resources and to utilize these resources to satisfy current needs.

Formal and informal organization are both important. Formal organization concerns the visible structure of an agency, which includes the hierarchy from the director to the lowest level of worker. Informal organization concerns matters outside the visible structure of the agency, particularly what occurs across the coffee cup and in other social situations.

[9]Joan Levin Ecklein and Armand A Lauffer, *Community Organizers and Social Planners* (New York: Wiley and the Council on Social Work Education, 1972), pp. 272–376.

Financing

Financing is the process of collecting, budgeting, and spending funds for community needs. Collection is usually carried out by the combined efforts of professionals, United Way drives, and private individuals.

Budgeting is usually done by a committee in a community agency that hears recommendations from its different members and then makes allocations for the coming year. These are related, of course, to the amount of money that can be collected through a United Way drive.

The way funds are spent depends on the individual community agency and its needs for the delivery of social services. Most funds are spent on agency salaries, but financial resources are also utilized for physical facilities.

Consultation

In consultation, an expert talks with administrators and workers. This person may be from a different professional discipline or a specialist within social work. Consultation is the process of acquiring professional information and guidelines from an expert whose knowledge can be helpful to staff.

Social work is using more consultants today than ever before, including those from such fields as psychiatry, psychology, nursing, and physical therapy. Social workers also are engaging other social workers in consultation in increased numbers. Many social workers are full-time consultants in the social service network.

Committee Operation

In one sense, committee operation is the essence of social work and community practice. Agencies organize committees to make studies, formulate proposals, make decisions, and implement policies and decisions.

Committee membership and activities significantly affect the efficiency and effectiveness of agencies. Administrators need to know about community committees and how to use them effectively (see Chapter 9).

Negotiation

Negotiation is a process of resolving conflicts, a neutral third party often acting as an intermediary. As individuals and groups differ on many policies and decisions, they often need an opportunity to get together, listen to one another, and come to an acceptable compromise.

Effective negotiation implies a coming together of administrators and/or workers with different points of view. The aim is not to prove who is right or wrong but to seek what is best for the agency and the services being provided. The basic premise of negotiation is that although differences exist, professionals can resolve them by working with rather than combating one another. This is a new field of emphasis in social work, encompassing principles, processes, and skills in social work administration. Negotiation is important within agencies, among the workers, as well as outside of them, where administrators from several agencies will talk, listen, and make compromises for the benefit of all.

Gibelman and Demone observe that negotiation is a powerful process and is needed more in today's world. They suggest that

> negotiating should be recognized and brought into social work as a skill and practice area. With the enormous growth of purchase of service contracting between public and private organizations, the growing number of interorganizational exchanges and mergers, the expansion of case management, and renewed interest in coordination, both public and private sector employees are increasingly involved in negotiating to achieve mutually desired ends.[10]

They conclude that the "ultimate objective of negotiation is for both sides to succeed."

Recording

Recording is the process of keeping an account of the considerations and actions of committees and other groups concerned with community problems and plans. Keeping minutes of committee meetings and staff meetings is essential in the administrative process and in community practice.

PROFESSIONAL ROLES

Certain roles have been found to be advantageous and applicable to community practice in social work. Administrators who understand these roles and utilize them well are likely to be more effective in their agencies as well as able to contribute to other community agencies and their services.

The Committee on Community Organization of NASW observed that

> method in the community organization practice is the orderly application of a relevant body of knowledge guided by social work values. The worker applies systematically and sequentially this coherent body of knowledge employing practice wisdom and learned behavior through characteristic, distinctive and describable procedures to help the community engage in a process of planned change toward community improvement.[11]

---

[10]Margaret Gibelman and Harold W. Demone, Jr., "Negotiating: A Tool for Inter-Organizational Coordinating," *Administration in Social Work* 14, No. 4 (1990), 41.

[11]*Defining Community Organization*, p. 15.

The committee also described the range of professional roles:

1. Enabling the community to engage in establishing goals and setting priorities
2. Helping community groups take effective action
3. Guiding the participants in the process through difficulties
4. Initiating action through education, demonstration or other similar techniques[12]

COMMUNITY SERVICE AGENCIES

Administrators of social work agencies must know the organization agencies in their communities so that they can tap their resources and work cooperatively with them to help deliver social services.

Community Welfare Councils

The London Charity Organization Society, established in 1869, was the first attempt made to coordinate community activities. An effort was made to eliminate duplication and fraud in relief administration, with the aim of improving total services in the community through better cooperation and coordination. In the United States, the first organized attempt to coordinate and systematize social services took place in 1877, with the founding of the Buffalo Charity Organization Society. Many private agencies existed at that time, and there was a considerable need to avoid duplication and to fill gaps in total services as well as to reduce competition.

The first community welfare councils were established in 1909 in Pittsburgh and Milwaukee. Called councils of social agencies, there are some 450 of them at present. These councils ordinarily have three main areas of concern: health, welfare, and recreation. Most have a delegate body representative of the agencies and diverse groups in the community. Usually a board of directors makes the policies and basic decisions of the agency and endeavors to represent the communities in which the board members are located.

The work of the councils is carried out by a professional staff with the assistance of volunteers. Committees are used extensively and usually include community leaders and council staff. The councils provide the following services:

1. Collect facts and information regarding community problems and plans of action.
2. Disseminate information to the various publics in the community, to increase their understanding of community problems and their solutions.
3. Formulate plans of action for the elimination of community problems and for supplying community needs.
4. Coordinate community services. The representatives of the various agencies that meet together through council auspices become better acquainted with total community services and can ordinarily cooperate and help one another avoid unnecessary duplication and fill gaps in services.

[12]Ibid.

5. Raise standards of community services through various interdisciplinary committees involving both professional and lay people. Councils, as a result of scientific studies and careful deliberations, often provide guidelines for improving and raising standards and services within the community.
6. Help facilitate referrals for people who need social services. Some communities have social service exchanges attached to the community welfare councils. Other councils provide community information services, operating mainly on a telephone basis, for answering inquiries and making referrals to proper agencies.
7. Help provide training services for both professional and lay leaders in the community. Welfare councils often sponsor institutes and workshops for this very purpose. A popular example is the sponsoring of institutes for volunteer workers who come together with professionally trained leaders to help them better understand the jobs they are to perform and how best to carry them out.[13]

United Way and Federated Financial Drives

Originally private agencies conducted financial drives on their own. As the number of individual agencies increased, the suggestion was made to organize a federated drive, for the benefit of all agencies. It was hoped that this would avoid competition and, with a coordinated, cooperative effort, would bring an increase in donations and funds. The first such federated drive took place in Liverpool, England, in 1873. Soon thereafter, in 1887, the first federated drive in the United States was conducted under the auspices of the Associated Charities of Denver, Colorado. The drive was relatively simple, compared to those today. Twenty-three agencies joined together and raised a budget of $20,000.

The name Community Chest became popular after World War I in designating federated fund-raising. Federated drives expanded, so that in 1978 the 2,300 members of the United Way in American communities raised more than a billion dollars for the support of 35,000 participating agencies; nearly 5 million volunteers were utilized in these united campaigns, and 40 million individual contributions were secured. The name United Fund replaced Community Chest, and today United Way, a more generic name, is used by most communities for their federated drives.

Administrators of social work agencies should know about federated drives for two reasons: (1) they may want to ask for funds or services from the federated drive, and (2) they will probably want to participate in the annual drive to collect money for building the community and reducing social problems.

Central Registration and Information Services

The Social Service Exchange was introduced during the latter part of the nineteenth century in an attempt to avoid duplication of services, particularly to

---

[13]Rex A. Skidmore and Milton G. Thackeray, *Introduction to Social Work*, 3rd ed. (Englewood Cliffs, NJ: Prentice Hall, 1982), p. 299. Copyright © 1982. Reprinted by permission.

reduce fraud and the misuse of funds. Its aim was to prevent an individual or family from getting funds from more than one agency. The basic plan was that all agencies would register their clients with the social service exchange, which could be used to avoid duplication.

In recent years, most social service exchanges have been abolished. The number in operation in the United States declined from 320 in 1956 to 42 in 1969, and there are fewer at present, for several reasons. Concerns of privacy, of giving a central agency information told in confidence to a particular agency, have been raised, as has concern about the inefficiency of a comprehensive single agency. In other words, it is impossible to register every client with a given agency.

Community information services have replaced social service exchanges in many population centers. Such services consist of a telephone service staffed by qualified persons who have a comprehensive knowledge of local community agencies and resources. They describe available resources and make referrals to appropriate agencies for those who ask for help.

There are other significant kinds of community organization agencies and services. In some communities, neighborhood councils, based on geographic proximity and common interests, have been instituted in an attempt to solve specific social problems. For example, coordinating councils have been established in several metropolitan areas on a neighborhood basis in an attempt to reduce juvenile delinquency. Some of these have been effective, whereas others have made little headway. Other councils establish or improve recreational facilities or resources for the homeless.

Various kinds of referral networks are now in operation that help agencies assist one another in the delivery of social services. Two or more agencies in a given field—for example, child welfare or corrections—work out a system for cross-referencing information about clients and services. This works to their mutual advantage. Other patterns include a larger network, such as a cluster of agencies that join together in a referral system.

PUBLIC RELATIONS

Administrators need to be cognizant of the importance of public relations, both for their own agency and its services and for the community as a whole. In the past, minimal interest was shown in public relations by the social work field or by individual administrators. Today the picture is changing, and competent administrators are trying to obtain effective public relations, either with their own social work staff or by hiring public relations experts.

Salient principles of successful public relations were suggested by Elizabeth Haglund, director of public relations at the University of Utah, to social work graduate students.

1. Know where and what your goals are. What are your targets?
2. Know who you want to reach. Who are your publics?

3. Evaluate resources, such as money, facts, manpower, and skills available.
4. Note how your benefits dovetail with those you reach. Give before you get.
5. Know specific techniques of public relations in regard to preparation and participation regarding advertising, publicity, and brochures. Ask the questions, who, what, where, why, and how much. For example, brevity is important. Ordinarily one to two pages for newspapers is ample, and probably half a page for radio and TV is optimal.
6. Be absolutely honest.
7. Thank people. Show appreciation.

Public Relations and the Media

Competent social work administrators utilize various ways of interpreting their agencies to the public and reaching community members. These include television, radio, newspapers, brochures, books, and personal contacts. Many radio and TV stations will make short announcements and broadcast case vignettes as a public service to help interpret what agencies do and how the public and the community might utilize them more effectively.

Newspapers often publish accounts of significant research and activities of agencies and give case studies as examples, while preserving the anonymity of those involved. These accounts help the community to understand what the agency is and what it can do; such information can also lead to increased utilization of the agency by local residents. Annual reports and brochures may be prepared for distribution among professional and lay leaders to inform them of the agency's services and resources.

Personal contacts, through individual conferences and workshops, can be used to advantage by administrators. Face-to-face contact with a community leader may result in additional support for the agency or use of the agency by the community. Talking to civic groups, to interpret the agency's policies and services to community leaders, may be helpful.

Brawley believes that social workers seem to be hesitant in using the resources of sound public relations, particularly the news media. He concludes that "whatever the reason for this reluctance, it constitutes a real barrier to the appropriate use of the media for vital community education purposes. It needs to be overcome if greater community understanding and support are to be generated for needed social programs and services."[14]

The following case illustrates how public relations helped in the problem of mental illness.

PUBLIC RELATIONS TO CHANGE
ATTITUDES TOWARD MENTAL ILLNESS _____

Mental illness constitutes one of America's most serious unrecognized public health problems. Very few citizens understand mental illness, and many regard

[14]Edward A. Brawley, "The Mass Media: A Vital Adjunct to the New Community and Administrative Practice," *Administration in Social Work* 9, No. 4 (1985/1986), 72.

it with less sympathy than any other disability. When labeled as mentally ill, a person is often feared, stigmatized, and shunned.

A community with a lack of awareness can set up barriers for treatment, housing, and employment. The stigmas attached to mental illness give rise to discriminatory health insurance benefits, inadequate research dollars, and financially starved public mental-health care systems.

Mental illness is not caused by moral weakness but rather by an individual's complex genetic makeup. Like diabetes or heart disease, mental illness encompasses biological, psychological, and social causes.

The goal of a competent social service administrator is to help mentally ill people function normally in society. To do so, the public misperceptions of mental illness need to be overcome through a carefully orchestrated public relations campaign.

In an effort to understand the public's perception of mental illness, a division of mental health in a western state commissioned a survey to study the attitudes, perceptions, and stigmas concerning mental illness. Two surveys were commissioned in 1988 and 1992 and were conducted by a university research center.

The two studies revealed that the attitudes and perceptions among the population had not changed in five years. Both surveys revealed that 32 percent of the people surveyed believed that mental illness was caused by sinning, and 61 percent believed that it was caused by bad parenting.

The poll was helpful in giving the division hard data to recognize that their public relations campaign to educate the public was not working. The division carefully analyzed the data and brought out several key points of the survey, which were written into a press release and distributed to the media.

Media calls inundated the executive director's office by local journalists, who were intrigued by the story. They were amazed at the public's extreme misperceptions of mental illness. Through the department's public information officer, the journalists received further information and were granted personal interviews with mental-health professionals and mentally ill clients.

The media campaign was successful because a competent social service administrator and public relations staff were able not only to educate reporters in the preparation of accurate news stories but also to address and perhaps to overcome the public's misperceptions concerning mental illness. The two major local daily newspapers ran the story on the front page, and significant television news stories were presented.

Throughout the next six months, the public relations staff continued their positive campaign by refocusing their educational efforts in the schools, with community groups, and with the media. They also continued to provide current statistics and reports on current medical research, legislative efforts, and the importance of early diagnosis and appropriate treatment. Public relations to alter attitudes toward mental illness had made a beginning.

SERVICES OF VOLUNTEERS

Competent administrators recognize that volunteers are a major resource. The volunteer movement has gained momentum, and millions of volunteers provide social welfare and related services in almost every kind of setting. For example, twenty-five members of a Junior League in a middle-sized city spend half a day a week assisting with activities in the local comprehensive mental-health center. They provide their own cars and transport clients to and from the center. They care for the children in the waiting rooms and spend time with clients, as friends, helping with routine problems and decisions. Similarly, the Medical Wives Auxiliary in a metropolitan area invites its members to spend half a day at one of the local hospitals, performing a variety of tasks that facilitate medical and social services. They work at telephone switchboards, care for children, and perform many other helpful services.

In 1965, the U.S. Department of Labor estimated that 16 percent of all people over fourteen years of age (22 million people) made contributions to some health, education, or welfare service on a volunteer basis. More than half of them were between twenty-five and forty-four. Sieder reported that a 1969 Gallup poll found 69 million adults who indicated they would donate time to solve problems in their own communities. She observed that this was "undoubtedly a conservative figure since it omits the large number of youthful volunteers.[15] In 1974 some 37 million men and women, one of every four Americans over thirteen, did some form of volunteer work.

In 1973 the United Way of America made a quantitative study of volunteer activities. It revealed that the United Way and its member agencies averaged an estimated 2.4 billion volunteer person-hours per year and that the largest percentage of volunteer activities (over 80 percent) was in the area of direct services rather than in setting policy or raising funds.[16]

According to Silver, there are 821,000 tax-exempt and church nonprofit organizations along with 6 to 7 million community organizations in the United States and "nearly half the people fourteen years or older in this country volunteer." According to a Gallup poll in 1985, 48 percent of the population volunteered an average of 3.5 hours a week.[17] In 1988 contributions to voluntary organizations exceeded $100 billion, and 80 million people volunteered a total of 14.9 billion hours, which is worth at least another $150 billion.[18] Competent administrators tap these volunteer resources when the services fit the needs of the agency.

Power Politics

Effective administrators understand the importance of power politics in community affairs. They know that decisions are often made long before committees meet or before formal legislative action on public issues is taken. Administrators recognize that they have to be well acquainted with the

[15]Violet M. Sieder, "Volunteers," *Encyclopedia of Social Work, II* (New York: National Association of Social Workers, 1971), p. 1,525.
[16]*A Study of the Quantity of Volunteer Activity of United Way and Its Member Agencies* (Alexandria, VA: United Way of America, 1974), p. iv.
[17]Nora Silver, *At The Heart: The New Volunteer Challenge to Community Agencies* (Pleasanton, CA: Valley Volunteer Center, 1988), p. 10.
[18]Brian O'Connell, "Our Open Hearts and Open Wallets," *Deseret News*, January 26, 1989.

power structure of the community and know the people who, publicly or privately, play key roles in the political network.

Effective administrators become personally acquainted with key people who possess power and prestige in the community, so that they can communicate with them, interpret agency needs, and obtain support for strengthening the agency. A competent agency administrator spends considerable time away from the office, gaining support for the agency program through contacts with community leaders.

Patti and Dear observe that legislative advocacy by social workers is a promising path to social change, especially in an era of budgetary constraints, tax rollbacks and reductions, and expanding human needs. They recognize the limitations of rational argument but reaffirm its importance in the legislative process. They suggest that the legislative advocate can be a significant resource in bringing about change, especially under the following conditions: (1) the information is timely, (2) it is balanced, (3) assistance is provided in response to requests, and (4) alternatives are provided when necessary.[19]

INTERAGENCY COORDINATION

Capable administrators recognize that other agencies in the community are major resources, often in many ways, and that agencies that work together can often benefit one another. Effective administrators know other agencies and also have the skills to help coordinate joint planning and action.

Certain principles underpin successful interagency collaboration and coordination. Effective administrators understand these principles and use them advantageously. Wimpfheimer, Bloom, and Kramer list four main working principles for interagency collaboration: (1) belief that everyone is a winner, (2) acknowledged responsibility for the problem, (3) realization of common risk, and (4) acceptance of limits.[20] These principles are illustrated by the case that follows.

NEGOTIATING ABOUT OVERLAPPING CLIENTELE _____

Agency A has operated a legally mandated crisis intervention service for school-aged children over several years. During this time, the agency has disseminated information about its services to relevant gatekeepers through personal visits to schools, PTA meetings, pediatricians, and the juvenile authorities.

Following the enactment of state legislation for certain areas of children's services, Agency B expanded its treatment facility to include preventive services to children and youth, including a crisis intervention service. They prepared their literature informing gatekeepers in the community about their service program, and this produced some confusion by referral sources because of the apparent overlapping functions with the crisis intervention service. Moreover,

[19]Rino J. Patti and Ronald B. Dear, "Legislative Advocacy: One Path to Social Change," *Social Work* 20 (March 1975), 108–114.

[20]Rochelle Wimpfheimer, Martin Bloom, and Marge Kramer, "Inter-Agency Collaboration: Some Working Principles," *Administration in Social Work* 14, No. 4 (1990), 93–95.

several cases "fell through the cracks"—each agency thought the other was going to handle the cases—resulting in some unfavorable publicity in the local papers about both agencies. Thus, there was pressure for the directors of these agencies to get together to iron out the problem.

Both directors, who had known each other professionally for several years, had ultimate decision making authority in their agencies. In addition, the two had worked together successfully on numerous committees and task forces and had developed a respect for each others' abilities (Authority and Influence). The director of Agency A called the director of Agency B regarding the problem, but initially met with resistance about a joint meeting. She recognized that B did not feel comfortable with the substantive issues, especially if they were to be discussed in a public forum, even though he had strong value commitments to children and youth. Director B had many other tasks to deal with and did not feel this merited immediate attention. But director A insisted that the legislative directive was not clear and that both organizations needed to come to some working agreement about this issue since it was potentially very risky to their agencies' reputations (Common Risk and Timing). Director B agreed to a very small gathering of the department directors and the unit directors in question (Mutuality). The focus of this meeting was to be the development of an interim plan until Agency B could get its policy and programming set (Creativity).

The interagency discussions were kept at a low key. They focused on the known facts, particularly on the several cases that had been poorly handled by both agencies. Both agency directors understood the need to cut overlapping services, but each director held strongly to his and her interpretations of their agency's function in this matter (Accept Limits). Director A thought it was her mandated service; and director B felt that this was part of his agency's traditional functions.

Both directors were aware of the possible risks involved if this interagency problem were not solved (Common Risk). So they both agreed to a compromise interim solution: All gatekeepers would be informed that crisis cases could be referred to either agency. Then each agency would inform the other and jointly respond to the crisis. When both workers were on the scene, they would determine which agency had the most appropriate resources for dealing with the crisis (Creativity). Although expensive, this temporary solution would minimize the number of cases where no one would respond (Acknowledging Responsibility). It would give Agency B some experience with these new kinds of cases. The director of Agency A felt confident that ultimately they would continue to deal with these crisis cases and so was willing to settle the difficulty in an amenable manner (Everyone a Winner).

Source: Rochelle Wimpfheimer, Martin Bloom, and Marge Kramer, "Inter-Agency Collaboration: Some Working Principles," Administration in Social Work 14, No. 4 (1990), 95–97. © By The Haworth Press, Inc. All rights reserved. Reprinted with permission. For copies of this work, contact Marianne Arnold at The Haworth Document Delivery Service (Telephone 1-800-3-HAWORTH; 10 Alice Street, Binghamton, N.Y. 13904). For other Questions concerning rights and permissions contact Wanda Latour at the above address.

Many strategies can be utilized to meet the numerous challenges and problems that face administrators in working with other agencies. Beatrice suggests the following as particularly significant in facilitating interagency coordination:

Identify and use the fact that agencies may want the same thing.
Get the priority for your program set at the top.
Highlight similar goals.
Generate attention and enthusiasm for your initiative.
Agree to help on an initiative of another agency in return for help with yours.
Develop personal relationships.
Structure your initiative so that benefits flow to agencies with whom you need to coordinate.
Act when the time is right.
Portray coordination as an investment to your possible partners.
Convince local or county subunits—or advocacy or constituency groups— to intervene with other agencies for you.
Recognize that new programs are a catalyst for coordination.
Require coordination.
Come together to meet a common threat.
Remember that little things mean a lot.
Take advantage of a crisis.[21]

SUMMARY

Community relations are highly significant in the successful administration of an agency. One of the unique aspects of social work is that its administrator should know the community and its resources and use them to help the disadvantaged.

Community organization, a cardinal social work method, is being utilized extensively by effective administrators. Its underlying principles are being used advantageously by administrators within the community. Knowledge about the basic processes in community practice is helpful to administrators. These include research, planning, coordination, organization, financing, consultation, committee operation, negotiation, and recording.

Community welfare councils are local bodies that attempt to coordinate all social service agencies within a given community. Federated financial drives have been instigated to bring about cooperative fund-raising, with reduced competition and duplication of effort.

Public relations is recognized as a great challenge and opportunity for top-level administrators. Knowledge of techniques for successful public relations is essential to successful administration.

QUESTIONS FOR DISCUSSION

1. Define, compare, and contrast the social work methods of administration and community organization.

---

[21]Dennis F. Beatrice, "Inter-Agency Coordination: A Practitioner's Guide to a Strategy for Effective Social Policy," *Administration in Social Work* 14, No. 4 (1990), 56–58.

2. Describe and illustrate two or three of the key principles of community organization.

3. How important is negotiation in community social work practice? Can you give an example?

4. Do you agree with the statement that sound public relations are becoming more important for social workers than ever before? Why or why not?

5. How might the news media be used to help bring about more and better social services?

6. Describe and illustrate the services of volunteers in helping disadvantaged people.

7. How important are power politics in the provision of social work services?

8. Describe and illustrate two or three strategies used in interagency coordination.

SPECIAL ACTIVITIES

1. Invite the director of the United Way or another agency in your community to describe some of its key community services to your group.

2. Present a panel discussion on strengthening social work public relations, with students assigned to focus on television, radio, newspapers, and magazines.

3. Interview a social work agency manager regarding his or her experiences with the news media and describe these experiences to your group.

SELECTED REFERENCES

AUSTIN, MICHAEL J. "Community Organization and Social Administration: Partnership or Irrelevance?" *Administration in Social Work* 10 (Fall 1986), 27–39.
BEATRICE, DENNIS F. "Inter-Agency Coordination: A Practitioner's Guide to a Strategy for Effective Social Policy." *Administration in Social Work* 14, No. 4 (1990), 45–59.
BRAWLEY, EDWARD A. "The Mass Media: A Vital Adjunct to the New Community and Administrative Practice." *Administration in Social Work* 9 (Winter 1985/1986), 63–73.
GIBELMAN, MARGARET, and HAROLD W. DEMONE, JR. "Negotiating: A Tool for Inter-Organizational Coordination." *Administration in Social Work* 14, No. 4 (1990), 29–42.
MERRITT, JO, and BERNARD NEUGEBOREN. "Factors Affecting Agency Capacity for Inter-Organizational Coordination." *Administration in Social Work* 14, No. 4 (1990), 73–85.
MIZRAHI, TERRY, and JOHN MORRISON, eds. *Community Organization and Social Administration.* New York: Haworth Press, 1993.
POPPLE, PHILIP R. "Negotiation: A Critical Skill for Social Work Administrators." *Administration in Social Work* 8 (Summer 1984), 1–11.
RUBIN, HERBERT J., and IRENE RUBIN. *Community Organizing and Development.* Columbus, OH: Merrill Publishing, 1986.
SKIDMORE, REX A., MILTON G. THACKERAY, and O. WILLIAM FARLEY. *Introduction to Social Work,* 6th ed., pp. 91–104. Englewood Cliffs, NJ: Prentice Hall, 1994.
WEIL, MARIE, and JEAN KRUZICH, eds. "Empowerment Issues in Administrative and Community Practice." *Administration in Social Work* 14, No. 2 (1990), 1–137.
WIMPFHEIMER, ROCHELLE, MARTIN BLOOM, and MARGE KRAMER. "Inter-Agency Collaboration: Some Working Principles." *Administration in Social Work* 14, No. 4 (1990), 89–102.

15

Staffing

Ms. J., a well-qualified social worker with a DSW degree, was hired on a federal grant by a graduate school of social work to bolster the group work curriculum. She was well liked by the students, the administration, and her colleagues. She taught classes and directed graduate theses successfully for six years. Then she was offered a teaching position at another university, with a promotion to assistant professor and a sizable increase in salary.

She had mixed feelings about accepting this offer, as the school year was nearly over and commitments had been made for the year ahead. She finally told her dean that she had decided to stay on in her current assignment.

Ten days later she announced that she was taking the new position. Apparently she had already accepted it and had put her house up for sale a few days before.

How much integrity did this show? And what administrative predicament did her action create at the school?

Staffing is a major administrative process that involves obtaining staff, maintaining and working with staff members, and terminating their positions when necessary.

Personnel actions and procedures make up a major part of the activity of administrators in social work agencies. Looking for staff, working with them, guiding them, helping them, listening to them—these and other related activities fill much of the typical day of an executive. The efficiency and effectiveness of an agency relate directly to staff—how they are hired, how they feel about their work, and what they do. These factors depend on staff relationships with the administration, which we shall consider next.

The importance of staffing is indicated by the following example. In a neighborhood house, there was virtually no system for maintaining agency morale through the effective selection and support of the staff. Little or nothing was done to allow for staff development or provide learning opportunities for the improvement of social services. Hiring was done on a hit-or-miss basis. What were the results? Obviously, morale was low and services suffered, particularly on a qualitative basis.

This chapter considers the key processes of staffing: recruitment, selection, appointment, orientation, appraisal, and termination. Each is described briefly, illustrated, and related to the operation of social service agencies.

STAFFING PROCESSES

Recruitment

The aim of recruitment is to employ staff members who are competent and also have the ability to get along well with clients and other members of the staff. Either attribute by itself is insufficient. Professional competency relates to training and previous experience. The ability to have good relations with others comes from experience and training, as well as from one's personality. No matter how competent people are, if they cannot get along with the administration and others on the staff, they will not improve an agency.

Several procedures are utilized in searching for a good staff: advertising, written announcements, letters to schools of social work and employment agencies, and personal contacts. Each may prove effective.

First, a variety of publications can be used for announcing positions, especially *NASW News* (appearing ten times annually), which is used extensively for listings of job openings. This publication reaches national and international markets. Advertisements in other professional magazines and in state publications may also bring results. A carefully written job analysis can be of the utmost significance in recruiting. It should be specific, clear, and describe the agency and tasks to be performed.

Second, a brief announcement, usually not more than a page or two, may prove effective. This should be clearly written and should list details about the position and agency, so that those who are interested in the opening will be sure to apply. Such an announcement may be distributed to members of NASW and to agencies in the area. It might also be sent to schools of social work throughout the country or simply within the local region. Undergraduate departments of social work can be contacted, depending on the nature of the opening. Also, many placement bureaus and employment agencies have on file résumés of candidates for social work positions. Universities have placement bureaus that perform such a service, and commercial employment agencies provide names and backgrounds of social workers who are seeking a position.

A third source is personal contact—talking, by telephone or in person, with contacts in agencies and schools of social work, telling them about the opening, and asking for suggestions and recommendations. Then those who appear to be qualified and might be receptive to an offer are interviewed.

Selection

There are various patterns for the selection of a new staff member, in which the administration and staff have different degrees of responsibility. In some agencies, the director is the sole decision maker; in others, the authority is delegated to a staff committee. In most agencies, the administration and staff work together to come to a final decision.

Common selection patterns are illustrated by the following two examples. In a school of social work, an appointments committee did the leg work in recruitment. It sifted carefully through the applications and narrowed them down to three or four, then turned the names over to the department head and the dean for a final decision. Actually, the department head became a temporary member of the committee, helping with the selection from the beginning. The dean and the department head discussed the choices, picked their candidate, and took the name to the entire faculty for final approval. Usually a faculty will concur with such a recommendation; however, occasionally, it will be voted down. Then another prospect has to be suggested, often the second person on the final list.

In a children's services agency that handled adoptions and foster placements, the director did the preliminary work and then recommended three prospects for consideration by the staff as a whole. After careful discussion, a joint decision was made, satisfying both the director and the staff.

The selection process involves many steps and procedures (see Figure 15–1). In staff selection, two factors are particularly important: the needs and expectations of the agency and the desires of the person being employed. Careful consideration should be given to the needs of the agency, particularly at the beginning of the recruitment process. It is usually advantageous to put job specifications in writing. These specifications should be listed in a job announcement, giving focus to the application process. The description might be written by a committee or by the director or by both working together.

In addition to obtaining written materials from the applicant that include training, experience, and other relevant data, a statement about his or her interest in joining the agency is helpful. Why does this applicant want the position? Usually feelings as well as background information surface, and they reveal much about an applicant that is germane to employment.

Ordinarily it is wise to personally interview applicants who are being considered seriously for a position. The interview should be relaxed, providing an opportunity to share ideas and feelings as well as questions. The direc-

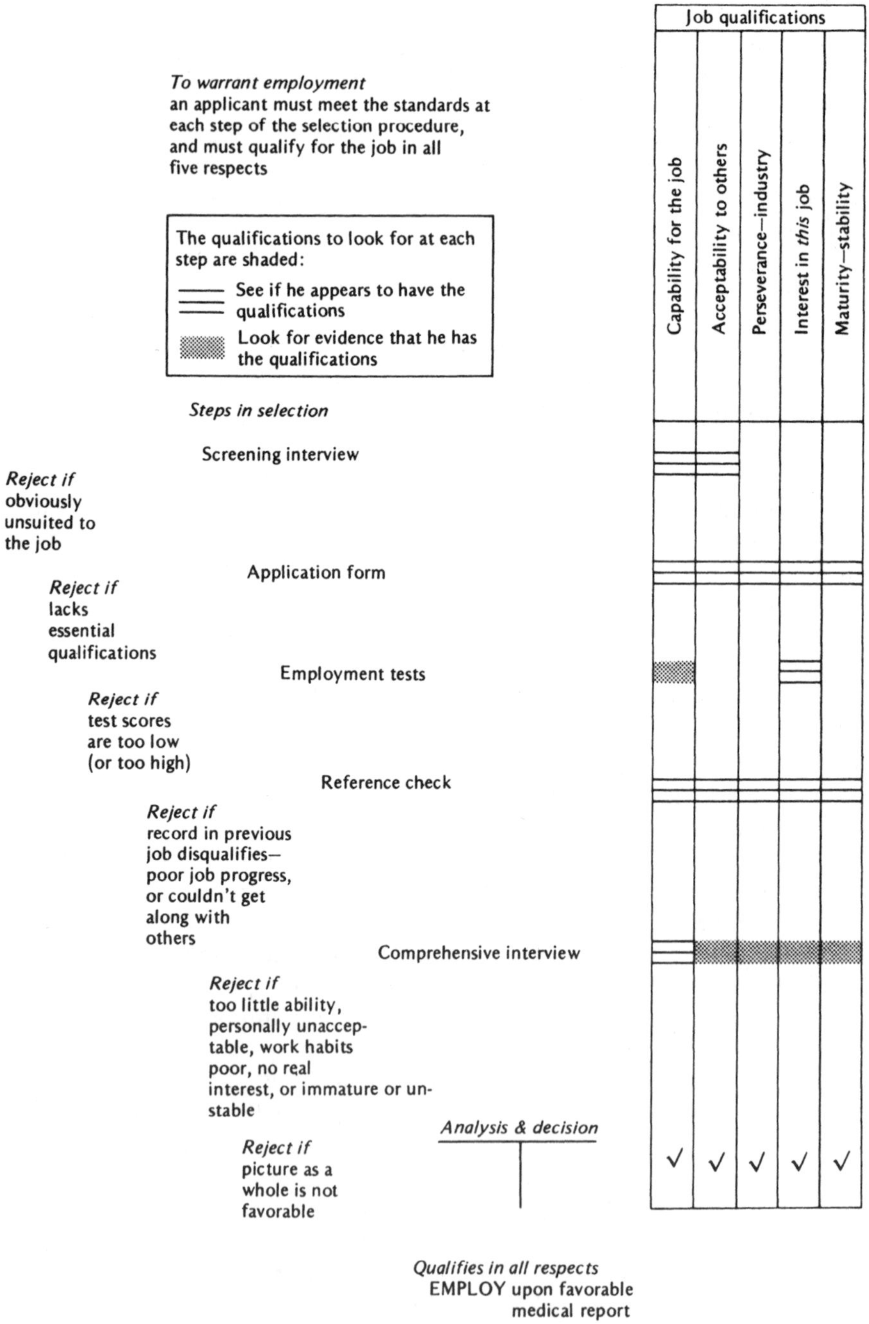

Job qualifications

Capability for the job | Acceptability to others | Perseverance—industry | Interest in *this* job | Maturity—stability

To warrant employment
an applicant must meet the standards at
each step of the selection procedure,
and must qualify for the job in all
five respects

The qualifications to look for at each
step are shaded:

—— See if he appears to have the
== qualifications

▓ Look for evidence that he has
the qualifications

Steps in selection

Screening interview

Reject if
obviously
unsuited to
the job

Application form

Reject if
lacks
essential
qualifications

Employment tests

Reject if
test scores
are too low
(or too high)

Reference check

Reject if
record in previous
job disqualifies—
poor job progress,
or couldn't get
along with
others

Comprehensive interview

Reject if
too little ability,
personally unaccep-
table, work habits
poor, no real
interest, or immature or un-
stable

Analysis & decision

Reject if
picture as a
whole is not
favorable

√ √ √ √ √

Qualifies in all respects
EMPLOY upon favorable
medical report

FIGURE 15-1 **Summary of a Selection Procedure.** From Milton M. Mandel, "The Employment Inter-
view," *Research Study No. 47* (New York: American Management Association).
Adapted and reprinted in Robert M. Fulmer, *The New Management*, 4th ed. (New York:
Macmillan, 1988), p. 174.

tor might well ask these questions: (1) Why are you interested in this position? (2) What are your professional goals? (3) How would you evaluate your contributions in your current position? (4) If married, how does your spouse feel about this job? (5) Why do you want to change positions at this time? Many interviews are now being conducted with the wife or husband of an applicant. In one sense, a family is hired for a position since, directly and indirectly, support from a mate will be significant in the success of a worker in an agency.

A candidate should be selected primarily on the basis of the needs of the agency, including loyalty to it. Competency and ability to get along well with the staff are considered in the final decision. The ability to care about the clients and the staff is essential. There are too many applicants who, although competent, are prima donnas. Such people will not last long in an agency because of their aggressive self-centeredness and unwillingness to share.

The three C's, competence, caring, and commitment, are essential if a social worker is to be effective. Competence derives from professional training and previous successful experience. Caring, so necessary in working with people, is manifested in both verbal and nonverbal communication. In social work, it is essential for a worker to convey to clients that they are important and that the worker wants to do everything possible to help. The third factor, commitment, involves a person's desire to make a contribution to agency services and the willingness to utilize his or her time and talents to do so, even if it means working overtime.

Appointment

Appointment to a position is another major part of the employment process. Approval by the agency's governing body is usually required. Such approval is mostly routine, especially if the preliminary work has been accomplished properly and the steps already discussed have been followed carefully. An appointment to a position provides an opportunity for administrators to enhance their relationships with their superiors by reinterpreting the goals and services of their agency or department as a new person joins the team. Each appointment offers a chance to interpret and explain the agency to its leaders, and a wise administrator takes advantage of it.

The appointment should be the best that can be offered in position and salary. Responsibilities and opportunities should be discussed with the new worker. Often these are not clearly defined, to the disadvantage of both worker and agency. Specific responsibilities of the new employee should be explained in detail. A new worker should be informed of the agency's goals, its organizational makeup, its staff, its board, and the community in which it operates. Also, the worker's specific duties and relevant information about the job need to be spelled out, including such items as salary, pay periods, fringe benefits, working hours, vacation policies, staff meetings, travel regulations, committee structure, staff development plans, and relationships with other community agencies, especially those in the same area of service.

A new appointee should be told about the opportunities and possibilities of the position. A director who speaks positively about the agency and its potential for service and achievement, both for the agency as a whole and for individuals, is helpful for new workers. Opportunities within the agency should be indicated, such as community resources, chances for writing and speaking, and ways to be creative. Help should be offered if an employee and family are moving. Sometimes the agency pays moving expenses.

Ordinarily, the level of the appointment should be as high as is commensurate with the background and experience of the applicant and is fair to other staff members. In an educational setting, the highest possible academic rank should be given. In an agency, a title should correspond with the level of employment.

Orientation

Orientation is the process of introducing a new employee to an agency, its services, and the community. It is the beginning step in becoming a full-fledged agency worker. Although an applicant is given some introduction to an agency by filing an application and having a personal interview, a more formal introduction is ordinarily advantageous. This may be made by the director of the agency or the supervisor under whom the new employee will work. It is best if the new worker is helped by both, in addition to assistance from other workers. Sometimes films, tapes, or written materials are helpful.

When a new employee arrives, it is best if the director indicates his or her personal philosophy, discusses the agency, and allows the person to ask questions. Getting answers from the person at the top is meaningful for an employee. The interview should be warm and personal. The administrator may take the new employee around the building and point out working quarters and relevant physical facilities. The administrator should explain the basic policies of the agency, its organization, its services, its board, its community relationships, and all other pertinent factors. The new worker should be given a copy of the policies and procedures manual.

Whatever the introductory method, the following are usually described in orientation:

1.   Agency history and services
2.   Basic policies, regulations, and procedures
3.   Agency organizational structure, including the level and position of the new worker
4.   Basic information about such items as salary, working hours, vacation, sick leave, and parking
5.   Office arrangements for the worker

6. Fringe benefits, including health and life insurance, retirement plans, and recreational facilities

7. Opportunities and challenges, including data about promotion, salary increases, and opportunities for creativity

A friendly introduction to the staff is significant. Although it depends somewhat on the size of the agency, it certainly should include personal introductions to those on the staff who will be working closely with the appointee. An opportunity should be provided for an interview with each key person. Again, these introductions should be positive and warm. In addition to personal interviews with key personnel, new employees might be invited to talk for a few minutes at a staff meeting, to indicate some of their experiences, ideas, and feelings.

New employees need to be introduced to the community also. This can be done at a lunch meeting with one or more key persons. Also, the first time new workers attend a community function, they should be introduced to the community leaders. Sometimes a special meeting, lunch, or dinner is held to introduce a new worker to the community. In addition to personal introductions, it is imperative that the new worker receive information about the key community agencies related to the work, including data about their services and personnel.

In an agency with an interdisciplinary staff it is particularly helpful to have a well-planned orientation. Abramson observes that an orientation in such a setting serves a variety of critical functions, including "establishing a social work perspective in the face of competing ideologies, building commitment to social work and to the organization, communicating supervisory expectations, and conveying the professional role."[1]

Promotion

Promotions are important in the functioning of an agency. Nearly everyone wants to move ahead, both in position and in salary. A sound administration will clearly define the procedures and standards for promotion. Some agencies spell out in detail the criteria for promotion, which should be based on the output of the worker—actual performance on the job. Every attempt should be made to objectify this process so that feelings and attitudes intrude as little as possible. Promotions should be made on a basis of merit only. When employees know that promotions are handled as fairly as possible, agency morale will be high. Although length of service is a factor, merit and quality of performance are becoming more significant in considering a promotion and/or a salary increase.

[1]Julie S. Abramson, "Orienting Social Work Employees in Interdisciplinary Settings: Shaping Professional and Organizational Perspectives," *Social Work* 38 (March 1993), 153.

Appraisal

Kahle suggests that "evaluation of the work of social work practitioners is an established and honored instrument for promoting professional development and has, in fact, been adopted by a number of other helping professions."[2] He also reports that the Committee on the Study of Competence of the National Association of Social Workers begins its *Guidelines for the Assessment of Professional Competence in Social Work* with the following statement: "One of the hallmarks of a profession is its willingness to set standards for its members and to have some mechanisms for designating individuals who are able to meet these norms." The report focuses on defining competence in service activities with individuals, groups, communities, and society at large.

Carlisle lists several significant purposes of performance appraisal: keeping subordinates informed on how they are doing, determining merit pay increases, uncovering training needs, identifying candidates for promotion, recognizing barriers or problems to improved performance, and discussing ways in which performance can be improved in relation to both the individual and the work unit.[3]

In a guide for executive evaluation, Kahle presents a comprehensive statement of factors to be covered in evaluation of staff.

I. The purpose of the evaluation (This section should state briefly why the evaluation is being conducted, at whose instigation, what it proposes to accomplish, and the time interval since the last evaluation.)
II. Responsibilities assigned and carried out (This section should include a summary of the basic job description that was provided by the board at the time it was recruiting the executive. It should also indicate any new or additional responsibilities that have been added or that have evolved since the beginning of his employment.)
III. General aspects of practice (strengths and weaknesses)
     A. What is the extent of his professional expertise? Does he attempt to increase his knowledge and keep himself informed of new developments in social work?
     B. Has he adequate working knowledge of the problems and structures and of key groups and individuals in his community?
     C. What are the quantitative aspects of his performance?
     D. How well does he organize and prepare his work?
IV. Specific (qualitative) aspects of practice (strengths and weaknesses)
     A. Service to the board or governing body
        1. Does he relate well to board members?
        2. Does he communicate his ideas clearly and is he receptive to communication from others?

[2]Joseph H. Kahle, "Assessing Executive Performance," in Simon Slavin, ed., *Social Administration* (New York: Haworth Press and Council on Social Work Education, 1978), p. 178.
[3]Howard M. Carlisle, *Management Essentials: Concepts for Productivity and Innovation*, 2nd ed. (Chicago: Science Research Associates, 1987), p. 389.

3. Does he involve board members meaningfully in planning, policy making, interpretation, and in the overall operations of the agency?
4. Does he keep the board adequately informed of his activities and of the affairs of the agency?
5. Is his general attitude acceptable to the board?
6. Does he provide leadership in board activities?

B. Service to the staff
1. How well does he relate to staff?
2. Does he understand their work and the problems that arise from their work?
3. Does he use personnel appropriately?
4. Does he delegate authority and responsibility appropriately?
5. Does he communicate well with staff?
6. Does he encourage and use staff participation in planning, policy making, and operations?
7. Does he contribute to staff development?
8. Is he fair in his actions relating to personnel practices?

C. Service to the community
1. How effective is he in his relations with funding bodies?
2. How effective is he in his activities with planning bodies?
3. How effective is he in his relations with other public voluntary organizations?
4. How effective is he in community and social action?
5. Is he effective in public relations and community education?
6. How is he viewed by his peers in other agencies?

D. Service to the agency program
1. Does he plan soundly?
2. Is he creative and innovative?
3. Does he assume the appropriate responsibility for making decisions?
4. Does he organize well?
5. Does he use agency resources well?
6. Is he effective in keeping the agency's program related to current community needs?
7. Does he demonstrate effective leadership of the agency staff?
8. Does he understand and use the budgeting process effectively?
9. Does he demonstrate ability in developing physical and financial resources?

V. Summary and recommendations (This section should provide a condensation of the total evaluation; it should indicate the executive's progress toward achieving agency goals, his strengths, his problem areas, and his deficiencies. It should make recommendations for specific changes and indicate when they are expected to be accomplished. The summary should clearly state the board's satisfaction or dissatisfaction with the executive's performance.)[4]

Various rating forms are utilized in the appraisal of performance. Carlisle presents a sample graphic form from the field of management that illustrates the basic factors considered in most evaluations of staff (see Figure 15–2).

Traditional appraisal methods have involved the study, observation, and rating of employees in terms of the traits they display on the job; in one

[4]Kahle, "Executive Performance," pp. 182–184.

	Circle appropriate rating				
	Unsatisfactory	*Fair*	*Good*	*Superior*	*Exceptional*
KNOWLEDGE: Extent of knowledge and practical know-how that relates to the job.	1	2	3	4	5
JUDGMENT: Capacity to analyze facts and to make reasonable decisions.	1	2	3	4	5
ATTITUDE: Cooperative and willing. Loyal to company and enthusiastic about job.	1	2	3	4	5
LEADERSHIP: Sets goals and motivates others to achieve them.	1	2	3	4	5
INITIATIVE: Works independently and strives to improve. Plans and follows through.	1	2	3	4	5
DEPENDABILITY: Trustworthy and reliable in carrying out assignments.	1	2	3	4	5
INTERPERSONAL RELATIONS: Gets along well with associates. Cooperative.	1	2	3	4	5
QUALITY OF WORK: Is accurate and thorough. Work requires little checking.	1	2	3	4	5
QUANTITY OF WORK: Accomplishes required work. Works quickly and achieves goals.	1	2	3	4	5

Name:_____ Job Title: _____
Department:_____ No. of months in position: _____

Comments and Recommendations:

Signed by rater: _____ Employee signature: _____
Date: _____ Date: _____

FIGURE 15-2 Sample Graphic Rating Form for Performance Appraisal. From Howard M. Carlisle, *Management Essentials: Concepts for Productivity and Innovation*, 2nd ed. (Chicago: Science Research Associates, 1987), p. 390.

sense, this is a kind of personality inventory. Carlisle suggests that many difficulties arise with this kind of evaluation:

> Ratings represent opinions and are, therefore, highly subjective and impressionistic. There are no clear standards or guides.
>
> The rater must evaluate the traits of an employee, a process where bias is naturally introduced. Attitudes are more likely to relate to sex, color, age, personality, and lifestyle than to accomplishments, measurable output, or productivity.
>
> Raters use different standards as norms. Just as certain professors grade hard and others easy, supervisors follow varied procedures in making evaluations. This creates difficulty in companywide comparisons for pay and promotion purposes.
>
> Ratings are generally higher than they should be. Some feel it is easier to give a subordinate an acceptable rating than force a confrontation. Justifying low opinions of another person's traits is difficult when objective measures do not exist.
>
> The halo effect appears, which is the tendency to rate someone high or low on all measures because of one dominating characteristic. For example, an employee who always obeys orders may receive a high rating on all characteristics because of the supervisor's preference for this trait.[5]

Recent methods of appraisal have tended to place more emphasis on results and less on personality traits. What has the worker been able to do, and what is that person doing now? Also, there has been a shift toward more individualization of evaluations, with less rigidity in regard to questions asked and answers obtained. Each person is unique, and each person's job is also unique in some ways that need to be recognized.

A common practice is to discuss with the worker the evaluation or appraisal that has been prepared. In some agencies, the worker is asked to initial the report and is given an opportunity to discuss it, indicating agreements or disagreements. It is hoped that these interviews will end on a positive note, with the supervisor indicating appreciation and encouragement and offering comments to improve the worker's motivation.

The worker's role in the process of evaluation is a significant one. Self-evaluation, in one sense, is the ultimate in staff evaluation. Competent, caring workers will know what they are doing and will be able to communicate this knowledge to the administrator concerned. The worker is responsible for continuous self-assessment and development. Written self-evaluations are often used in staff appraisal systems. These are then discussed with the supervisor to the mutual advantage of both parties.

New evaluation systems appear often. Current major approaches to evaluate worker performance have been summarized by Pecora and Austin and include: (1) Essay/Narrative; (2) Graphic (Trait) Rating Scales; (3) Ranking Techniques; (4) Forced-Choice Rating; (5) Management by Objectives and

[5]Carlisle, *Management Essentials*, p. 391.

Results (MBO/MOR); (6) Work Standards; (7) Behaviorally Anchored Rating Scales (BARS); (8) Weighted Checklist; (9) Critical Incident; (10) Assessment Center; (11) Forced Distribution; and (12) Field Review.[6]

Termination

Termination may be looked on with great anticipation or dread, depending on individual circumstances. It may occur as a result of retirement, change of position because of advancement or new interest, or being fired.

Termination should be handled by the administrator with maturity and sensitivity, for the benefit of both the individual and the agency. Usually a lunch or other activity is helpful in assisting an employee to depart, even though the reasons for leaving may vary. The occasion is usually more meaningful if it is arranged by a committee of staff members than by an executive. A gift, contributed by the staff, is meaningful too. Such an occasion need not take much time, but it should include an opportunity for one or two tributes to the person and to the services he or she provided and for a brief response by the recipient.

If an employee leaves because of retirement or for a better position, usually he or she feels positive about the departure. If the employee is forced out, this may be a different matter. Every attempt should be made to alleviate problems before a person is fired. Such action should be fair to both the agency and the individual. Talking with an employee who is not functioning well will often alter the situation. Further interpretation and clarification of the employee's position may make a difference. Sometimes additional staff development or individualized training may be the answer.

It takes courage to fire a staff member. After all steps to help an employee change have been taken and change has not occurred, termination must take place. Before this action, however, a wise administrator will check its legal ramifications so that the agency is protected in case a protest is lodged, whether informal or legal.

Every effort should be made before employees leave to talk with them and endeavor to make them understand and accept the situation. Often an administrator can guide people to jobs more suited to their abilities and may even offer references. Of course, this offer must be genuine.

AFFIRMATIVE ACTION AND MINORITIES

Affirmative action programs are almost universal because of legislation. Consequently, jobs are open to all persons, without regard to race, color, religion, sex, national origin, physical handicap, age, or marital status. Affirmative action is a major factor in social work employment, as in other areas of work.

[6]Peter J. Pecora and Michael J. Austin, *Managing Human Services Personnel* (Newbury Park, CA: Sage Publications, 1987), pp. 63–64.

The pioneer legislation in this area includes three federal laws and one executive order: Title VII of the 1964 Civil Rights Act, the Equal Pay Act of 1963 as amended, Title IX of the educational amendments of 1972, and Executive Order 11246 as amended by 11375.[7]

Title VII of the Civil Rights Act covers employers with fifteen or more employees and makes it unlawful to discriminate against an individual in hiring or firing or with respect to compensation, terms, conditions, and privileges of employment because of race, color, religion, sex, or national origin. The 1972 amendments expand the jurisdiction of the Equal Employment Opportunity Commission to include educational employers, major educational public elementary and primary school systems, and public and private institutions of higher education. The Equal Pay Act of 1963 prohibits sex discrimination in wages or fringe benefits, and in 1972 this act was amended to cover executive, administrative, and professional workers.

Executive Order 11246, amended by Executive Order 11375 in 1968, includes sex discrimination. Under the executive order, all employers with federal contracts of more than $10,000 must take affirmative action to eliminate all discriminatory practices against women and minorities and eliminate underutilization of women or minorities in their work force.

Various laws have been added and changed to bring about fairness and equality for minorities in employment. Problems still exist in varying degrees because legislation is often slow to go into effect and sometimes laws are disregarded, often in subtle ways.

Arguello made a limited review of publications exposing specific factors of ethnicity that influence not only entry into management but also efficiency and effectiveness. He concluded that there is sufficient information to concede that minority administrators' "ascendance to top management positions continues to be blocked by numerous barriers attributable to their ethnicity. Many of these barriers are invisibly rooted in long-held attitudes and beliefs about the inferiority of minority group members. Many are residual vestiges of the overt oppression to which minority groups were exposed. Most of these barriers have yet to be addressed in the mainstream of organization and management education."[8]

Minorities need to be given equal consideration in the hiring of new staff, and every attempt should be made to keep them in an agency. Everyone is aware that in the past, minority administrators in social work or in other professional groups have been sparse. However, Herbert reports that progress has been made in many areas for minority administrators. For example, federal employment data reveal that despite continued decline in total

[7]Shirley M. Buttrick, "Affirmative Action and Job Security: Policy Dilemmas," in Simon Slavin, ed., *Social Administration: The Management of the Social Services*, 2nd ed., Vol. II, *Managing Finances, Personnel, and Information in Human Services* (New York: Haworth Press, 1985), pp. 230–231.

[8]David F. Arguello, "Minorities in Administration: A Review of Ethnicity's Influence in Management," *Administration in Social Work* 8 (Fall 1984), 26.

federal employment, minority employment continued to increase. "Total minority employment (20.4 per cent of the federal work force) expanded 1.9 per cent for the period May 1972–May 1973."[9] McNeely participated in an ongoing, multisite study designed to assess factors associated with the job satisfaction of human service workers. Based on the data gathered, it appears that "the racial status of respondents does not act directly to suppress or enhance job satisfaction in human services work."[10]

Minority-group social workers do not need to work only with minorities. Numerous studies reflect that membership in a minority group is generally not of major significance in social work relationships, although a few persons claim otherwise.

Although the number of women administrators in social work has increased in recent years, many inequalities based on sex exist in various aspects of management and administration appointments and processes. Hanlan suggests that we may reduce the inequalities for women in administration if we follow these guidelines: (1) The notion that male administrative enclaves ought to be protected should be firmly and unequivocally rejected; (2) there should be specific training of women for managerial positions; (3) thought should be given to the possibilities of differing career patterns and their applicability to managerial and administrative positions.[11]

Odewahn and Ezell made a questionnaire study of 299 randomly selected men and women managers in state public welfare agencies listed in the *Public Welfare Directory* (1989). The instrument included three major sections—the initial movement of women into managerial positions, women functioning as managers, and the promotion of women in the management hierarchy. The results of the study strongly suggest "that since 1980 improvements in the attitudes toward women managers have taken place in human service agencies. On the other hand, there continues to be a persistent dichotomy in the views of men and women on each of the variables studied." The results also suggest that the "most productive avenue for narrowing the existing gaps in perceptions between men and women lies in two areas: (1) actions to deal with differential perceptions of organizational power, and (2) actions to increase the perception of equal assess to promotion to high-level management positions."[12]

[9]Adam W. Herbert, "The Minority Administrator: Problems, Prospects, and Challenges," in Simon Slavin, ed., *Social Administration: The Management of the Social Services*, 2nd ed., Vol. I, *An Introduction to Human Services Management* (New York: Haworth Press, 1985), p. 213.

[10]R. L. McNeely, "Race and Job Satisfaction in Human Service Employment," *Administration in Social Work* 13, No. 1 (1989), 92.

[11]Mary S. Hanlan, "Women in Social Work Administration," in Simon Slavin, ed., *Social Administration: The Management of the Social Services* (New York: Haworth Press and Council on Social Work Education, 1978), p. 202.

[12]Charles A. Odewahn and Hazel F. Ezell, "Attitudes Toward Women Managers in Human Service Agencies: Are They Changing?" *Administration in Social Work* 16, No. 2 (1992), 53.

SUMMARY

Significant processes in staffing social service agencies include recruitment, selection, appointment, orientation, appraisal, termination, and working with minorities.

Recruitment ordinarily involves public advertisements as well as personal contacts and requests. Selection of personnel should encompass the needs of the agency as well as the abilities and loyalty of the applicants being considered, including competency, caring, and commitment.

Appointees need to be told the responsibilities and opportunities of the position in the agency. Orientation must be provided for the new staff member, including orientation to the agency, the staff, the building, and the community.

Termination is sometimes a difficult process and should be handled sensitively and justly for both the individual and the agency.

Special efforts should be made to employ minorities and women, keep them in social work positions, and provide equal opportunities and salaries for similar work.

QUESTIONS FOR DISCUSSION

1. What are some of the significant resources for recruiting capable staff members in social work agencies?

2. If you were the director of a mental-health center in your community, what would you consider to be essential characteristics for a new staff member?

3. Do you agree with the statement that a new staff member should never be given a salary higher than that of present staff members for a position of similar standing? Explain your answer.

4. Why is a comprehensive orientation so important for a new staff member?

5. Evaluate Howard Carlisle's rating form for the appraisal of staff.

6. What suggestions do you have for reducing discrimination against minorities for social work administrative positions?

7. What might be done to increase the number of women in top administrative positions in social work agencies?

SPECIAL ACTIVITIES

1. Role-play the first interview of an agency director of a marriage and family counseling center with a new staff member who is an experienced caseworker. Discuss the pros and cons of what occurred.

2. Invite an agency administrator to talk to your group about the importance of staff performance and appraisal and how they should relate to salaries and promotions.

3. Have a panel discussion on how to increase the number of minorities and women in top administrative positions in social work agencies.

SELECTED REFERENCES

ABRAMSON, JULIE S. "Orienting Social Work Employees in Interdisciplinary Settings: Shaping Professional and Organizational Perspectives." *Social Work* 38 (March 1993), 152–157.

ARGUELLO, DAVID F. "Minorities in Administration: A Review of Ethnicity's Influence in Management." *Administration in Social Work* 8 (Fall 1984), 17–27.

FERNANDEZ, HAPPY CRAVEN. "'Family Sensitive' Policies Can Attract Employees to Human Service Organizations." *Administration in Social Work* 14, No. 3 (1990), 47–66.

HERBERT, ADAM W. "The Minority Administrator: Problems, Prospects, and Challenges." In Simon Slavin, ed., *Social Administration: The Management of the Social Services,* 2nd ed. Vol. I, *An Introduction to Human Services Management,* pp. 212–224. New York: Haworth Press, 1985.

MCNEELY, R. L. "Race and Job Satisfaction in Human Service Employment." *Administration in Social Work* 13, No. 1 (1989), 75–94.

MUNSON, CARLTON, E., ed., *Social Work Supervision.* New York: Free Press, 1979.

ODEWAHN, CHARLES A., and HAZEL F. EZELL. "Attitudes Toward Women Managers in Human Service Agencies: Are They Changing?" *Administration in Social Work* 16, No. 2 (1992), 45–55.

PECORA, PETER J., and MICHAEL J. AUSTIN. *Managing Human Services Personnel.* Newbury Park, CA: Sage Publications, 1987.

PILOTTA, JOSEPH J. *Women in Organizations: Barriers and Breakthroughs.* Prospect Heights, IL: Waveland Press, 1983.

RIVAS, ROBERT F. "Perspectives on Dismissal as a Management Prerogative in Social Service Organizations." *Administration in Social Work* 8 (Winter 1984), 77–92.

SCHWARTZ, SANFORD, and PATRICK DATTALO. "Factors Affecting Student Selection of Macro Specializations." *Administration in Social Work* 14, No. 3 (1990), 83–96.

SLAVIN, SIMON, ed. *Social Administration: The Management of the Social Services,* 2nd ed. Vol. II, *Managing Finances, Personnel, and Information in Human Services.* New York: Haworth Press, 1985.

VELASQUEZ, JOAN. "GAIN: A Locally Based Computer System Which Successfully Supports Line Staff." *Administration in Social Work* 16, No. 1 (1992), 41–54.

16

Supervision—A Two-way Process

Two medical educators were discussing their curricula and training programs. One remarked, "I think we ought to have more supervision of our students and also encourage more supervisory services when our graduates start in practice."

The other observed, "I think I agree. I'd like to suggest we talk to some social workers and get their suggestions. From what I've heard, their supervision system is tops."

Since formal social work education began, at the turn of the nineteenth century, supervision has been a basic component of both the educational process and social work practice. It has been recognized as one of the unique characteristics of social work and is generally regarded positively. It is an integral part of most social work agencies in the delivery of social services. It is worth noting that several current textbooks in management do not even list supervision in their contents or indexes, let alone cover it in their presentations. Social work has developed a meaningful administrative process—supervision.

Robinson's pioneering work in 1936 did much to stimulate interest in understanding the supervisory process and using it effectively. She observed that *supervision* had become a technical term in social work "with a usage not defined in any dictionary." She explained, "Supervisors in a social agency are responsible for 'overseeing' the job in the generally understood meaning of the word, but they have, in addition, a second function of teaching or training workers under their supervision. This teaching function is developing in importance as schools of social work become surer in defining the place of supervised field work in the whole professional training." Then she observed,

"I have set myself the problem . . . of lifting supervision out of its confusing entanglement with the case work process in order to see it as a unique teaching process which has grown up inside of case work, indigenous to it, but different from it in important ways."[1]

Evidence of the interest in supervision in social work was reflected in the publication in 1979 of *Social Work Supervision*, a book that attempted to provide an overview of relevant literature, systematically interrelating representative articles that had appeared in recent years.[2] It cited eighteen pages of bibliographical references relevant to social work supervision.

In the last several years, some differences of opinion regarding supervision in social work have developed. Most practitioners, however, reaffirm that adequate supervision is an essential part of sound administration and social work practice. A few claim that social workers have become "snoopervisors," that less supervision is needed, and that workers should be given more independence.

PURPOSES OF SUPERVISION

Supervision in social work is concerned with helping staff members use their knowledge and skills to do their job efficiently and effectively. In the etiological sense, the word *supervision* means "oversight, control, surveillance." In social work it is used, ordinarily, to describe the function that one individual, the supervisor, assumes in relation to a worker, a supervisee. Interaction between supervisor and supervisee aims to bring about worker competence. It is a teaching-learning process, educational as well as administrative and enabling. It may be accomplished in a group as well as on a one-to-one basis.

The supervisor's role is to support, encourage, impart information, and listen to workers, particularly to new and inexperienced ones. Capable supervisors point out knowledge gaps and deficiencies in skill and help workers control their biases. They help alleviate anxiety and give support by showing interest and understanding. They are professional models for new workers and a bridge to the agency for experienced workers who have come from other agencies.

Supervision encompasses three main functions: teaching, handling administration, and enabling. Teaching is aimed at helping workers increase their knowledge and understanding to deepen their professional attitudes. It also involves assisting workers to increase and improve their social work practice skills. Ordinarily, workers learn by doing; they then discuss what has gone well and what has been difficult.

---

[1]Virginia P. Robinson, *Supervision in Social Case Work* (Chapel Hill: University of North Carolina Press, 1936), p. xii.

[2]Carlton E. Munson, ed., *Social Work Supervision: Classic Statements and Critical Issues* (New York: Free Press, 1979).

According to Kurland and Salmon, supervisors, along with classroom teachers, field instructors, and consultants, need to recognize the unusually stressful nature of social work practice and the frequent "sense of pervasive hopelessness felt by practitioners." They describe five areas that need special emphasis in courses on practice and in in-service training and supervision:

1. Helping workers set realistic goals in their work while encouraging them to recognize and appreciate the small successes that are achieved by their clients
2. Developing positive norms and setting limits
3. Working with open-ended groups and with individuals and groups where attendance is sporadic
4. Dealing with differences and conflict, especially racially based conflict
5. Using activities to help clients express their thoughts and feelings and work cooperatively with others[3]

In administration, the supervisor directs and guides workers and helps with management matters such as salaries, promotions, assignment of cases, and appointments to committees. The supervisor ensures some uniformity of quality and quantity in the work of the staff.

The enabling part of supervision aims at facilitating the work of the supervisees so they can do their part in the delivery of social services. It means opening doors for the utilization of their abilities and skills. Bunker and Wijnberg, who studied organizational climate and its impact on outcomes in public social service organizations, suggest that supervisors may play important roles as climate mediators or buffers, enabling the workers to adjust to the organizational structure of the agency:

> Supervisors provide the most direct and sustained expression of organizational characteristics to the worker. They can either intensify or soften even those aspects of the worker's experience of which they are not a part. We propose an active, counter-climate model of supervision as the approach most likely to compensate for the most severely abrasive features of the model PSSO (public social service organization) climate. This approach provides the often missing ingredients of goal interpretation, task support and team development that make successful performance more likely.[4]

Watson summarizes the teaching functions and materials to be learned through supervision as follows: "(1) social work philosophy and the history and policy of the agency, (2) social work knowledge, techniques, and skills, (3) self-awareness, (4) available resources in the agency and in the community, and (5) the priorities of case service and the management of time." He states that the administrative component can be broken into six functions: "(1)

---

[3]Roselle Kurland and Robert Salmon, "When Problems Seem Overwhelming: Emphases in Teaching, Supervision, and Consultation," *Social Work* 37 (May 1992), 241.

[4]Douglas R. Bunker and Marion Wijnberg, "The Supervisor as a Mediator of Organizational Climate in Public Social Service Organizations," *Administration in Social Work* 9 (Summer 1985), 71.

communications linkage, (2) accountability for performance, (3) evaluation, (4) assignment of cases and distribution of work, (5) emotional support of workers, and (6) utilization by the agency of each worker's experience."[5]

In an article published in 1960, Levy discusses with sensitive insights the pros and cons of supervision in social work and describes some of its contributions:

> The social work supervisor, by virtue of the role to which he is assigned in the agency and by virtue of the relationship through which he activates that role, helps his supervisee to do a better job for the agency and to become a creative and proficient social worker in his own right. Through the supervisory process, the social work supervisor helps the supervisee become equipped to undertake greater or different responsibilities within the same agency or in another agency. Through the supervisory process, the social work supervisor encourages the supervisee to participate in research and otherwise to make his practice the medium for the conscious examination not only of his own practice but social work practice in general, and for the development of social work theory. These gains are not designed for the advancement of the agency's purposes alone, but they will accrue to the agency just as the social worker, who comes to the agency after a salutary development experience in another agency, will bring his gains with him to the advantage of the clientele he will be serving in the new setting.
>
> There is a good and sufficient reason to reemphasize and further elaborate the developmental aspects of the supervisory task, not only because it serves the agency, but because it serves a significant professional end.
>
> The challenge is not to dispense with supervision—not yet at least—but to realize its true potential. What richer resource is there than the experienced, professionally educated social worker, particularly if agency clients are still so fortunate as to have access to his services, and he is so fortunate as to have a skilled and imaginative supervisor to stimulate him toward further and more significant and more professional achievement?[6]

Kadushin attempted to ascertain opinions of supervisors and supervisees in practice, particularly significant implications for social work education. In 1973 he sent a questionnaire to 750 supervisors and 750 supervisees randomly selected from a listing of 2,600 casework supervisors and 5,300 casework supervisees in the 1972 NASW Directory. Usable returns were received from 469 supervisors and 384 supervisees. It was ascertained that supervisors were responsible for an average of 4 to 5 workers each; only about 30 percent of the supervisees had MSW degrees. The largest percentages of both groups indicated that they were satisfied with the current supervisory situation. About 60 percent of the supervisees reported being "extremely satisfied" or "fairly satisfied" with their supervisor; 73 percent of

---

[5]Kenneth W. Watson, "Differential Supervision," *Social Work* 18 (November 1973), 81.

[6]Charles S. Levy, "In Defense of Supervision," *Journal of Jewish Communal Service* 37 (Winter 1960), 201.

TABLE 16-1. **Sources of Supervisory Power as Perceived by Supervisors and Supervisees**

SUPERVISOR'S SOURCE OF INFLUENCE WITH RESPECT TO SUPERVISEE	AS PERCEIVED BY SUPERVISORS (PERCENTAGE)	AS PERCEIVED BY SUPERVISEES (PERCENTAGE)
Expert power	95.3	65.5
Positional power	2.6	21.1
Coercive power	.6	5.5
Reward power	.2	3.1
Referent (relationship) power	.6	2.1

Source: Alfred Kadushin, "Supervisor-Supervisee: A Survey," *Social Work* 19 (May 1974), 290. Copyright © 1974, National Association of Social Workers, Inc.

the supervisors were "extremely" or "fairly" satisfied with their role as supervisor. Conversely, 6 percent of the supervisors were "fairly" or "extremely" dissatisfied with their assignment, and 15.4 percent of the supervisees were "fairly" or "extremely" dissatisfied.[7] Table 16–1 compares the sources of supervisory power as perceived by supervisors and supervisees.

Expert power is regarded by both supervisors and supervisees as the main source of influence over the latter. However, the supervisors claim that their expertise is much more important than do the supervisees, 95.3 percent and 65.5 percent, respectively. Also, the supervisees feel more than do the supervisors that supervisors attain their influential role because of position, coercion, and reward. Supervisees are probably more realistic than supervisors in ascertaining the actual sources of power. Supervisors need to recognize that the importance of their expertise may be overrated.

That there is a genuine need for supervision in social work education and practice is axiomatic. No social worker reaches optimum competence. It is hoped that each student and worker is accomplishing, approximating, and moving ahead, but none can fully realize all goals in education or in the delivery of social services.

The justification for supervision is based on the premise that people who are well trained and experienced, who have developed competencies, knowledge, and professional attitudes, can be helpful to beginning workers and to one another. Why shouldn't experienced, competent workers share their knowledge, skills, and techniques with those who are just beginning? Why not help others to avoid some of the possible pitfalls and become more efficient and competent as they move ahead in their social work career?

Supervision in the field, or practicum, has been recognized as essential from the beginning of formal social work education. It is still considered vital, although a variety of patterns and procedures have developed, which include person-to-person supervision, group supervision, and peer supervision.

[7]Alfred Kadushin, "Supervisor-Supervisee: A Survey," *Social Work* 19 (May 1974), 289–291.

In practice many changes have occurred, although supervision is regarded as an essential component of the administrative structure and functioning of an agency. In some agencies, considerable independence is encouraged, with a minimum of supervision. In others, particularly as new workers come to a job, a major emphasis is placed on the supervisory process. Generally, some kind of supervision takes place, formal, informal, or a combination of both, and it is a challenge to offer the program that will be most helpful and effective in developing a competent agency staff. In other words, the concern is not with too much or too little supervision but with enough to be meaningful for a particular worker at a particular time. The amount of supervision may well vary from worker to worker. The quality of supervision should always be high.

In a desire for autonomy and professionalism, some social workers maintain that supervision should be terminated after graduates have been in practice for some time. Wax exemplifies this point of view when he states that "lifelong supervision is a vestige of the sub-professional past. Social workers do come of age. They can be proud of their training and confident of their skill."[8] He recommends that workers should terminate supervision after two years if the following conditions exist:

> (1) The supervisee is a graduate of an accredited school of social work and has the incentive, capacity, and opportunity to be a competent professional; (2) the supervisor has sufficient command of supervisory skills to be able to complete the task in two years; and (3) the agency has confidence in the competence of its practitioners and supervisors, is prepared to have administrative personnel shoulder the administrative aspects of the supervisory job, and is prepared to provide a planned staff development program to meet the ongoing developmental needs of staff.[9]

CHARACTERISTICS OF EFFECTIVE SUPERVISORS

The following is a brief consideration of several characteristics of successful supervisors.

Knowledgeability.   Knowledgeability is an essential characteristic of an effective supervisor. This means professional knowledge as well as knowledge about the agency in which practice is taking place. Supervisors need comprehensive knowledge, professional attitudes, and practice skills and should be able to tie them in with the organization and services of their

---

[8]John Wax, "Time-Limited Supervision," in Carlton E. Munson, ed., *Social Work Supervision* (New York: Free Press, 1979), p. 120.
[9]Ibid., p. 111.

agency. Supervisors should also be acquainted with the current professional literature in order to refer their supervisees to further study.

Practice Skills.   Practice skills are essential for competent supervisors. This may mean professional competency in a particular social work method or methods, with general abilities in all basic social work methods. Such abilities would depend on what the supervisors are doing, in which area they are working, and on the needs of students or workers.

Open-door Policy.   Having an open-door policy is highly desirable. This means the supervisor can be reached in emergencies and that the door is usually open for the supervisee to come in, ask questions, and be given guidance when necessary. It does not mean that the door is open at all times. Usually a weekly interview between supervisor and supervisee takes care of most questions and problems.

Commitment to Supervision.   A genuine conviction of the need for effective supervision is essential. Capable supervisors have a dynamic interest in the agency, in themselves, and in their supervisees. This should not be artificial or superficial. The supervisee can tell whether this interest is genuine. A sustained concern can be a positive motivating factor and can help to increase the supervisee's knowledge and skills.

Openness.   Effective supervisors are open-minded. This means that although they ordinarily have answers to the questions that may be raised, they will admit it when they do not know the answer to a problem or question and they will acknowledge their mistakes when they make them. Supervisors who recognize that they are human are the ones most likely to reach their workers.

Showing Appreciation and Giving Commendation.   New workers in particular hunger for commendation and appreciation. Such positive reinforcement can increase motivation and professional development. W. I. Thomas, a social psychologist, suggests that recognition is one of the four fundamental wishes of people throughout the world. Supervisors who fail to show appreciation limit their effectiveness, slow down professional development, and decrease the competency of supervisees. Scherz lists the major responsibilities of a casework supervisor:

> (1) He has the degree of competence in casework practice that is required to facilitate the work of casework staff; (2) he is able to transmit knowledge effectively; (3) he is capable of assessing the performance and the professional developmental needs of casework staff; (4) he has a body of knowledge about

differential supervisor methods which he can apply discriminatingly; and (5) he understands authority and uses it appropriately.[10]

BASIC PRINCIPLES OF SUPERVISION

The following five principles offer a broad framework for the supervisory process in social work:

1. Social work supervisors teach principles and skills about their organization and services and then allow the supervisees basically to govern themselves.
2. Workers govern themselves mainly by selecting goals and objectives that are consonant with the principles and knowledge indicated by their supervisors.
3. Supervisors are prepared and available to help workers when needed, in addition to providing regular teaching and learning experiences.
4. Workers call on their supervisors for help when needed.
5. Workers give an account to their supervisors of their activities, and together they set goals for the future.

A major role of a competent supervisor in social work is to teach principles and skills, particularly those relating to agency services. Ordinarily, this reaffirms what workers have learned in their education, formal and otherwise, and previous experience. Knowledge and skill can be shared on an informal, often one-to-one basis. Theoretically, the supervisor helps the supervisees to increase their knowledge and skills in the organization and services of the agency in which they work. Then supervisees are invited to govern themselves and operate in the way they choose. Workers will be masters of their own destiny in an agency, as long as their performance is consonant with agency policies and goals. Basically, it is believed that the supervisees have the ability to do competent work, particularly if they are given the confidence and guidance of a supervisor to accompany and bolster previous experience and education.

The second principle of supervision, that supervisees govern themselves through the development and selection of goals consistent with supervisory principles, means that workers, not supervisors, decide what they will do. Workers must clarify their personal goals in the agency. They need to think of the objectives they would like to achieve as staff members, both individually and for the agency as a whole.

Once workers formulate these goals, they must evaluate them and put them in some order. Which are most important and which are least important? Which need to be achieved regularly and immediately, and which might be worked on occasionally and irregularly? These objectives should be consonant with the organizational policies and procedures of the agency.

[10]Francs H. Scherz, "A Concept of Supervision Based on Definitions of Job Responsibility," in Carlton E. Munson, ed., *Social Work Supervision: Classic Statements and Critical Issues* (New York: Free Press, 1979), p. 72.

The third principle concerns the availability and involvement of the supervisor. That is, supervisors accept their significant role in the agency and have a deep respect for its importance in the effective delivery of social services. Rather than being regarded as a burden, this role is seen as a way to offer service and benefit the individual worker as well as the agency. This means that although a weekly conference is scheduled, there is a clear understanding that the supervisor's door is open if and when the supervisee is confronted with an emergency or believes the supervisor can be helpful. Supervisees respect the privacy of the supervisor and do not overuse this privilege. They realize that at times the supervisor's door must be shut to everybody.

The fourth principle recognizes the actual desirability of asking the supervisor for assistance—both at regular weekly conferences and at other times. Assistance may be given during a visit to the office of the supervisor or by telephone, depending on the physical setup of the office and the size of the agency. The important factor is that the worker is able to get in touch with the supervisor when help is needed. Too many supervisees let problems continue and put off decisions; they are not taking advantage of the supervisory process. Supervisees recognize that time is valuable. They are prepared for their meetings with the supervisor, so that time is utilized effectively.

The fifth principle of supervision involves evaluation and accountability. Today, the delivery of social work services is no longer immune from objective scrutiny. The weekly supervisory conference is a convenient, traditional way to give an account of a worker's actions. Annual or semiannual written evaluations by the supervisor and self-evaluations by the supervisee are part of the procedure as well. A self-evaluation can be a true educational process, particularly for the supervisee. As a result of such a self-evaluation, the supervisor can teach additional principles and skills to the worker.

The five principles just described are based on the assumption that workers have the ability to carry out their role effectively and make most of their own decisions. However, the supervisory process provides an opportunity for setting guidelines and interacting on a regular basis with someone who is experienced and competent, especially when problems, fears, or uncertainties arise.

THE SUPERVISORY PROCESS

Based on a research study of supervisors in continuing education workshops and of beginning students in a social work master's degree program, Cohen and Rhodes identified the essential components of effective supervision:

> (a) Setting individual and group objectives for task allocation and implementation; (b) implementing shared decision making; (c) directing group process (including agenda building); (d) planning work and case management; (e) developing communication networks; (f) evaluating performance; (g) motivating workers; (h) case consultation and professional support; (i) team building;

(j) worker and client advocacy; (k) conflict management; and (l) planned change at dyadic, team, and intergroup levels, with particular attention to coalescing separate interests into collective interests on behalf of employees and clients.[11]

To achieve the educational and training objectives suggested for effective supervisory practice, they identified the following helpful approaches: role playing, development exercises focusing on a particular supervisory or organizational process, and simulations.[12]

Kadushin conducted a national survey among social work supervisors and supervisees that reflected their opinions and reactions regarding the supervisory process and its functions.[13] Although there were some shared opinions, there were also some differences (see Table 16–2). Although both supervisors and supervisees agreed that supervisors play major roles in teaching, administration, and enabling, the supervisees indicated that the administrative functions of the job were more important and the teaching functions of the supervisors less important to the supervisees than they were to the supervisors. Also, the supervisees' description of the activities occupying the supervisors' time was closer to the truth than the supervisors' descriptions.

This study reflects the attitude of some supervisors, who do not perceive themselves as part of the administrative process in an agency and do not feel comfortable in an administrative role. Apparently there is need for additional study of supervision to assist supervisors in recognizing that they are an integral part of the administrative process and that sound administration is essential for sound practice in an agency.

Directly and indirectly, the supervisor has considerable influence over the personal and professional life of the worker. Levy enumerates the following sources of power:

1. The supervisor has administratively assigned and sanctioned authority over the supervisee.
2. The supervisor mediates the relationship between the supervisee and the agency.
3. The supervisor usually has a role to play in hiring and firing the supervisee.
4. The supervisor controls the supervisee's salary increases and promotions and determines the kind of entries that will appear in his record.
5. Although the supervisor is not inevitably more professionally competent than the supervisee, he almost invariably knows more than the supervisee about some things. To the extent that he does, he has power to influence the supervisee.

[11]Neil A. Cohen and Gary B. Rhodes, "Social Work Supervision: A View Toward Leadership Style and Job Orientation in Education and Practice," *Administration in Social Work* 1 (Fall 1977), 289–290.

[12]Ibid., p. 290.

[13]Kadushin, "Supervisor-Supervisee," p. 292; see also Alfred Kadushin, *Supervision in Social Work* (New York: Columbia University Press, 1976), pp. 41–90.

TABLE 16–2. Supervisors' and Supervisees' Reactions to Supervisory Functions

FUNCTIONS	REGARDED AS MOST PREFERRED BY SUPERVISORS (PERCENTAGE) N = 469	REGARDED AS MOST IMPORTANT BY SUPERVISEES (PERCENTAGE) N = 384	OCCUPIED MOST OF SUPERVISORS' TIME (PERCENTAGE) N = 469
Teaching the supervisee the casework aspects of the job—the knowledge, skills, and attitudes he needs for effective job performance.	26.8	18.0	18.2
Case consultation—analysis and planning of client contact with supervisees.	21.7	14.8	15.4
Preparing for and conducting staff meetings and training sessions with supervisees.	15.5	5.4	3.4
Reading and reviewing case records in preparation for individual conferences.	6.5	3.4	5.4
Facilitating the work of supervisees by coordinating their work with others in the agency and arranging for the availability of clerical help, case aides, consultation, etc.	5.8	9.8	7.5
Teaching the supervisee the administrative aspects of the job—agency policy, procedures, regulations, forms, caseload management.	5.5	11.0	13.4
Acting as a channel of communication from administration to supervisees and from supervisees to administration.	5.1	11.8	10.7
Helping the supervisees with morale problems related to the job.	3.3	5.4	5.7
Holding evaluation conferences with supervisees.	3.1	5.4	1.8
Reading and reviewing case records for assignment to supervisees.	2.1	3.4	5.9
Checking and sanctioning supervisees' decisions, regarding clients, procedures, budgets, reports.	1.5	4.6	7.6
Other (specified).	3.1	7.0	5.0
Totals	100.0	100.0	100.0

Source: Alfred Kadushin, "Supervisor-Supervisee: A Survey," *Social Work* 19 (May 1974), 292. Copyright © 1974, National Association of Social Workers, Inc.

6. The supervisor expects, if not requires, the supervisee to reveal much about himself in the supervisory relationship.
7. The supervisor's influence extends beyond the supervisee's tenure on the job.[14]

LOGISTICS OF SUPERVISION

Place

Ordinarily, conferences and other meetings between a supervisor and supervisee are held in the latter's office. Sometimes the supervisor goes to the supervisee. In some agencies, separate offices are reserved for supervisory conferences. Privacy is required, so that whatever the two talk about will be kept confidential. Sometimes negative feelings arise, and privacy is essential for discussions about them.

Time

The length of supervisory conferences varies. Although some supervisors prefer an hour, others feel they need two. Both supervisor and supervisee should feel comfortable with the time schedule.

Written Materials

Most supervisors ask for written documentation that can be used as a basis for discussion in supervisory conferences. Sometimes supervisees are invited to record some cases, which can then be studied and evaluated together by the supervisor and the supervisee; at other times, a highlighted summary of a case might be utilized. Also written self-evaluations that consider the supervisee's work over a given period of time can be helpful, as can copies of letters and reports submitted to the agency.

SUPERVISION MODELS

There are many kinds of supervision. Some agencies use a variety of approaches, and others only one. Watson describes six models of supervision used by the Chicago Child Care Society:

1. *Tutorial model.* A supervisor and a supervisee are in a one-to-one relationship.
2. *Case consultation.* This system involves a worker and a consultant and may be on a one-to-one basis or with other staff members to increase their learning or seek their contributions or both.

---

[14]Charles S. Levy, "The Ethics of Supervision," *Social Work* 18 (March 1973), 16–18.

3. *Supervisory group.* This model involves a supervisor and a group of supervisees and is, in a way, an extension of the tutorial model.
4. *Peer-group supervision.* There is no designated supervisor, and all group members participate as equals.
5. *Tandem supervision.* This pattern developed out of the peer-group model, with two workers who function by themselves supervising each other.
6. *The team.* Membership is deliberately varied as much as possible within the agency. The agenda is proposed in advance by members, and decisions about a case are reached through peer interaction.[15]

Peer Supervision

Traditionally, supervision in social work has been on a one-to-one basis, and a supervisor, an experienced person, has helped a newer worker. However, different patterns have now developed. One of the most interesting and challenging is peer supervision.

Many social workers have moved into private practice, partly out of a desire for more independence and less supervision. Mandell suggests that traditional, individual supervision has been questioned as no longer the most efficient way of training and socializing new personnel, or of "assuring the stable continuation of organizational patterns." She observes that "peer group supervision, consultation, and inservice training are potentially more democratic training methods than individual supervision, and could encourage self-confidence and creativity."[16]

Fizdale described a peer-group supervision plan in operation at the Arthur Lehman Counseling Service, where there were no casework supervisors or consultants and no regularly scheduled individual conferences between the administrator and staff members. The workers assumed the basic responsibility for their own cases and were free to consult and interact with other staff members about them. Matters pertaining to casework practice were dealt with at two weekly staff conferences. In addition to the group meetings, individual consultation among the workers was common.[17] This pattern is one in which coworkers help one another in a supervisory capacity, utilizing the basic processes and mechanics already described but varying them to fit the appropriateness of a group operating in a cosupervisory capacity.

There are advantages and disadvantages to peer-group supervision. Workers who are helping one another are ordinarily sensitive to the problems, decisions, and uncertainties inherent in their position. It seems easy to identify with other workers of about the same age and experience. The main

---

[15]Watson, "Differential Supervision," pp. 83–86.

[16]Betty Mandell, "The 'Equality' Revolution and Supervision," *Journal of Education for Social Work* 9 (Winter 1973), 43.

[17]Ruth Fizdale, "Peer-Group Supervision," in Carlton E. Munson, *Social Work Supervision: Classic Statements and Critical Issues* (New York: Free Press, 1979), pp. 122–132.

disadvantage of such supervision is that inexperienced workers may not have the knowledge and skills necessary to answer some of their questions, solve some of their problems, or make decisions.

Supervision by Objectives (SBO)

One of the newer developments in social work has been the introduction of Management by Objectives (MBO) principles and procedures in the supervisory realm. A number of agencies have experimented with this managerial approach, and the results have been varied. Some reports have been very positive; others have raised questions about its applicability to the delivery of social services.

Granvold suggests that Supervision by Objectives (SBO) is the social work supervisor's "contribution to accountability and the legitimation of 'achievement' in the delivery of social services." He discusses two kinds of objectives in social agencies: *performance objectives* and *personal development subjectives*.[18]

Performance objectives are formulated to *maintain* a desired level of unit productivity in agency services, for example, "to sustain the rate of foster home licensing at 100 homes per year" or "to provide 500 hours of direct counseling services per month." Performance objectives can also be formulated to *improve* the level of unit productivity in key areas, for example, "to increase by 20 percent the number of foster homes licensed this year over last year's 85 homes licensed."

Personal development subjectives differ in that they are addressed to the individual's skill development or professional interest. They are statements of specific, verifiable, measurable events or activities, which if accomplished presumably lead to the achievement of a desired result. A supervisor might write a subjective for professional growth as follows: "To develop grantsmanship through successfully completing a series of three grant-writing courses through the Center for Labor and Management" in one year's time. An example of a supervisor's commitment to worker development might be the following subjective: "To ensure that all unit social workers attend one continuing education course each 6 months." An illustration of a subjective for his or her own improvement might be this: "To gain competency in interviewing through the development of microcounseling skills by March 1."

Granvold states that the "process of implementing SBO: (a) provides the worker with an opportunity to participate in goal setting and in the establishment of criteria for performance appraisal, (b) contributes to the quality of the interaction between supervisor and workers, and (c) provides a mechanism for the definition of measurable outcome criteria for job tasks."[19]

---

[18]Donald K. Granvold, "Supervision by Objectives," *Administration in Social Work* 2 (Summer 1978), 199–209.

[19]Ibid., pp. 202–203.

Granvold concedes that there are both advantages and disadvantages in using SBO. "The major advantages of SBO are related to accountability. The method is designed to facilitate reciprocal accountability between worker and supervisor in which there is explication of expectations and jointly predetermined criterion measures of performance appraisal." He observes that the predominant disadvantage of SBO is the "expenditure of time and energy in developing, revising, and reviewing objectives. The paper work itself may be a frustration to supervisor and staff."[20] He concludes that "the SBO method, with its inherent disadvantages, has the potential to enhance the managerial effectiveness of the social work supervisor. The viability of the method has received significant support; the effectiveness of its implementation rests with the supervisor."[21]

In 1974 the Work Planning Performance Appraisal/Evaluation System, an MBO form of supervision, was adopted on an agency-wide basis by the Durham County Department of Social Services, in Durham, North Carolina. This agency had 270 employees, including clerical, and service workers and supervisors. The system was adopted on a limited basis but was not completed within the original time frame. Bloom's evaluation of the program reflects some limitations of this kind of supervision.

The most frequent criticism was the program's inability to measure the quality of work.
Another frequent objection to the plan was the feeling workers had of being constantly monitored and "harassed."
Work planning treated workers as if they were dull, irresponsible individuals who required lists of tasks to be accomplished.
Work planning was devoid of flexibility.
"Busywork" was a frequent comment.
Work planning paid little attention to the supervisory relationship.

Bloom concluded that there is insufficient evidence that MBO can provide more efficient and productive use of resources and that further research is needed.[22]

Group Supervision

Some agencies combine individual and group supervision. Abels indicates that groups can be used successfully in the supervisory process.

In group supervision, the major supervisory tasks (teaching, administration, and enabling) are carried on in and with the group. Supportive teaching opportunities such as individual evaluations, staff meetings, and individual conferences are essential. The responsibilities for teaching and content become those

[20]Ibid., p. 206.
[21]Ibid., p. 209.
[22]Allan A. Bloom, "Pitfalls of a Managerial Approach to Supervision in a Public Welfare Agency," *Administration in Social Work* 2 (Winter 1978), 482–487.

of all the instructional group members, and not only the formal supervisor. The latter's authority comes from the institution and his competence; the learner's authority to teach comes primarily from the instructional group, but also from his formal supervisor.[23]

Supervision on Wheels

Another interesting development is supervision on wheels, a system of taking the supervisory process to sparsely populated areas where there is a minimum of supervision or none at all. Sharlin and Chaiklin describe an innovative plan to provide supervision in rural areas in the north of Israel. After a needs survey was made, supervisors went to small towns along the Lebanese border, met with workers, and provided selected supervisory services. Although there were limitations, this was a bona fide attempt to reach social workers who had been previously neglected in the supervisory process.[24]

Task Supervisors

Pawlak, Webster, and Fryer suggest that *task supervisors*, individuals who do not have an MSW degree but do have an area of specialized expertise, may be used to advantage in training administration students in the field. Task supervisors might be used in placements that have a social service program but no MSW staff member, such as in the United Mine Workers; a sheltered workshop; a housing authority; and in nontraditional settings, the Tennessee Valley Authority—Tributary Area Development, a utilities company, health or regional planning, manpower training, a state legislature, or a city manager's office. A faculty field instructor is used to facilitate planning, coordination, and leadership.[25]

The tasks students perform in such field placements include assisting in writing a grant application, aiding in social work problem and needs analysis, developing a management information system, designing and implementing a program and acting as its coordinator, assisting with budget analysis, participating in program evaluation, developing personnel management policies and procedures, helping to staff a committee, serving as a staff member for a community group, and assisting with staff development and training.[26]

[23]Paul A. Abels, "On the Nature of Supervision: The Medium Is the Group," in Carlton E. Munson, *Social Work Supervision: Classic Statements and Critical Issues* (New York: Free Press, 1979), p. 134.

[24]Shlomo Sharlin and Harris Chaiklin, "Social Work Supervision on Wheels," in Carlton E. Munson *Social Work Supervision: Classic Statements and Critical Issues* (New York: Free Press, 1979), pp. 166–175.

[25]Edward J. Pawlak, Stephen Webster, and Gideon Fryer, "Field Instruction in Social Work Administration and Planning: Roles, Tasks, and Practices," *Administration in Social Work* 4 (Summer 1980), 90–92.

[26]Ibid., pp. 91–93.

Adaptive Supervision

Another approach is adaptive supervision. Latting, for example, has derived a theoretical model of adaptive supervision in social work on the underlying premise that supervision is most effective if the supervisor's leadership "is based on the worker's level of professional development, yet conveys a concern for both service delivery and the developmental needs of the worker." She recognizes the importance of the expressive (people-oriented) and the instrumental (task-oriented) components of their jobs. She presents a four-quadrant normative model for conceptualizing the relationship between the supervisor and his or her workers.

Latting suggests that the supervisor may utilize the proactive mode (to influence the worker's attitudes and behavior) or the reflective mode (in which the worker takes the lead in the interaction, the supervisor becoming a sounding board), and she observes, "The supervisor chooses to be proactive or reflective based on the worker's level of professional development." She names four supervisory actions: instruct, collaborate, encourage, and entrust. She concludes, "The goal is to enable the worker to function as independently as possible."[27]

Live Supervision

Another current model in social work supervision is live supervision. Rickert and Turner describe this innovative process:

> Live supervision employs a one-way mirror and a telephone to give immediate supervision to the trainee. Typical live supervision involves a session with one student interviewing and another present with the supervisor behind a one-way mirror. The supervisor has three alternatives for directing a trainee: telephoning, convening a brief conference outside the training interview, or entering the training interview. Before and after the training interview, there are brief teaching and planning sessions.[28]

SUPERVISION OF VOLUNTEERS

Millions of volunteers make valuable contributions to social service agencies. Many have some competencies in helping people; many others do not. Most volunteers care about people and want to provide meaningful services. An agency can tap the resources of volunteers and help develop their potential through supervision.

[27]Jean E. Latting, "Adaptive Supervision: A Theoretical Model for Social Workers," *Administration in Social Work* 10 (Spring 1986), 22.

[28]Vernon C. Rickert and John E. Turner, "Through the Looking Glass: Supervision in Family Therapy," in Carlton E. Munson, *Social Work Supervision: Classic Statements and Critical Issues* (New York: Free Press, 1979), p. 157.

The two main ways of supervising volunteers are to work with them within the agency and outside of the agency. Within the agency, a particular staff member or members might be designated to develop a supervisor-supervisee relationship with the volunteers, teaching knowledge and beginning skills and helping to engender professional attitudes. The five basic principles mentioned earlier in this chapter also apply to volunteers. Volunteer workers have the potential to help others if they are given some guidance in social work knowledge, attitudes, and skills. They are likely to be most helpful and effective if they are basically allowed to govern themselves within the agency framework.

Outside of the agency, various institutes and workshops can be meaningful to volunteers. For example, in a metropolitan area with a population of about half a million, an institute was held with the theme Responsibilities and Opportunities for Administrative Volunteers. More than one hundred volunteers from different community agencies participated in this one-day institute, sponsored by the local Community Welfare Council. Professionals and volunteers shared knowledge, ideas, and suggestions for improving their services.

Supervision for volunteers is essential, to reduce or prevent the problems that might arise when people, trying to help because they care, do not have the knowledge or skills adequate to assist others.

IMPROVING SUPERVISION

Education for Supervision

One problem in social work supervision is that few supervisors have received specific or adequate training for this important position. Patti and Austin state that a serious challenge "facing schools and agencies is the anticipatory preparation of the thousands of direct service practitioners (both students and graduates) who will, in short order, become first- and second-line supervisors, project managers and coordinators, residential supervisors, and the like."[29] They suggest the following guidelines to strengthen educational planning:

1. Develop an opportunity for students to experience an in-depth, intensive exposure to supervisory roles.
2. Develop opportunities and requirements for students to assess their own potential for supervisory management by standardized tests and otherwise.
3. Intensive reexamination of the instructional and supervisory processes is required of instructors and administrators to maximize learning.[30]

[29]Rino J. Patti and Michael J. Austin, "Socializing the Direct Service Practitioner in the Ways of Supervisory Management," *Administration in Social Work* 1 (Fall 1977), 267.
[30]Ibid., pp. 278–279.

Specific classes on supervision are offered in schools of social work, helping students to gain knowledge and develop skills that will be of value if and when they become supervisors in agencies. These classes also benefit all students, making them knowledgeable about supervision so they will be effective participants in this two-way process.

Handling Role Conflicts

Supervisors often experience conflicts in their daily practice role. Erera conducted research in role conflict among public welfare supervisors in four urban New York state agencies. The results "strongly indicate that supervisors' role conflict is highly associated with the state's external control in the form of incompatible policies." Erera recommends that the first action to be undertaken to improve services and reduce conflict "should aim at mitigating the destructive effects of state policies, particularly as regards the feeling of powerlessness that results from them. It is, therefore, suggested that social worker leaders should involve themselves more greatly in determining policies in the human services, in order to enhance their coherence and congruity."[31]

Supervision and Ethics

Levy explains that supervisors need to focus on what is morally right in situations involving their supervisees, and he reaffirms the importance of ethical behavior.

> Ethics are important in all phases of the supervisory relationship, including before it is formally initiated and after it has ended, insofar as its consequences follow the supervisee. Ethics in supervision need not imply a favorable result for the supervisee, only a just consequence for him. The outcome need not be beneficial to the supervisee, only appropriate. Ethics need not result in special advantage for the supervisee, only equity for him. They need not provide the supervisee with preferential opportunities, only safeguards against the genuine hazards he faces because in so many respects he and the supervisor are not equals.[32]

CONSULTATION

Consultation is one of the newer administrative processes in social work agencies. It is closely related to supervision, yet it is a process that stands alone. Formal consultation is the process by which a well-qualified person, in

[31]Irit P. Erera, "Role Conflict Among Public Welfare Supervisors," *Administration in Social Work* 15, No. 4 (1991), 47.

[32]Levy, "Ethics," p. 20.

social work or an allied field, who is competent and caring meets with individuals or the entire staff in a social work agency. Such an individual helps to answer questions, assists in solving problems, and aids in planning and decision making, particularly that related to the future.

The consultant is a resource person, not a line officer. Such people do not tell administrators or staff workers what to do. They describe, to the best of their knowledge and ability, what the possibilities are, suggest various alternatives, and endeavor to help the agency reach sound decisions. Consultants are invited from psychiatry, psychology, nursing, educational psychology, and other related disciplines. Social workers now call on other competent social workers to act as consultants. Some social workers now work full time in this capacity. For example, a California school district hired two recent MSW graduates to work full time in the school system as consultants. They were to be available to the principals, supervisors, and teachers, to help them increase their knowledge and skills in working with students, families, and the community and in utilizing administrative processes.

According to Kevin, "There are three major approaches through which consultants can influence the consultation group. There can be a primary focus on the feelings and attitudes of the consultees; on the interaction between individual consultees and the consultant; or on the involvement of the consultees in an interchange of problems and solutions."[33]

The many significant roles of a consultant are described by Ferguson:

1. Capture data.
2. Scan for troubled interfaces.
3. Promote psychological bonding.
4. Be a linking agent between people and/or groups.
5. Serve as a communications conveyor belt.
6. Suspend animation and analyze process.
7. Assist in the diagnostic formulation and reformulation of issues.
8. Raise relationship problems and feeling data for consideration
9. Use clinical skills to help make communication more congruent (effective).
10. Encourage feedback.
11. Serve as a plumber and/or obstetrician (give gentle assists and help with the birth of developments).
12. Promote the spirit of inquiry.
13. Analyze ongoing problem-solving meetings.
14. Set up opportunities for mutual coaching and team building.
15. Assist in the management of conflict.
16. Help promote a proper psychological climate.
17. Take calculated risks because one is expendable.[34]

[33]David Kevin, "Use of the Group Method in Consultation," in Lydia Rappoport, ed., *Consultation in Social Work Practice* (New York: National Association of Social Workers, 1963), p. 77.

[34]Charles K. Ferguson, "Concerning the Nature of Human Systems and the Consultant's Role," in Warren G. Bennis, Kenneth D. Benne, and Robert Chin, eds., *The Planning of Change*, 2nd ed. (New York: Holt, Rinehart & Winston, 1969), pp. 412–417.

On the cutting edge of growth and development in social work administration is practice in industry. "Shadow consultation," an innovation offered by social workers for the business world, has many possibilities for the future. It involves a qualified social worker spending a typical day with a business manager, observing everything he or she does, from specific planning to telephone calls to interviews. At the end of the day, the social worker and manager discuss what has occurred, how it has occurred, and specific ways in which improvement may take place in the "manager's effectiveness in relating to and directing his or her associates and team."[35]

SUMMARY

Supervision is recognized as a unique process in social work education and social work practice as well as in agency management. It is desirable to have the right amount of supervision, not too much or too little. Supervision is an integral part of the educational system, especially in practicum experiences.

Competent supervisors in social work are knowledgeable, able to teach their skills, interested, available for consultation, and able to admit their limitations. They provide appreciation and commendation when appropriate.

Five basic principles of supervision are the following:

1. Social work supervisors teach knowledge, principles, and skills and then allow the workers basically to govern themselves.
2. Social workers govern themselves by selecting goals and objectives consonant with the those of the agency.
3. Supervisors are available for help when needed.
4. Social workers call on their supervisors for help when necessary.
5. The workers give an accounting to their supervisors periodically.

Peer supervision has proven effective in a variety of settings, and the supervision of volunteers is an essential aspect of effective agency services.

Consultation is being utilized increasingly by social work agencies, and growing numbers of social workers are acting as consultants. Federal and state government contracts are supporting this development.

QUESTIONS FOR DISCUSSION

1. Define, describe, and evaluate the importance of supervision in social work practice.

---

[35]Hy Resnick and Josephine King, "Shadow Consultation: Intervention in Industry," *Social Work* 30 (September–October 1985), 447.

2. What are the major characteristics of successful supervisors?

3. Describe and illustrate the five basic principles of supervision in this chapter.

4. What is your opinion of peer supervision?

5. What would be some advantages of group supervision? Some disadvantages?

6. Compare and contrast the supervision process with volunteers and agency social workers.

7. Define, describe, and evaluate the social work process of consultation. Why is it increasing in use?

8. Do you agree with the statement "The supervisory process is one of the very positive processes in social work practice"? Why or why not?

SPECIAL ACTIVITIES

1. Role-play an interview between a supervisor in a private mental-health agency and a caseworker who has been employed for a year.

2. Present a panel discussion on the topic "Values and Dangers of Supervision."

3. Interview a supervisor in an agency of your choice to learn what allows successful supervision.

SELECTED REFERENCES

BUNKER, DOUGLAS R., and MARION WIJNBERG. "The Supervisor as a Mediator of Organizational Climate in Public Social Service Organizations." *Administration in Social Work* 9 (Summer 1985), 59–72.

ERERA, IRIT P. "Role Conflict Among Public Welfare Supervisors." *Administration in Social Work* 15, No. 4 (1991), 35–51.

GRANVOLD, DONALD K. "Supervisory Style and Educational Preparation of Public Welfare Supervisors." *Administration in Social Work* 1 (Spring 1977), 79–88.

HIMLE, DAVID P., SRINIKA JAYARATNE, and PAUL A. THYNESS. "The Buffering Effects of Four Types of Supervisory Support on Work Stress." *Administration in Social Work* 13, No. 1 (1989), 19–34.

JAYARATNE, SRINIKA, HOWARD V. BRABSON, LARRY M. GANT, BIREN A. NAGDA, ANUP K. SINGH, and WAYNE A. CHESS. "African-American Practitioners' Perceptions of Their Supervisors: Emotional Support, Social Undermining, and Criticism." *Administration in Social Work* 16, No. 2 (1992), 27–43.

KADUSHIN, ALFRED. *Consultation in Social Work.* New York: Columbia University Press, 1977.

KADUSHIN, ALFRED. *Supervision in Social Work.* New York: Columbia University Press, 1976.

KURLAND, ROSELLE, and ROBERT SALMON. "When Problems Seem Overwhelming: Emphases in Teaching, Supervision, and Consultation." *Social Work* 37 (May 1992), 240–244.

LATTING, JEAN E. "Adaptive Supervision: A Theoretical Model for Social Workers." *Administration in Social Work* 10 (Spring 1986), 15–23.

MUNSON, CARLTON E., ed. *Social Work Supervision: Classic Statements and Critical Issues.* New York: Free Press, 1979.

PECORA, PETER J., and MICHAEL J. AUSTIN. *Managing Human Services Personnel.* Newbury Park, CA: Sage Publications, 1987.

PERLMUTTER, FELICE DAVIDSON, and SIMON SLAVIN, eds. *Leadership in Social Administration.* Philadelphia: Temple University Press, 1980.

RUSSELL, PAMELA A., MICHAEL W. LANKFORD, and RICHARD M. GRINNELL, JR. "Administrative Styles of Social Work Supervisors in a Human Service Agency." In Simon Slavin, ed., *Social Administration: The Management of the Social Services,* 2nd ed. Vol. I, *An Introduction to Human Services Management,* pp. 150–167. New York: Haworth Press, 1985.

YORK, REGINALD O., and THOMAS HASTINGS. "Worker Maturity and Supervisory Leadership Behavior." *Administration in Social Work* 9 (Winter 1985/1986), 37–46.

17

Staff Development

A brief portrait of two social work agencies follows:

Agency 1. All staff members have an appropriate number of assigned cases and do their work individually. Staff meetings to decide policies and handle agency business are held weekly, for an hour. No other get-together is offered for the group as a whole.

Agency 2. As in agency 1, staff members are assigned an appropriate number of cases and attend and participate in weekly staff meetings. In addition, two hours each week are spent in staff development, including talks by guest lecturers, role playing, films, tapes, and informal discussions.

Which agency would be likely to develop better services, with a high esprit de corps?

Staff development includes a variety of activities and learning experiences with the aim of increasing the staff's knowledge, deepening its professional attitudes, and increasing its skills and ability to work with and help people. Staff development is usually made possible by an administration that is sensitive to change and wants to keep abreast of the new knowledge explosion and skills that are reported regularly in the literature or by professional associates.

PURPOSES OF STAFF DEVELOPMENT

We live in a world in which knowledge is constantly being added at a geometric rate. Current research and study in social work results in new and innovative presentations at professional conferences and in many books and journal articles. In fact, so many publications are available today that no one worker can begin to read all the current literature about social work and its services. For an agency to be up to date, it is imperative for its staff members to have some knowledge of current developments. Change in social work practice is inevitable, and agencies should try to keep abreast of developments so that they can provide better and more effective social services.

Some forecasters have projected that by A.D. 2000, a typical social work administrator and staff may be spending a day a week in staff development—20 percent of their time. The results of staff development activities seem to substantiate the need to expand them.

Staff development is important because it can help workers increase their knowledge and understanding of human behavior and social relationships, which puts them in a better position to help clients. Staff development can also provide increased understanding of professional attitudes; this, too, can make a difference. Perhaps most important, staff development can provide an opportunity for social workers, no matter how long they have been on the job, to stay abreast of developments in technique and methodology.

Staff development can be important for seasoned staff members as well as for neophytes. Capable educators and practitioners know that if staff members do not have a chance to study and are not motivated, they tend to stagnate and become less effective in their practice. The axiom "He who rests, rusts" well applies.

Staff development not only provides an opportunity for increasing knowledge, deepening professional attitudes, and improving skills in working with people but also directly and indirectly helps to increase the effectiveness of an agency through the greater understanding of others, the result of the interaction of staff members. As staff members talk, explore feelings, and act together, they enhance their understanding of the agency, its services and resources, and improve their delivery of services.

For the social-service system to fulfill its mission, according to Weiner, all staff members must be involved and informed. Staff development can help to achieve agency objectives, which are twofold. First, and traditionally, staff development has been concerned with enhancing skills and knowledge. Second, it is intended "to foster improved communication and work group cohesion in regard to clinical, case management, and administrative issues. Central to this is the understanding by staff of program objectives and client population characteristics, subjects which represent excellent topics for initial staff development seminars."[1] Weiner recommends a variety of activities for effective staff development, including staff meetings, case conferences, training seminars, and supervisory conferences.[2]

METHODS OF STAFF DEVELOPMENT

There is a variety of methods for staff development. Which ones are used depends on the particular agency, the administrators, and individual staff members. The following are brief descriptions and illustrations of effective methods.

Lectures

The lecture is a common tool for staff development. A staff member or an outside guest is invited to deliver a presentation on a specific topic related to knowledge in social work, attitudes, a skill, or a combination of skills. For example, a lecture might be given on behavior modification, task-centered casework, gestaltism, AIDS, or sexual harassment. After the lecture, time should be allowed for questions and discussion, particularly if the guest meets with the staff.

Case Presentations

The presentation of cases is a common method of staff development. Ordinarily presentations are made by staff members, in turn, providing variety and enriching the learning process. Besides helping to improve the understanding and abilities of staff members, case presentations are usually helpful in case planning and the consideration of intervention techniques. The discussion of a difficult or complex case involving family dynamics might help others involved with similar cases. Thirty to forty-five minutes are generally allowed for the caseworker to explain the case, and then several minutes are spent in discussion and evaluation, including possible intervention alternatives. Staff members are asked not to discuss these cases elsewhere, thus maintaining professional ethics.

A popular version of the case presentation is the case-incident approach, which focuses on a particular action or series of events in detail, attempting to help those present understand a particular dynamic, technique, or principle in working with an individual, family, or community. Sometimes a series of case incidents may be presented at a staff development meeting, all related to a particular principle, professional attitude, or specific technique or skill.

[1] Harvey Weiner, "Administrative Responsibility for Staff Development," in Felice Davidson Perlmutter and Simon Slavin, eds., *Leadership in Social Administration* (Philadelphia: Temple University Press, 1980), pp. 231-232.

[2] Ibid., pp. 230-248.

Role Playing

Role playing and psychodrama are used in many agencies for staff development. Staff members assume roles, to act out what might have happened, what is happening, or what might happen in problematical relationships. Situations are dramatized to make them come alive. Role playing can be an enjoyable activity—even a humorous one—as well as a sound learning experience. Usually staff members are invited to volunteer to assume a role. Although some prefer not to be involved in role playing and even resent being called on, most favor this kind of activity.

Role playing often brings out feelings as well as ideas that are relevant to a given situation. It is just one step away from reality. In an attempt to understand the dynamics of a family, including two teenage daughters, for instance, four staff members might be invited to assume the four roles. Sometimes acting the part of someone of the opposite sex is helpful in stimulating new viewpoints.

Self-development Programs

One of the newer methods of staff development is self-development or self-study programs, which involve programmed learning. Printed materials are included, with detailed instructions for solving problems and supplying answers or opinions as requested. This is intended to help staff members increase their knowledge of themselves; their abilities, goals, and alternatives; and how they might attain them. Self-development programs often involve values in decision-making situations.

Dedicated staff members also keep abreast of current developments by reading recent books and journal articles. This is still one of the best ways to improve practice abilities.

Another effective staff development resource is writing. Staff members who prepare and submit articles for publication learn much in the process. Other workers may write for themselves, keeping notes or case histories, perhaps submitting to their colleagues materials they consider valuable.

Group Actions

A variety of group approaches is utilized in staff development. Sensitivity training with "T" groups is sometimes used in social service agencies. This approach, pioneered at Bethel, Maine, attempts to provide an open, accepting climate for members of a small group so that they will reveal their thoughts and feelings and react to the revelations of others. The aim is to help staff members increase their understanding of themselves, particularly of their own feelings and how these affect their decisions and other actions in the delivery of social services.

Staff members may participate in a retreat, which takes place away from the office. An example of a successful retreat involved a state hospital with a professional social work staff of nineteen. Plans were made for the staff to spend two days and nights at a canyon resort. The objective was to improve their understanding and use of group work skills. A nationally known leader in group work was engaged to lead the retreat. Meals were shared. Evenings were utilized for brief learning sessions and informal social activities. The days were given over to informal lectures, group discussions, films, and role playing. At the end, the event was summarized. Evaluations indicated that nearly all who attended felt that their group work skills were improved. They concluded that this experience was not only educationally effective but also socially enjoyable. As a side effect, staff members became better acquainted and were freer to interact. Staff relations were genuinely improved.

Another kind of group action is the marathon, in which a group of workers, perhaps even the entire staff, spends twenty-four, thirty-six, or forty-eight hours together. Ordinarily this provides an open, relatively free emotional atmosphere. It is expected that participants' feelings and thoughts will be articulated so that they understand themselves better and improve their ability to understand others and work more effectively with them.

Game Exercises

A whole gamut of games have been devised to provide simulated experiences in solving social problems. For example, a game may provide experience in being a member of a committee or a planning group that is trying to reduce juvenile delinquency in a large metropolitan area. Some of these games are complicated, requiring several hours of preparation and many hours of operation to reach their objectives and teach problem-solving techniques. For example, a game on budget formulation might provide background data on three or four alternatives and require the participants to become knowledgeable about one another, to weigh the likely results of each alternative, and to reach a sound decision. Computers are used in some of these games.

Library Facilities

Most social work agencies provide library materials for their staff. These include books, selected social work journals, and tapes and films germane to social work practice. Ideally, a separate room is available for study.

Continuing Education

Several opportunities for staff development exist outside of social agencies. Many social work practitioners take credit or noncredit refresher courses to improve their understanding of people and of ways to help clients with personal, family, and community problems. Several schools of social work offer part-time training facilities so that full-time practitioners can complete their work for an advanced degree. In a sense, this is the ultimate in staff development. Some agencies provide leaves for workers to return to school full time and complete a degree program. In educational settings, sabbatical leaves make this possible.

Summer or evening classes offer additional opportunities for staff members to remain in touch with developments in the field. Many state regulatory bodies now require that social work staffs spend time in classwork or have other appropriate training to maintain their licenses. One state, for example, requires ninety hours of classwork or other approved training every three years to maintain an active clinical license.

A variety of workshops provide opportunities for practitioners to advance professionally and academically. For example, workshops or institutes might be held on topics of current interest such as task-centered casework, ego psychology, transactional analysis, staff burnout, time management, strategic planning, or sexual harassment.

Formal credit and noncredit classes or seminars may be offered at an agency or educational institution. Teachers may be from a school of social work, from other disciplines, or from the agency staff. Topics vary considerably but are usually relevant to the agency and its needs.

Exchanges

Some agencies and schools of social work provide an opportunity to exchange staff and positions for three months, six months, or longer. This introduces new knowledge and skills to agency staff. It also enriches the curricula of schools of social work.

Visiting experts from other states and foreign countries often make valuable contributions to staff development in schools of social work and agencies, as do agency workers teaching part time in a school of social work, on either the undergraduate or graduate level. Practitioners may be invited to teach a particular class in either a method or knowledge area. Besides enriching the training of prospective social workers, it provides a learning experience for the agency worker who prepares such a class.

EFFECTIVE LEARNING

Learning is a complex phenomenon, involving many factors. Staff development sessions need to be built on learning experiences that are meaningful and effective. To benefit the staff and the agency, (1) specific objectives should be set, (2) preassessment should be sensitive, (3) planning should be effective, (4) learning experiences should be appropriate, and (5) evaluation should be adequate.

Specific Objectives

Often staff members get together, intending only "to improve our skills and increase our knowledge." Such a goal is too vague. Specific, observable, measurable objectives are needed. The more specific the target, the more likely the results will be desirable.

Preassessment

Before detailed plans are made for staff development, the knowledge and skill levels of the staff have to be carefully assessed. Backgrounds and abilities should be known. A short questionnaire to ascertain the level of understanding about a particular topic may be administered.

Planning

The third step in effective learning involves formulating an organizational system by putting in charge either a staff member for whom this is part of his or her regular duties or an ad hoc committee.

Learning Experiences

It is common knowledge that experiential learning is effective learning. Educational sessions that actively involve the staff are usually preferable to the passive kind.

Dale suggests a *cone of learning experiences* that illustrates various effective teaching methods (see Figure 17–1). The base of the cone represents firsthand experiences, which are the foundation of learning. Such experiences in social work might include an interview with a client or a presentation at a community meeting. The learning takes place by doing. Contrived experiences are provided through models and mockups, which help learners to overcome the limitations of direct experience. For example, the model of a city area could be useful in studying city planning.

Dramatized experiences are used in staff development, including such exercises as role playing or psychodrama. Demonstrations, study trips, exhibits, educational television, motion pictures, recordings, radio, videotapes, and still pictures are additional resources. Visual symbols include chalkboard communication, flat maps, diagrams, and charts. The verbal symbols, in one sense the pinnacle of the cone, allow for abstract thinking, which is essential for social workers. As we increase our knowledge and understanding of principles and concepts, we enlarge our resources for helping people.[3]

[3]Edgar Dale, *Audiovisual Methods in Teaching*, 3rd ed. (New York: Holt, Rinehart & Winston, 1969), pp. 107-135.

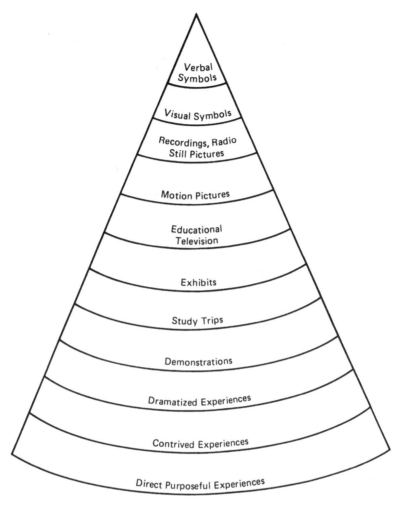

FIGURE 17-1 **The Cone of Experience.** From Edgar Dale, *Audiovisual Methods in Teaching*, 3rd ed., p. 107. Copyright © 1946, 1954, and 1969 by Holt, Rinehart, and Winston, Inc. Reprinted by permission of Holt, Rinehart, and Winston, CBS College Publishing.

Dale suggests that in education a variety of sensory experiences should be provided and that each can be meaningful. His teaching goal is applicable to social work practitioners: to nurture their "higher mental processes through a continuing interaction of the concrete and the abstract, the specific and the general, the particular and the universal."[4]

[4]Ibid., p. 134.

Evaluation

The fifth step in learning, evaluation, should include both positive and negative aspects of the learning experience. What went well? What were the limitations of the experience? Objective evaluations, if periodically introduced, can enable staff development experiences to be effective in the future.

TRAINING PROGRAMS

A few schools of social work train their students to become teachers in schools of social work or to coordinate agency staff development. For example, at the University of Utah, a major objective of the DSW program is to train a selected group of students for leadership positions as social work educators. Social work teachers are trained to teach in graduate schools of social work, undergraduate social work programs, and staff development programs in agencies. Several graduates have been employed to assist with staff development in social service agencies. One graduate became the director of staff development for a private comprehensive mental-health center. He coordinated and guided an educational program in an agency with 130 professional workers from various disciplines, including social work, psychiatry, psychology, and nursing.

Another area of growing importance is staff development for the faculty in schools of social work and undergraduate departments. A study of 150 institutions of higher learning revealed that faculty members from 142 institutions were "overwhelmingly negative" in their response to the question of whether their institutions provided effective faculty development systems.[5]

However, educators have made major efforts to improve the quality of teaching in social work. Previous efforts have focused largely on academic content, professional skills, and attitudes to be taught, rather than on the teaching skills per se. A significant effort to lay the groundwork for enhancing teaching effectiveness was the Faculty Development Project, sponsored by the Council on Social Work Education (CSWE) and supported by a grant from the National Institute of Mental Health.[6] Initiated in 1965, the project made an extensive review of the literature, took three surveys, and ran two workshops. The surveys were directed to administrative heads of schools of

[5]Kenneth Eble, *Career Development of the Effective College Teacher* (Washington, DC: American Association of University Professors, 1971), p. 3.

[6]Joseph Soffen, *Faculty Development in Professional Education* (New York: Council on Social Work Education, 1967), pp. xi-xviii.

social work, faculty members designated as having responsibility for faculty development or improvement of instruction, and 300 faculty members.

It was concluded that the project surveys were lacking in rigor; therefore, few specific conclusions were drawn. However, emphasis was placed on the apparent need for organizing and expanding faculty development programs and enhancing those efforts through administrative supports. Moreover, it was recommended "that the CSWE undertake leadership responsibility in strengthening practices for the continuing development of social work faculty."[7] CSWE has indeed assumed a leadership role in providing consultation and sponsoring workshops for its constituent schools; but within the individual schools progress has been slow, and many faculty development programs have been largely ineffectual.

To achieve the goals of a faculty development program, maximal involvement of the total faculty is essential, for two basic reasons. First, the optimal climate for professional growth is based on the tenet that all faculty members not only bear responsibility for "becoming" in their own professional development but also are given the responsibility and opportunity to assist their colleagues in becoming effective and productive scholars and educators. In the absence of a growth climate, some faculty members are prone to stagnate; others may continue to grow but fall far short of achieving their potential. Such a climate can be achieved only gradually, but a viable faculty development program can play a major role. The consequent atmosphere of sharing and involvement is in marked contrast to the competition and pettiness in many institutions of higher learning, including schools of social work.

The second reason for involving the faculty in its development is pragmatic in nature: to exploit to the fullest the diversity of knowledge and expertise embodied in the faculty as a whole. The proliferation of knowledge, the broadness of the field of social work, and the constant and rapid changes in the domains of practice and education make it difficult for social work educators to remain up to date. Obsolescence is a constant threat to faculty members and schools of social work. An effectively functioning faculty development program, however, supports individual faculty members in their attempts to keep abreast of developments within as well as outside of their specialty. The coordinated planning of faculty development activities taps the diverse knowledge, interests, and expertise of individual faculty members and makes these available to the faculty as a whole.

Time Management

Time management is of growing interest to many social workers in our pressurized world. Many administrators are focusing on relevant principles and

[7]Ibid., p. 146.

practices in their staff development sessions. This movement is particularly significant for female leaders and managers, because many of them combine work at an agency with family responsibilities. Nichols suggests that planning, organizing, and controlling time are the core concepts in a curriculum unit on time management. She observes that analysis of ways in which agencies and universities can modify their structures and programs (related to time expectations) to be more responsive to the life situations of many women is highly significant.[8]

STAFF DEVELOPMENT MANAGERS

One development in agency organization is the surfacing of staff development managers or other personnel designated to lead staff development programs and activities. These, of course, are established to build the quality of agency services and to strengthen knowledge and skills.

Doueck and Austin, in a systems focus, believe that new roles for staff development personnel are very important. They identify specific roles in the context of analytic and interactional functions on a continuum. On the analytic side they include the "policy analyst" and the "interpreter," and on the interactional side the "staff advocate" and the "organizational change facilitator." They conclude that the blended approach "seeks to assure workers that their concerns and dilemmas will be shared with other levels of the agency's hierarchy. While changes might not always be forthcoming, at least the worker will have a sense that they have had some input into the problem-solving and decision-making processes of the organization."[9]

Roles of staff development managers are developing and shifting rapidly. Austin, Brannon, and Pecora suggest that these roles include "*translator* of training needs into learning objectives, *orchestrator* of training experiences, *facilitator* of the learning process, and *change agent* in relationship to individual and organizational needs."[10]

SUMMARY

Staff development is becoming an integral part of the internal operation of social work agencies. It can benefit individual workers and improve agency

[8]Ann Weaver Nichols, "Teaching Time Management: A Gender-Sensitive Perspective," *Administration in Social Work* 7 (Spring 1983), 84.

[9]Howard J. Doueck and Michael J. Austin, "Improving Agency Functioning Through Staff Development," *Administration in Social Work* 10 (Summer 1986), 36.

[10]Michael J. Austin, Dianne Brannon, and Peter J. Pecora, *Managing Staff Development Programs in Human Service Agencies* (Chicago: Nelson-Hall Publishers, 1984), p. 129.

services. Staff development is needed to keep staff members up to date in professional attitudes and new areas of knowledge, skills, and techniques.

Numerous methods are available for staff development within the agency, including lectures, case presentations, case-incident studies, role playing, self-development programs, group activities, and games. Outside of the agency, beneficial activities include continuing education, workshops, institutes, teaching, and exchanging positions with workers in other agencies and schools of social work.

Staff development may be enhanced by five steps:

1. Set specific objectives.
2. Preassess staff.
3. Make effective plans.
4. Offer appropriate learning experiences.
5. Evaluate outcomes.

QUESTIONS FOR DISCUSSION

1. What are the main purposes of staff development?

2. What are the advantages and limitations of role playing as a method of staff development?

3. What guidelines would you suggest for effective case presentations in weekly staff development sessions in a social work agency?

4. List and evaluate five main experiences or processes that are meaningful for successful learning.

5. Describe and evaluate Dale's "cone of experience" as it relates to social work staff development.

6. Who should be responsible for staff development in a social work agency?

7. If you were director of a large social work agency in family services and you wanted to hire a staff development manager, what criteria would you use in making your selection?

SPECIAL ACTIVITIES

1. Invite a social work administrator to talk to your group about the importance of staff development in providing effective social services.

2. Role-play a hypothetical staff problem in a hospital to illustrate the advantages and disadvantages of role playing as a staff development process.

3. Present a debate on the following statement: For providing effective services, social work agencies should spend about 10 percent of their working time in staff development activities.

SELECTED REFERENCES

Austin, Michael J., Dianne Brannon, and Peter J. Pecora. *Managing Staff Development Programs in Human Service Agencies*. Chicago: Nelson-Hall Publishers, 1984.

Dane, Elizabeth. "Continuing Education in Administration: The Job-Related Principle." *Administration in Social Work* 7 (Summer 1983), 79–89.

Dane, Elizabeth. "Managing Organizational Relationships in Continuing Education Programs: Is Loose Coupling the Answer?" *Administration in Social Work* 9 (Fall 1985), 83–92.

Doueck, Howard J., and Michael J. Austin. "Improving Agency Functioning Through Staff Development." *Administration in Social Work* 10 (Summer 1986), 27–37.

Hartford, Margaret E. "Faculty Development: The Continuing Preparation of the Social Work Education Teacher." *Journal of Education for Social Work* 11 (Spring 1975), 44–51.

Martinez-Brawley, Emilia E., and Sybil M. Delevan. "Centralizing Management and Decentralizing Services: An Alternative Approach." *Administration in Social Work* 17, No. 1 (1993), 81–102.

Pecora, Peter J., and Michael J. Austin. *Managing Human Services Personnel*. Newbury Park, CA: Sage Publications, 1987.

Pecora, Peter J., Steven Paul Schinke, and James K. Whittaker. "Needs Assessment for Staff Training." *Administration in Social Work* 7 (Fall/Winter 1983), 101–113.

Resnick, Herman, and Rino J. Patti, eds. *Change from Within: Humanizing Social Welfare Organizations*. Philadelphia: Temple University Press, 1980.

Stein, Herman D., "Board, Executive, and Staff." In Simon Slavin, ed., *Social Administration: The Management of the Social Services*, 2nd ed. Vol. I, *An Introduction to Human Services Management*, pp. 191–204. New York: Haworth Press, 1985.

18

Future
Administrative
Developments

Ortega y Gasset depicts the complexity of the perception of reality with a parable:

"Peary relates that on his polar trip he traveled one whole day toward the north, making his sleigh dogs run briskly. At night he checked his bearings to determine his latitude and noticed with great surprise that he was much farther South than in the morning. He had been toiling all day toward the North on an immense iceberg drawn southward by an ocean current."[1]

What is the reality of social work administration? Where is it now? Where will it probably be in A.D. 2025?

We live in an uncertain world, which is constantly changing. Problems in human relations exist everywhere, in nations, communities, neighborhoods, and families. Social work is being called on to help meet many needs. What is in the offing? Will social work services be available by phototelephone? Will there be increased problems in human relationships, and will innovative skills and techniques be devised for coping with them? What will social work administration be like at the turn of the century? In A.D. 2025? Of course, no one knows for sure, but there are indications of interesting future developments.

[1]José Ortega y Gasset, *Meditations on Quixote* (New York: W. W. Norton, 1961), p. 104.

LIKELY DEVELOPMENTS

New Administration Positions

During the past few decades social workers have been rather quiescent in the area of leadership. Today the situation is changing and tomorrow augurs well for increased leadership positions. Social work administrators are gaining positions as directors of mental health centers, state hospitals, state training schools, youth development centers, residential treatment units, and other agencies and organizations. It is recognized that social workers have a breadth of knowledge and skill in the larger community, as well as in human relations, that can be useful in leadership positions.

On the political scene social workers are moving into elected positions and are gaining hard-earned status in government councils and legislative bodies. In educational circles social work administrators are becoming presidents of colleges and universities, vice-presidents, and deans for student affairs. In the business world requests are on the increase for social work consultants. It is likely these trends will continue.

An example of a top educational appointment was that of Leon H. Ginsberg, former social work dean and commissioner of the West Virginia Human Services Department, who was named chancellor in 1984 of the West Virginia Board of Regents, which administers the state's sixteen colleges and universities.

In 1990 Patricia A. E. Rodgers was named director of VISTA, guiding the destinies of more than 3,000 volunteers in this domestic peace corps. Currently, social workers serve in the U.S. Congress, in numerous state legislatures, and in other important government and community positions, and it is likely these numbers will increase.

Bargal and Karger recognize that the world is changing economically in so many ways and that occupational social work can play a significant role in the reindustrialization of America: "Specifically, social workers are in a unique position to effect change because of their relative proximity to both management and workers. As such, social workers can help shape the new industrial reality by helping to make certain that economic reorganization takes into account the human cost of economic change."[2]

Shift from "Pyramid" to "Circle" Pattern

Historically, administration in social work followed the basic pattern of a pyramid, with a chief executive officer (CEO) at the top, staff with decreasing

---

[2]David Bargal and Howard Jacob Karger, "Occupational Social Work and the New Global Economy," *Administration in Social Work* 15, No. 4 (1991), 108.

authority and responsibilities going downward, and more numbers on each level. The bottom level usually had the largest number of employees, the line workers. Under an administrator were supervisors and then a staff of case-workers, group workers, and others.

Authority patterns have been shifting, providing more power and more responsibilities for staff members in the planning and implementation of agency policies and services. Today, three groups often share power and responsibility for agency operation: administrators, staff, and clients. In many agencies, administrative operations are becoming more of a circle, with these three groups intertwined—interacting, interplanning, and joining together to provide services.

The power and involvement of these three groups vary from agency to agency, but their working together for the benefit of the agency seems to be increasing and is likely to continue in the years ahead. Significant inputs from staff members and clients are bringing many changes in agency organization, planning, decision making, and overall provision of social services.

There has been a considerable shift from authoritarian to participatory management between administrators and staff. Although various patterns still exist, this allows for the involvement of all employees and tends to create interacting team members within the working circle of management. Also, in many agencies, opinions, feelings, and suggestions are being received from clients as never before. Their evaluations, often obtained in both formal and informal discussions, are playing a vital part in the formulation of agency policies and in the provision of services. Consumer satisfaction is a powerful force in today's world.

Increased Private Practice

Traditionally social work practice has been housed mainly in agencies, public or private, which have allowed for supervision and guidance of social workers. During the last several years, however, there has been a definite increase in private practice, for many reasons: higher income, more individuality and independence, opportunity for part-time practice, and meeting specialized needs of people who have problems in social relations. This development is likely to increase in the future.

The increase in private practice has been gradual, in both full-time and part-time positions. Consequently, social work students are seriously considering these career choices. A study of students in a New York State master's of social work program reveals that two-thirds intended to enter private practice sometime during their careers.[3]

---

[3]Amy C. Butler, "The Attractions of Private Practice," *Journal of Social Work Education* 28 (Winter 1992), 52.

Increased International Cooperation and Collaboration

Wendell Wilkie's "one world" has become a reality as never before. Administrators are recognizing that social work knowledge and skills have no concern for national boundaries. Numerous leaders in human services are traveling to countries around the world, acting as consultants for government agencies and social work leaders, both public and private. This movement is a two-way process, and social work administrators in countries abroad are also being used as consultants in the United States and in other New World countries.

How far can an MSW take you? How about India, Pakistan, Poland, or Hungary? "Two social workers at the World Bank in Washington, D.C., are using their social work skills as they study entrepreneurs establishing businesses in former communist countries and help develop clean water projects in rural areas of Bangladesh."[4] Many other social workers, both administrators and clinicians, are serving abroad, helping to improve human services in countries all around the world.

Another example of active international cooperation in human relations is the Alliance of Universities for Democracy, a consortium of ninety-four universities from central and eastern Europe and the United States. It was established in 1990 to enhance the role of universities in promoting democratic institutions, economic development, education, philanthropy, and human rights in the newly established democracies of central and eastern Europe. In 1992, it expanded its mission to include the republics of the former Soviet Union. During 1994 it will extend membership to universities in western Europe.

The alliance promotes collaborative work among universities, drawing on social workers for participation. For example, since 1991 Dr. Kay L. Dea, dean of the Graduate School of Social Work at the University of Utah, and Dr. Ben Granger, director of the School of Social Work, Colorado State University, have codirected a project to develop grassroots volunteer associations in Bulgaria, Poland, and Romania. Eight universities have been associated with this project. At a meeting held in Budapest in November 1993, Dean Dea was elected to the Board of Directors and the Executive Committee of the Alliance of Universities for Democracy.

Increased Involvement of Women

Historically women have not held their share of important positions in social work administration, and their salaries and status have been lower than those of men. Although some current changes have been positive for women as administrators, many inequities still exist.

[4]*NASW News*, April 1993, p. 5.

One improvement has been the appointment of women to top federal positions by President Clinton, which seems to be bringing a favorable response across the country. Another innovative move was the establishment of a course entitled Women in Social Welfare Administration in one school of social work. Healy, Havens, and Chin made a follow-up study of students who had taken the class, reporting that 66.77 percent indicated that the course had helped motivate them to pursue an administrative position. Based on the results of the study, the researchers recommended that women's issues in administration "be addressed both in required administration concentration courses and in a separate elective for students wanting more emphasis."[5]

Advanced Technology

More and more social work administrators and agencies are tapping the resources of computer networks and other technologies for recording, planning, and implementing social services. Almost daily, new technological advances are becoming available to both public and private agencies, thereby requiring social work administrators to be knowledgeable about these innovations, which can improve the efficiency and effectiveness of agency services, often at reduced cost.

In practice, advanced technology is offering many resources for clients. Schoech, Cavalier, and Hoover, recognizing that technology enhances the opportunities for work and independent living for people with disabilities, give the following examples: a child with cerebral palsy communicating for the first time with a speech synthesis device; a bedridden person living independently with the help of computer-controlled doors and appliances; a person with quadriplegia earning money by programming a computer through a mouth stick and using electronic communications to send and receive business mail. The researchers state that it has been a struggle to locate the appropriate experts in technology, acquire the appropriate technologies, and provide the necessary follow-up services. They also observe that the "integration of technology into service delivery is an important but difficult goal for both professionals and consumers."[6]

Development of Theoretical Frameworks

Administrative theory is inadequately developed in the delivery of social services, as it is in other helping disciplines. Creative social work administrators are beginning to formulate theoretical bases for management and other

[5]Lynne M. Healy, Catherine M. Havens, and Alice Chin, "Preparing Women for Human Service Administration: Building on Experience," *Administration in Social Work* 14, No. 2 (1990), 91.

[6]Dick Schoech, Al R. Cavalier, and Betts Hoover, "Using Technology to Change the Human Services Delivery System," *Administration in Social Work* 17, No. 2 (1993), 32.

aspects of the administrative process. The future is likely to bring numerous theoretical constructs.

Illustrative of development in this area is Slavin's theoretical framework for social administration. He identifies three elements in the social services: the client/consumer, the practitioner or provider of service, and the service agency.[7] He views the administrator's task as "that of 'orchestrating' these diverse constituencies, with their different, and often conflicting, interests and needs."[8] In his theoretical framework, Slavin proposes a proactive view of the administrator's role, which includes an advocacy stance encompassing case advocacy, program advocacy, and policy advocacy. He summarizes his position as follows:

> The administrator of a social agency always functions in a dynamic field of forces in which conflicting constituency interests contest for attention and response. The varying pressures and demands that result place powerful constraints on administrative authority. Power and influence tend to be unequally distributed among constituencies and make purely rational behavior by administrators problematical. Organizational-maintenance needs contend with the perceived requirements of clients and practitioners.
>
> The administrator must bring these differing needs and interests into some form of balance or equilibrium—to orchestrate these diverse constituencies.[9]

In educational circles there is a movement to tie together social welfare administration and social policy, to integrate them into a single social work major, both in education and in practice. It is recognized that administrators are involved in understanding and formulating social policies and that social policies affect the activities and leadership skills of administrators in many ways.

Neugeboren points out that in education there is an increasing emphasis on administration, that such programs in schools of social work have increased from 30 percent in 1966 to 50 percent in 1975, and that deans of schools of social work in 1977 "revealed that 80 percent of the schools have been able to develop a program in social welfare administration." He then provides empirical data for a conceptual framework for field education in administration based on the integration of social policy and administration: "The evidence supports the assumption that field education that is concerned with the *goals* of social programs is more effective than one focused on the administrative *means*."[10]

[7]Simon Slavin, "A Theoretical Framework for Social Administration," in Felice Davidson Perlmutter and Simon Slavin, eds., *Leadership in Social Administration: Perspectives for the 1980's* (Philadelphia: Temple University Press, 1980), pp. 3–21.

[8]Ibid., p. 3.

[9]Ibid., p. 13.

[10]Bernard Neugeboren, "Field Education for Social Welfare Administration: Integration of Social Policy and Administration," *Administration in Social Work* 4 (Summer 1980), 63.

More Focus on Accountability
in the Delivery of Social Services

Accountability is required more than ever before. Legislators and community leaders are asking, "Are social work services justified?" "Can we afford them?" "What actually happens in clinical and community practice?" Answers to these questions will arise only as we utilize new techniques to consider objectively what we are doing, how we are doing it, and what the outcomes are. The future undoubtedly will require more accountability of the social work profession.

However, accountability may be overstressed. Looking at the role of the social service administrator, Lewis lists three anticipations that should be avoided.

1. There is a view, tied in with our initial age of accountability, of seeing only what is wrong in what social service workers do and only what seems right in what nonsocial service administrators do.
2. We should not limit the roles we play in administration, but should allow functions to be defined by administrative roles that evolve in time.
3. We need to avoid ambiguities and theories that promise neutrality in partisan situations. Values and ethical behavior are essential in the social work arena.[11]

Wilson suggests that the amount of information required by administrators in social administration appears to be increasing exponentially and that numerous skills are now needed. He concludes, from a study of values and technology as foundations for administrative practice in the social services, that "the employment of recent graduates of social work schools' administration specializations is presented as the most cost-efficient alternative for upgrading important aspects of administrative accountability technology while promising to retain a sensitiveness to social work values and an administrative advocacy stance."[12]

Social work's probable response to the demand for more accountability is noted by Fischer, who observes that a quiet revolution has been taking place in relation to how social work develops and uses knowledge for practice. The profession is gradually shifting from vague and haphazard formulations to scientifically or empirically based practice. According to Fischer, a basic point in the new thrust toward objectivity is "that social workers can use clear, specific, systematic, and rational criteria to select the techniques they use in practice."[13]

[11]Harold Lewis, "The Future Role of the Social Service Administrator," *Administration in Social Work* 1 (Summer 1977), 120–121.

[12]Scott Muir Wilson, "Values and Technology: Foundations for Practice," in Felice Davidson Perlmutter and Simon Slavin, eds., *Leadership in Social Administration: Perspectives for the 1980's* (Philadelphia: Temple University Press, 1980), p. 120.

[13]Joel Fischer, "The Social Work Revolution," *Social Work* 26 (May 1981), 201.

Computers, videotapes, and other mechanical devices are being utilized by various agencies in an attempt to analyze their organizations and to help improve services and accountability. Many agencies are now computerized, so that nearly every significant action or service is recorded and can be reported and studied. It is likely that the computer will become even more important as a tool for recording and improving services.

More Use of Professional Teams

Within the past few decades, professional teams have begun to work together in an attempt to solve human problems and provide therapy. A team usually includes a psychiatrist, social worker, psychologist, and sometimes others, depending on the service and the particular needs of an agency. Undoubtedly we will see an increasing use of the professional team in the delivery of social services.

The professional team is effective for several reasons. It provides for a sharing of knowledge and skills, which increases understanding and improves therapy. It provides additional motivation for workers who are trying to solve human problems. It offers an opportunity to combine resources in conducting research—to ascertain etiological factors about human behavior and the effectiveness of treatment methods.

Social workers are working more in teams, and this trend is likely to continue. Often the social worker acts as coordinator and facilitator for the professional team. At staff meetings, the social worker may conduct the meeting and pull the loose ends together as the team looks at a case and plans for its solution.

Improved Staff Development Programs

Another significant move is the increased emphasis on staff development in social work agencies. Today, there is an increase in staff development programs, and it is likely to continue in the future. The aim is to improve staff members' understanding of themselves and to increase their skills so that they will be more effective helpers.

Some agencies, both public and private, employ full-time social workers whose major assignment is to strengthen and further staff development. In one community mental-health center, a worker with a DSW degree works full time to coordinate, strengthen, and direct development for the total professional staff of 150, including psychiatrists, social workers, and psychologists. Weekly meetings are held for two hours. Evaluations indicate that these meetings are helpful in formulating specific goals for the staff members and the agency. In other agencies, part-time workers assist with staff development, and this is likely to increase. Given the increase in knowledge about human behavior and in skills, it is imperative for social workers in practice to keep up to date.

More administrators and boards are agreeing with Weiner, who suggests that staff development can facilitate the achievement of program objectives, both in singular and multidisciplinary settings, and that "staff development presents an opportunity to improve morale and motivation while fostering a consensus treatment philosophy and enhancing work group cohesion."[14]

Another likely development is an increase in staff development programs, some of which are already in existence, in schools of social work. Social work educators must keep up to date to help their students become skillful practitioners.

Austin, Brannon, and Pecora observe that recent actions of federal, state, and local governments to curtail expenditures for social welfare programs signals a significant shift in societal priorities. They suggest that although tightening of funds is deplorable in the light of needs, "it appears that creative staff development program management could become the new fringe benefit for the 1980s and 1990s."[15]

More Use of Community Processes

A few decades ago, casework was almost synonymous with social work. In the 1930s, the group work method became an integral part of social work practice. The introduction and application of community organization, the last of the three major methods of social work, is even more recent.

Most social workers today acquire some training in working with individuals, groups, and communities, but it is evident that there will be an increase in working with and through communities. There is a unique power in group interaction and behavior that can be utilized in the planning process. Competent administrators are increasingly tapping community resources.

Wilson recognizes the need to integrate two approaches in the coordination of health services—the structural and the case coordination. In the past, the lack of such a connection has hampered the delivery of health services. Wilson suggests that social work is expanding its role in mobilizing community networks for greater coordination of health-care services. This expanded role includes the development by social workers of new functions: information broker, opinion maker, and definer of issues.[16]

[14]Harvey Weiner, "Administrative Responsibility for Staff Development," in Felice Davidson Perlmutter and Simon Slavin, eds., *Leadership in Social Administration: Perspectives for the 1980's* (Philadelphia: Temple University Press, 1980), p. 247.

[15]Michael J. Austin, Dianne Brannon, and Peter J. Pecora, *Managing Staff Development Programs in Human Service Agencies* (Chicago: Nelson-Hall Publishers, 1984), p. xv.

[16]Paul A. Wilson, "Expanding the Role of Social Workers in Coordination of Health Services," *Health and Social Work* 6 (February 1981), 57–64.

Improved Public Relations

In the past, social workers have had limited training and experience in public relations. Today, there is a greater focus on public relations, and some training is available, particularly in administration and community practice. A few schools offer courses in public relations and community affairs.

In the future, there will undoubtedly be more emphasis on both training and practice for administrators in public relations, as well as for all social work students and for those who may want to specialize in this area. Also, social work administrators will probably hire full-time or part-time experts in public relations from the fields of business, communications, public administration, or psychology. Both approaches are likely to be used increasingly in the future because there is a need to improve the image of social work to correct various misconceptions and to make it known that social work needs the financial, psychological, and political support of community leaders and citizens.

Emphasis on Leadership

In recent years, there has been an emphasis on developing more qualified leaders for social work practice. Classes in leadership and lab experiences are likely to increase in the future. The profession needs competent leaders who are able to participate in the planning and decision-making processes of the government and other institutions. Social workers no longer can let leaders from other fields make plans and decisions about social problems, a process that has traditionally left social workers to pick up the pieces. Social workers are beginning to move into positions in government and community life that will call on their leadership abilities.

Capable administrators are also making significant contributions in preventing personal and social problems as well as providing guidelines for the enrichment of daily living for all people. The future holds many opportunities for such creative actions.

More Effective Communication

Most administrators in social service agencies are aware of the need for better communication among staff members to improve organization and functioning. More emphasis will undoubtedly be placed on ways to improve communication among staff members and with clients. There is likely to be a move toward clarity and simplicity in messages and an attempt to minimize psychological interference.

Effective communication makes it possible for clients to take a bigger part in the planning and decision making of an agency. Clients will be able to convey their impressions of the effectiveness of social work services, and staff members will probably feel freer to make suggestions to administrators.

Warfel, Maloney, and Blase devised a consumer feedback system, using the *Teaching-Family Model*, to get feedback from the youths (clients), parents, school teachers, social service and juvenile court personnel, and the board of directors of a home. They conclude that "effective consumer feedback systems can provide immediate benefits to managers and clients of human service programs."[17]

Peters, author of the popular book *Thriving on Chaos*, also emphasizes the importance of listening to those who are involved in total management and services: "Today's successful leaders will work diligently to engage others in their cause. Oddly enough, the best way, by far, to engage others is by listening—serious listening—to them. If talking and giving orders was the administrative model of the last fifty years, listening (to lots of people near the action), is the model of the 1980s and beyond."[18]

Increase in Research

Millions of dollars are being expended annually for research about human relations and social problems and their solutions. We are just beginning to be able to answer some of the questions. It is likely that there will be an increase in quality research in both public and private agencies. The hope is, of course, that research will bring an increased understanding of human behavior and social problems, enabling us to solve them more effectively than we do at present. Another challenge for researchers is to study methodology and therapy, including specific skills and techniques, to ascertain and evaluate results. It is possible that future research projects will discover knowledge and skills that administrators can use to influence the lives of millions of people.

FUTURE EDUCATIONAL PATTERNS
FOR SOCIAL WORK ADMINISTRATORS

More Emphasis on Administration

As mentioned earlier, about 15 percent of graduate students in schools of social work are presently majoring in administration or are pursuing a combined major that includes administration. In the future, more students will probably major in administration, anticipating their roles as leaders in agencies and in communities.

It is likely that there will be an increase on two fronts in schools of social work: (1) more administration courses and labs for all graduate students and (2) more opportunity for specialization in administration. Several schools of

[17]David J. Warfel, Dennis M. Maloney, and Karen Blase, "Consumer Feedback in Human Service Programs," *Social Work* 26 (March 1981), 151.

[18]Tom Peters, *Thriving on Chaos: Handbook for a Management Revolution* (New York: Knopf, 1987), p. 434.

social work require one or more administration courses for all graduate students in social work, recognizing that they may become either administrators or members of an administrative team. In addition, more schools are offering a major or concentration in administration.

Administration labs for graduate social work students will undoubtedly be offered more and more. The University of Washington at Seattle, the University of Utah, and a few other schools have been doing pioneering work in this area, which offers graduate students in administration an opportunity to test the theories and skills they acquire in the classroom. Lab experiences include movies, filmstrips, and videotapes related to administrative principles, skills, and problems. Vignettes portraying critical incidents in administration are used to provoke discussion. Games, simulations, and role playing are utilized to give students firsthand experience in administrative decisions.

A likely development in the future is increased planning and implementation of training for social work administrators. Many social workers advocate more use of the managerial skills of business to strengthen administrative services. For example, Hart suggests that "social administrators and teachers should use the next twenty-five years to define further an integrated, comprehensive, but specific business approach to nonprofit management. The government's nonprofit sectors constitute 20% of the GNP and an even larger component of our country's employment. We need enhanced conceptual, theoretical, and skill bases with which to work."[19]

Patterns of Social Work Education

There is no uniform educational pattern for training social work administrators. Developments in the future are likely to build on current models, with some new combinations, both on the master's and doctoral levels. Current patterns include the following:

1. *Two-year graduate programs.* Some graduate schools select those who wish to major in administration at the beginning of graduate training. The students spend two full years in classwork and practicums focused on administration, in addition to the basic training received by all students. This program provides a maximum of time for acquiring the knowledge, attitudes, and skills for management and administration.
2. *One-year-concentration programs.* In these programs, the first year of graduate work is generically based, with classes and field experiences shared with the other students. The second year offers opportunities to specialize in administration, both in class and in the field.
3. *Modified plan.* A few schools offer a modified pattern, which provides for one or two quarters or one semester of generic social work training before the students move into their concentration in administration for the remainder of two academic years.

[19]Aileen F. Hart, "Training Social Administrators for Leadership in the Coming Decades," *Administration in Social Work* 12, No. 3 (1988), 9.

4. *Doctoral programs.* Some doctoral programs include an emphasis on administration, and most provide some training for those pursuing postmaster's work. In fact, many of those who are awarded DSW or Ph.D. degrees each year are employed in administrative positions, either full or part time. The advanced work includes graduate seminars and offers opportunities for dissertations in administration.

Innovative training programs for social work administrators will undoubtedly develop in the future. It is likely that additional courses will be offered on all levels, from the undergraduate to the doctoral, in administrative training.

Patterns of Fieldwork

Since emphasis on administration is relatively new in social work training, the opportunity for fieldwork or a practicum is still rather limited. Although there are many kinds of placements for graduate students, there is a paucity of excellent field settings in many areas, although expansion is likely to be forthcoming in the years ahead.

Cox and Paulson suggest that an increased concern for educating social work administrators is bringing many curriculum changes. They describe several models of field education, including some that allow schools to recruit and train full-time employees of social service agencies. They conclude that

> it is especially important in light of the need of social work as a profession to maintain and increase its role in the planning and administration of social services, that field work education help guide this process. Models that allow access to part-time students, access to undeveloped settings, multi-disciplinary experience, and closer working relationships between schools and agencies can contribute to this goal.[20]

PREVENTION

Some administrators in social work have crusaded for more preventive services in their programs. Isn't "an ounce of prevention worth a pound of cure" true in social work as well as in medicine or nursing? In the monumental 1959 curriculum study of the Council of Social Work Education, prevention was described as one of the three primary functions of social work. Since that time, various practitioners and educators have endeavored to push for the study of prevention in schools of social work and for devoting more of agencies' efforts to preventive social work practice.

Social work administrators of the future are likely to spend more time on prevention than administrators do at present. The hope is that through

[20]Enid O. Cox and Robert I. Paulson, "Field Placement Alternatives in Social Welfare Administration/Management," *Administration in Social Work* 4 (Summer 1980), 84–85.

preventive work, social problems may be reduced. Another current development that is likely to increase in the future is the establishment of specific courses on prevention. Several schools find this offering of considerable interest to students and of value to the profession of social work.

THE JOB MARKET OF THE FUTURE

Two significant developments have appeared in administrative positions in social work. Qualified social workers have been offered leadership positions that they would not have been offered in the past, such as director of a mental-health center or superintendent of a state hospital or state training school. At the same time, graduates from the related fields of psychology, business, public administration, and sociology have been hired for administrative positions in social services previously limited to social workers. This means that social workers will need a good deal of training in administration in graduate school. It also means that social workers will be competing with other professionals for many key positions in the community.

ENRICHMENT IN LIVING

The future undoubtedly will show an increase in social work programs with an emphasis on enrichment in living. Traditionally, social work has been clinical and therapeutic, with some attention paid to prevention. Now forward-looking agency administrators say that enrichment or personal fulfillment in living is imperative for the profession of social work. We need to share with all people our knowledge about human relationships to bring increased satisfaction and mental well-being.

This may mean an increase in premarital counseling—helping couples contemplating marriage to understand more about the potentials as well as the pitfalls of marriage. On the community level, family-life education may increase, with social workers conducting institutes and seminars on such topics as successful parenting, handling stress, understanding emotions, and enriching husband-wife relationships.

There will probably be more opportunities for social workers to participate in planning educational programs to help groups of citizens understand more about human values. Such values as acceptance, love, and appreciation, as well as the intrinsic worth of individuals and the potential personal satisfactions in human relationships, may receive special consideration.

In addition, new social work settings are providing opportunities for increasing knowledge about human relationships. For example, many social workers are beginning to be employed in business and industry. Although much of their practice is clinical in nature, some of it involves employees and their families and includes lectures and discussions on such topics as preventing divorce, creative parenting, and using conflict for growth. A genuine effort is being made to help people understand how to achieve satisfying human relationships.

REACHING FOR QUALITY

Traditionally, social work administrators have provided services for persons in need, especially for those with problems in social relationships. Many quantitative reports have been issued to describe the numbers of people aided. The aim has been to provide helpful services with efficiency. Today there is a growing recognition of the importance of providing not only quantity but also quality.

According to Martin, top-quality management (TQM) is rapidly shaping up as today's new managerial wave. Many large corporations have initiated TQM programs in the past few years. Martin also suggests that it is just a matter of time "before this new management wave washes over human service organizations. In anticipation of this eventuality, human service administrators may find it in their best interest to begin exploring the concept of TQM."[21] Of course, a major element in this new approach is its emphasis on quality as the primary organizational goal.

SUMMARY

In the years ahead, emphasis on administration as a method of practice is likely to increase both in education and in practice. The need for capable social work administrators is critical.

Rapid social changes, including increased knowledge about human behavior and solutions of social problems, will require an increase in the effectiveness of administration in social agencies.

Probable trends and developments in the future include the following:

New administrative positions
Administration shifting from "pyramid" to "circle" pattern
Private practice increasing
More international cooperation and collaboration
More women as administrators
More technology
Development of theoretical frameworks in administration
Greater focus on accountability in the delivery of social services

[21]Lawrence L. Martin, "Total Quality Management: The New Managerial Wave," *Administration in Social Work* 17, No. 2 (1993), 1–2.

Greater use of team relationships
Improved staff development
Greater use of community processes
Improved public relations
Emphasis on leadership
More effective communication
Increase in research and evaluation
Greater emphasis on training for administration in schools of social work
Shifting patterns in social work education
Competition in the job market
Increased interest in prevention
Advances in agency enrichment programs
Reach for high-quality services

QUESTIONS FOR DISCUSSION

1. What is meant by the statement "Social work administration is changing from a 'pyramid' to a 'circle'"?

2. Can you describe relatively new positions in which social workers have become the administrators?

3. What is the professional role of the social worker as he or she works with administrators from related disciplines?

4. What approaches might be utilized in staff development to sensitize staff and administrators to issues of diversity that might affect their relationships?

5. How might modern technology be used to improve the delivery of social services in a mental-health center?

6. Evaluate some of the reasons why private social work is increasing.

7. What suggestions do you have for reducing discrimination against women in administrative roles, both in salaries and lower status?

8. Why is the developing emphasis on quality in social services so important for the profession of social work.?

SPECIAL ACTIVITIES

1. Debate the following statement: Women administrators should receive the same salary as male administrators for the same level of position.

2. Interview a successful social work administrator and ask what two or three trends in professional social work will be found at the end of the century. Why?

3. Role-play a situation to illustrate the importance of prevention in the delivery of social services.

SELECTED REFERENCES

BARKER, ROBERT L. *Social Work in Private Practice*, 2nd ed. Silver Spring, MD: NASW Press, 1992.

BUTLER, AMY C. "The Attractions of Private Practice." *Journal of Social Work Education* 28 (Winter 1992), 47–60.

CARLISLE, HOWARD M. *Management Essentials: Concepts for Productivity and Innovation*, 2nd ed., pp. 497–586. Chicago: Science Research Associates, 1987.

FULMER, ROBERT M. *The New Management*, 4th ed., pp. 499–514. New York: Macmillan, 1988.

GARVIN, CHARLES D., and JOHN E. TROPMAN. *Social Work in Contemporary Society*. Englewood Cliffs, NJ: Prentice Hall, 1992.

GOWDY, ELIZABETH A., CHARLES A. RAPP, and JOHN POERTNER. "Management Is Performance: Strategies for Client Centered Practice in Social Service Organizations." *Administration in Social Work* 17, No. 1 (1993), 3–21.

HASENFELD, YEHESKEL. "The Changing Context of Human Services Administration: Implications for the Future." In Simon Slavin, ed., *Social Administration: The Management of the Social Services*, 2nd ed. Vol. I, *An Introduction to Human Services Management*, pp. 357–370. New York: Haworth Press, 1985.

MOR-BARAK, MICHAL E., and MARGARET TYNAN. "Older Workers and the Workplace: A New Challenge for Occupational Social Work." *Social Work* 38 (January 1993), 45–55.

PETERS, TOM. *Thriving on Chaos: Handbook for a Management Revolution*. New York: Knopf, 1987.

RESNICK, HERMAN and RINO J. PATTI, eds. *Change from Within: Humanizing Social Welfare Organizations*. Philadelphia: Temple University Press, 1980.

SCHOECH, DICK, AL R. CAVALIER, and BETTS HOOVER. "Using Technology to Change the Human Services Delivery System." *Administration in Social Work* 17, No. 2 (1993), 31–51.

Author Index

Subject Index